THE
CHIPILLY
SIX

Lucas Jordan grew up in Burekup in Western Australia. He holds a PhD in history from the Australian National University. Lucas spent more than a decade teaching and researching in the Kimberley, Cape York and central Australia. He worked for Amnesty International as a researcher and fieldworker and co-wrote Amnesty's global report '"The land holds us": Aboriginal peoples' right to their traditional homelands in the Northern Territory', which was based on six years of collaboration and camping with the Alyawarr and Anmatyerr people. Lucas is currently a leading teacher at Western English Language School, a secondary school for new arrivals and refugees in Melbourne, and occasionally consults on history projects. He is the author of *Stealth Raiders: A few daring men in 1918*. Lucas lives in Lara, Victoria, with his wife and two sons.

THE CHIPILLY SIX

UNSUNG HEROES OF THE GREAT WAR

LUCAS JORDAN

NEWSOUTH

A NewSouth book

Published by
NewSouth Publishing
University of New South Wales Press Ltd
University of New South Wales
Sydney NSW 2052
AUSTRALIA
https://unsw.press/

 A catalogue record for this book is available from the National Library of Australia

ISBN   9781742238098 (paperback)
        9781742238784 (ebook)
        9781742239729 (ePDF)

Internal design Josephine Pajor-Markus
Cover design Peter Long
Cover images Wrecked buildings in a section of the war-ruined village of Chipilly, 10 August 1918 (Australian War Memorial, H15934); two diggers of the 5th Division (Australian War Memorial, E02819)
Printer Griffin Press

*To Madeline and Ken Jordan
(Mum and Dad)*

CONTENTS

Then out spake brave Horatius,
The Captain of the Gate:
'To every man upon this earth
Death cometh soon or late
And how can man die better
Than facing fearful odds,
For the ashes of his fathers
And the temples of his gods.'

TB Macaulay, *Lays of Ancient Rome*
(A staple of Australian schoolbooks
of the 1890s.)

MAP OF THE WESTERN FRONT

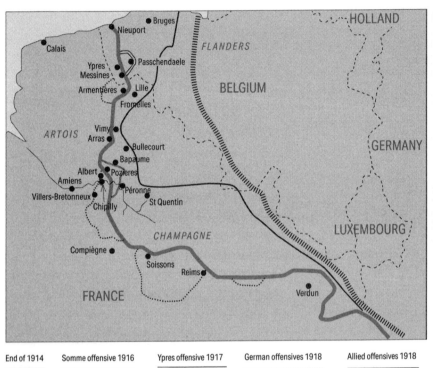

End of 1914   Somme offensive 1916   Ypres offensive 1917   German offensives 1918   Allied offensives 1918

MAP OF CHIPILLY SPUR

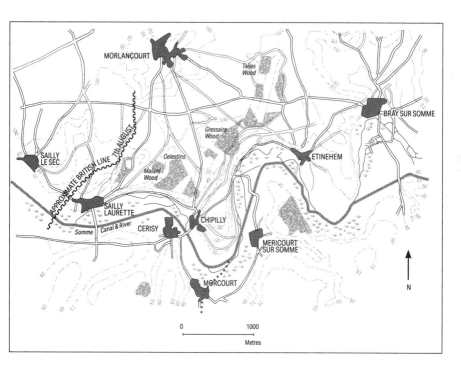

Map of Chipilly Spur, a vast peninsula of high ground bounded
by the Somme River and Gressaire Wood to the north.

INTRODUCTION

On 9 August 1918 at Chipilly Spur on the Somme River, six Australians carried out one of the finest, yet least known, feats of arms in Australian military history. The 'Chipilly Six' were Company Quartermaster Sergeant Jack Hayes, Sergeant Harold Andrews, Privates Billy Kane, George Stevens, Richard 'Dick' Turpin and Albert 'Jerry' Fuller. What these men did was truly remarkable: the six diggers achieved what an entire British corps of 30 000 men supported by artillery and tanks could not, rousting the Germans from their positions on the heights of the spur. Their intelligence, bravery and initiative settled the outcome of the Battle of Amiens – one of the most decisive battles of the First World War.

There is an old saying that the generals are the first to write the history books. In the case of this story that is true. Commanding officers, including Lieutenant-General John Monash, were quick to take the credit for what happened at Chipilly Spur and the Chipilly Six were largely forgotten.

In 1919 Monash was the first to write an account of the capture of Chipilly Spur. In a statement in the London *Sunday Times* spruiking his new book, *The Australian Victories in France in 1918*, Monash claimed Chipilly Spur was captured on his orders by the 131st American Regiment and the Australian 13th Brigade, 50th Battalion.[1]

Monash's claim provoked an immediate reproach from Captain RJ Martin, former adjutant of the 2/10th London Battalion, whose D Company, led by Irishman Captain Jack Berrell, played such a prominent part in the battle, capitalising on the crucial gains first made by the Chipilly Six. In a letter to the *London Times*, Martin took aim at Monash:

> Sir John Monash was very unfortunate in [making] quite untrue statements regarding the capture of Chipilly Spur ... It was bad enough having the British press during the war joining in the eternal chorus of praise of the work of the Colonial troops. It is still worse when an eminent Australian general, who had not troubled to verify his data, makes untrue statements and false charges about our divisions. We all know that the Australians and Americans won the war, but surely credit should be given for any minor successes won by English troops.[2]

Martin referred Monash to Berrell's citation in the *London Gazette* in February 1919 for the award of the Distinguished Service Order, second only to the Victoria Cross, which credited the 2/10th London Battalion with the capture of Chipilly Spur.[3] According to the citation, Berrell 'signalled to the assaulting troops, and leading the remainder of his party over the spur, established himself at the final objective' – which the Chipilly Six had already captured!

Unfortunately, Martin mistakenly referred to Berrell as Captain Beneer, thereby adding more whitewash to the names of the men who were actually there.[4] The mistake is understandable. At the time of the Battle of Amiens, the 58th London Division had just been brought up to strength. It consisted mostly of conscripts and experienced officers drawn from various units across the British Army. Berrell, usually a lieutenant in the 7th Battalion, Royal Fusiliers, was transferred to the 2/10th Battalion on the eve of the battle. Two weeks after the fight for Chipilly Spur, Berrell was gassed at 'Happy Valley' near Peronne, and took no further part in the war. It is unlikely that Martin had met him.

The tone of Martin's criticism fuelled a tempest of letters. Some in favour of Monash returned fire on Martin, others agreed with Martin. The publicity was all good for Monash. He returned a desultory barrage in reply to Martin's criticism, but did not press home a counter-attack. He was content to let the story sell his book.

The controversy quickly made its way to Australia via the cable service. In January 1920, local newspapers in major towns and cities around Australia ran articles quoting Martin under the headline 'Attack on Monash, English Defended: Who Took Chipilly?'

In December 1919, Frederick Cutlack, assistant to the official war correspondent Charles Bean, wrote a response to the newspaper controversy in which he corrected English, American and Monash's accounts of the capture of Chipilly Spur. In an article entitled 'Chipilly Spur … Clearing Up Discussion', and in a chapter in his subsequent book *The Australians: Their Final Campaign in 1918*, Cutlack gave honour where honour was due and acknowledged the Chipilly Six. The story of their epic raid behind enemy lines had gone through the lower ranks of the AIF like wildfire. Cutlack described Jack Hayes' patrol as 'sheer daring adventure'. He politely suggested that Monash had his spurs mixed up, and that Monash's comments 'allude rather to the capture of Etinehem Spur … than to the Chipilly Spur incident'.[5] This was the next ridge to the east, which fell with little resistance to Australian and American troops fighting under Monash on 10 August 1918. The damage to the German defence of the Somme had already been done at Chipilly.

The English Captain Martin's contempt for Monash's snub is understandable. The 58th London Division suffered around two and half thousand casualties in the fighting on 8 and 9 August 1918.[6] In 1926, senior officers of the 58th London Division commissioned the French artist Henri Désiré Gauqué (1858–1927) to sculpt a memorial to the division in the village of Chipilly. The site was chosen because the Battle of Amiens was the fiercest fighting the Londoners endured on the Western Front, and the memorial trust committee, headed by Major-General Frank William Ramsay, the divisional commander, believed the capture of Chipilly and Chipilly Spur was the division's proudest achievement of the war. Carved in white marble and featuring a soldier cradling his dying warhorse, the memorial is one of the most memorable on the Western Front. It stands almost exactly where Jack Hayes, Harold Andrews, Billy Kane, George Stevens, Dick Turpin and Jerry Fuller led Captain Berrell and his Tommies (as English soldiers were known) into the village under fire. By following the road north from the memorial – the Rue d'Etinehem – to the crest of the spur, the battlefield visitor will be in the footsteps of the Chipilly Six and Berrell's men.

The real issue over who took Chipilly Spur was that neither Monash's book nor the published histories of the 58th London Division corrected the record by acknowledging the Chipilly Six. Monash, who seldom went near the front, can be excused for not knowing anything about the role the Six played in the capture of Chipilly Spur, but his assertion that the spur was captured under his orders is wrong. Martin was right to criticise Monash on this point, but the histories of the 58th London Division (III Corps) were equally flawed for omitting the Chipilly Six.

The history of the 2nd City of London Regiment includes the following statement taking credit:

> Then, in a flash, the situation suddenly changed. The 2/10th Londons ... succeeded in clearing the village [of Chipilly]. Having gained a footing on the southern end of the spur, they began to clear out the machine-gun nests on the terraces that had so long delayed the advance of the Brigade ... by 11p.m. the ridge was ours.[7]

The US 131st Regiment records did note the presence of the Australians. Dale Van Every, in his history *The AEF in Battle*, wrote that American infantry of 'Company K of the 3rd Battalion' attacked through Gressaire Wood and

> Joined the 10th London Battalion in renewing the assault ... The Australians down on the Somme gladly joined ... and climbed the steep slopes from the south to assist in stamping out the machine guns.[8]

Twenty-two American soldiers received gallantry awards of various kinds for their role in the capture of Chipilly Spur.[9] The commanding officer of the United States Army 131st Regiment, Colonel Joseph Sanborn, a sixty-two-year-old veteran of the Spanish-American War and the Mexican border wars, was awarded the Distinguished Service Order – the first given to an American in the war. Corporal Jake Allex, also known as Jake Allex Mandusich, a Serbian-American of Chicago, Illinois, working alone captured a machine gun and fifteen prisoners after killing five Germans with his bayonet and the butt end of his rifle. For his bravery in Gressaire Wood, Allex earned the Congressional Medal of Honour.[10]

In his after-action report, Colonel Sanborn wrote that the Americans could not have captured Gressaire Wood were it not for 'a British detachment [which] mopped up the town of CHIPILLY, captured about 300 prisoners and the machine-gun commander … and his guns along the ridge.'[11] This was the Chipilly Six leading Berrell's Londoners. Most German accounts confirmed that the capture of Chipilly Spur was due to an outflanking movement from the south.[12]

But Jack Hayes did not receive the Victoria Cross to which his former platoon commander, Lieutenant Bob Traill, thought he was entitled. Colonel Bertie Stacy, who was not with the battalion at the time, signed a recommendation for the Distinguished Conduct Medal for Hayes and Andrews.[13] This was the second-highest award for gallantry a soldier from the ranks could receive. There is no evidence of bitterness in any of the Australian records that the Victoria Cross was not recommended. Did Stacy recommend the lesser award because he had a strained relationship with Hayes, and because the stunt originated while Hayes and Andrews were absent without leave, souvenir-hunting in the midst of a major battle? The response of Jack Hayes' close friend, Sergeant Archie Barwick, is illuminating. On 4 September 1918 he wrote:

Heard last night that one of my greatest cobbers Jackie Hayes had been … recommended for the D.C.M. for a fine piece of work he did, captured nearly 80 Germans single handed & quite accidentally for Jackie true to the old days went souveinering [sic] in Chipilly the village that held the Tommies up … there will be no one more pleased than I if Jack gets this for he is a splendid chap & he has been badly treated by the Military.[14]

Hayes' citation commended his 'great gallantry, initiative and devotion to duty'. The Chipilly Six were officially credited with the capture of seventy-one prisoners and nine machine guns.[15] These figures were quoted in Bean's *Official History*, but Harold Andrews did not accept them. He believed there was a 'discrepancy in the official reports', representing the number of walking wounded prisoners, and stretcher-cases 'not taken into account'. Not to mention the unknown numbers killed or wounded as the Six bombed their way through the German dugouts and fired 'from the hips' as they ran across the spur.[16]

A worthy comparison with Jack Hayes is Sergeant Alvin York, United States 328th Infantry Regiment. In the midst of a major battle in the Meuse-Argonne a couple of months later, on 8 October 1918, York and a few men captured a similar number of men, machine guns and ground as did the Chipilly Six. York was awarded the Medal of Honour, French Croix de Guerre and Legion of Honour, the French Médaille Militaire, the Montenegrin Silver Médaille pour la Bravoure Militaire and Italian Croce al Merito di Guerra, making him the most decorated American soldier of the war. York also had several books and a Hollywood movie made about him.[17] American historians and public memory-makers embraced the god-fearing Sergeant Alvin York. Yet recently, Australian historians – and the institutions that shape public knowledge of the war and the extraordinary part played by Australian soldiers in 1918 – have been far less inclined to celebrate the absent-without-leave, souvenir-hunting larrikin Jack Hayes and his mates, in favour of more orthodox and often high-ranking heroes like Monash.

For the award of a VC, the action must be witnessed by an officer. At Chipilly that would have been the Londoners' Captain Berrell, and no doubt his note commending the men 'for their conspicuous work and magnificent bravery with me to-day' led to such medals as were awarded. It seems too that Britain's political leaders and generals needed a victory by English and American troops. The diggers and the Canadians claimed they were doing the lion's share of the fighting and complained, as the Chipilly Six's officer Bob Traill did, that 'in the papers there was no mention of the Aussies' work, but plenty about the dash of the blasted Tommies!'[18]

A few days after the capture of Chipilly Spur, the correspondents Charles Bean and Keith Murdoch went to see generals Birdwood and White. They wanted to trigger some action so that the diggers would get full credit publicly for what they had done and were still doing. Bean's biographer, Dudley McCarthy, wrote that 'Both felt bitterly that this was not happening.' They met an unfavourable reception; White, a well-respected and high-ranking Australian, believed that the British people needed the stimulus of the present success and that the matter of credit to the Australians was a lesser one. The fact that the AIF was doing so well with so few men was embarrassing when viewed alongside the failure of the English III Corps to capture Chipilly Spur on 8 August 1918. Bean and Murdoch also worried privately that Monash sought personal fame rather than credit for 'the magnificence' of the ordinary digger.[19]

Was Jack Hayes robbed of a VC? Had Monash known about the Chipilly Six and acknowledged their action, it would have taken nothing away from his stature to acknowledge them. Indeed, it would have been the crowning glory of the AIF's achievements in 1918 – a fitting tribute to the initiative and skill of the digger at the peak of his powers.

*

This book tells the story of the Chipilly Six's role in the Battle of Amiens north of the Somme River. I have been able to recreate the battle through first-hand accounts written by members of the Chipilly Six, private papers held in archives in Australia and Britain, AIF records in the Australian War Memorial, and official records including AIF enlistment papers and Repatriation Department files in the National Archives of Australia.

While the events of one hundred years ago might seem like 'ancient history', they are not to anyone interested in Australian culture or history. It is also not 'ancient history' to the children and grandchildren of the Chipilly Six, some of whom contributed to this book. When families tell and retell the stories of their ancestors, important dynamics shift. Memory takes on new and different meanings with each retelling. Some of the most important stories of the past are coded in silence. I asked the daughter of one of the Chipilly Six, 'Do you know how your dad earned his gallantry medal in the First World War?'

She replied: 'He told us he got it for polishing the officer's boots.'[20]

I could not accept that these men's lives had fallen through the gaps of our history or that their life stories only merited an obituary in a newspaper. I found a wealth of sources, stories, artefacts, photographs and memories. The Chipilly Six were born into the economic depression of the 1890s, saw war, a pandemic (the Spanish flu), experienced the Roaring Twenties (some more than others) and the Great Depression. The Second World War took their sons to new battlefields, and some of the Six would fight in that war too.

Also of note are the significant roles women played both in these men's lives and more broadly. This needs to be acknowledged, and I have done my best to honour these women.

This book corrects many previous versions of what happened at Chipilly Spur. It aims to bring to life what these quintessential larrikin diggers could not put into words. This is the story of the Chipilly Six and how their families have lived with their legacy.

PART ONE
THE SIX

CHAPTER 1
JACK HAYES

Jack Hayes – Jackie to his friends – was born in Hay in country New South Wales and grew up in Bathurst. The Hayes family traces its ancestry to Cork, Ireland, where Jack's great-grandfather once removed, Sir Henry Brown Hayes, had been a knight and sheriff of the city. But on 22 July 1797, the family fortunes took a plunge. Sir Henry was arrested for the abduction of a wealthy heiress named Mary Pike in an armed hold-up of the type bushrangers like Ben Hall made famous in Australia. Twelve eminent judges, once Sir Henry's peers, condemned him to death. The sentence was commuted to transportation for life to New South Wales on 4 September 1801.

Sir Henry became the wealthiest convict in the colony. He built Vaucluse House (now one of Sydney's 'living museums') and gained notoriety as the founder of the colony's Freemasons Lodge. By most accounts, he was the bane of Governor King's life and a suspected incendiary of the Castle Hill Rebellion of 1804 – the greatest battle between Irish convicts and soldiers of the Crown on Australian soil. Hayes served his time in New South Wales at Vaucluse House and with stints at Norfolk Island and Coal River (Newcastle), where the most troublesome convicts were sent. He returned to Ireland by ship in 1813, surviving a shipwreck off the Falkland Islands. He has since been the subject of many books and articles, but Frank Clune's *Radicals, Ruffians & Rebels of Early Australia* supplies the most appropriate adjectives to describe his wild and mercurial life.[1] According to Clune, Hayes' motto was *Erin Go Bragh* – Ireland forever.

In 1879 Sir Henry's great-grandson, Ottiwell John Shaw Hayes, Jack's father, migrated to a very different Australia. Most of the family money was gone (not all because of Sir Henry's indiscretions). Ottiwell, known to his Aussie mates as John, set about forging a new life in a new land of opportunity. He married Blanche Louisa Rogers, the daughter of a hotel manager, in October 1892 in the town of Hay on the low-lying saltbush plain of the western Riverina. Eight children followed. Jack, christened John Charles Ottiwell Hayes, the second eldest, arrived on 12 June 1895. The Hayes family managed the Bridge Hotel on the Murrumbidgee River, and later the Black Horse Brewery in Hay.

Brewing was in the blood on both sides of the family. Much of the fortune Sir Henry inherited came from his father's brewing interests in Cork. Blanche, who grew up on the goldfields in central Victoria, knew how to handle the shearers and bushmen who frequented the bar. But the boom years of the gold rushes had already passed when Ottiwell arrived in Melbourne in 1879, and in the 1890s gave way to an economic depression. The shearers' strikes and drought meant fewer workers and less business at the hotel. The family faced bankruptcy. They moved to Bathurst, a small inland city with big ambitions. The hardworking John and Blanche recovered. John got work as a clerk for the railways and accountant for the *National Advocate*, the Labor-leaning daily newspaper whose title declared the city's goal to be the capital of the newly federated Commonwealth of Australia. The family lived on the corner of Piper and Havannah streets (today the Railway Heritage precinct). Their neighbours included a young engine driver named Ben Chifley, a future prime minister of Australia. Jack went to the Superior Public School, where he enjoyed compulsory military training and sports.

The constant coming and going of locomotive traffic, the shunting of goods carriages and the steam and ash clouds of the coal-fired engines were a feature of Jack's boyhood. A career in the railways seemed inevitable. A railway job was 'akin to joining the services, with its strict hierarchy of different ranks, its own disciplinary code and its requirement to remain on duty each day until stood down'.[2] The politics of the engine yards were familiar, too. The Hayes family were Australian nationalists and dyed in the wool Labor people. Like many of that era, that did not prevent them also being committed to the British Empire. The *National Advocate* reported on 9 September 1912 that Jack finished 'a close second' in the highly competitive British Empire League rifle-shooting competition: 'Hayes had particularly bad luck, a rain squall, which almost obscured the target, coming up just as he was firing his last shots.'[3]

Just before the war, Jack and his older brother Harry got work at the busy railway workshops at Eveleigh, near Sydney's Redfern station. The Hayes family left Bathurst for 23 Margaret Street, Enmore. Jack started as a shop boy and was quickly promoted to railway engine cleaner. By this time, John and Blanche's family had grown to eight children. The terrace house on Margaret Street still stands today, though Enmore has become more of a middle-class suburb. The Hayes family crammed into the narrow two-storey home, making provision for their youngest boys, Noel and William, who were still babies; their school-age children, Eileen, Ottiwell and Charles; and their eldest daughter Isabel. In summer Jack and Harry slept outdoors on the narrow veranda. The economic future of the family was tied to Jack and Harry's career prospects. A job in the railways offered the best means for a working-class lad to achieve advancement. The Eveleigh workshops were the biggest in the Southern Hemisphere and introduced Jack to the world of men, union loyalty and blue-collar work. The cleaner was a type of apprentice to an engine driver, the typical job progression being shop boy, cleaner, fireman, then driver.

The war interrupted all that.

*

Two days after war was declared, Jack went to Victoria Barracks and enlisted. Harry enlisted soon after. Jack would later tell his son that he enlisted for the adventure. Harry, on the other hand, had run into trouble with the police. He faced a charge of 'affiliation' and might have joined the army to avoid gaol. Jack was a good horseman and hoped to join the Light Horse, but was told they had enough men. Perhaps at five feet seven inches (170 centimetres), he was considered too short. In August 1914, class and physical dimensions still played a part in recruitment. Jack found himself in the 1st Battalion: the 'Pride of the Line', as he would call it for the rest of his life.

A photograph of Jack and friends in uniform in August 1914 shows a fair-haired youth of nineteen, cigarette in hand, leaning on an improvised mess bar under canvas at

Kensington Racecourse. Beside him is a bottle of beer and a double-barrelled shotgun. Signs behind the bar read, 'Man with wooden leg wanted to mash potatoes' and 'Leave your guns at the BAR'. He also left a girl in Bathurst who called him 'Micky Dripping' – a reference to his Irish ancestry. But he never told her that he fancied her, and she married while he was at the war.

Tough physical training and a military drill in Egypt followed before he landed at Gallipoli on 25 April 1915 and was wounded shortly afterwards – 'a little shrapnel in the knee'. From the Second General Hospital, Mena House, beside the pyramids, Jack wrote to a friend in Bathurst:

> I suppose you have heard about our baptism of fire … They seemed very wild at us for paying them a visit so early on a Sunday morning, but our boys did not seem to mind them in the least. I happened to stop a bit of their Turkish delight … The doctor said he will let me go back to Gallipoli as soon as some of the others are ready. The hospital will drive me off my head if I have to stop here long. Fancy only stopping in the field for 5 hours! Hard luck, eh. I'll bet I stop there a bit longer next time.[4]

He did. He was back in the trenches in May – reassuring his mother in a letter that he felt 'as lively as a cricket again', and had been promoted to lance corporal.[5] He fought at Lone Pine, which his friend Sergeant Archie Barwick described as a 'frightful battle … our boys & the Turks lay 3 & 4 deep, & on top of these we had to fight for our lives'.[6] Jack remained on Gallipoli until the evacuation and left the peninsula a corporal.

He was promoted to sergeant in July 1916 when the battalion was at Vignacourt in northern France on their way to attack Pozières. Jack was twenty-one and already a veteran. He kept a diary in which he laid bare his attitude on the eve of the battle: 'Feeling confident but a bit shaky continue this after the push.'[7] When the battalion went over the top that night, Jack organised five men who had been separated from their units in no man's land. The patrol headed for the second German trench system. They 'encountered 33 square heads … had a little scrap … we stuck one [with a bayonet] who was giving a bit of cheek [and] took the rest [prisoner]'.[8] He admitted to a case of shell shock at Mouquet Farm in August 1916, which he reckoned he managed to sleep off.[9] He kept up his diary throughout 1916 and 1917. By the time of the Chipilly 'stunt' in August 1918, he was one of only a few dozen original men left in the battalion, and had either given up writing or his 1918 diary has been lost.[10] 'Originals' like Jack Hayes were the custodians of the battalion's fighting spirit and ethos. After Pozières he wrote: 'our people … stuck it like the old boys'.[11] This was a reference to the standards set at Gallipoli.

In September 1916 Jack was promoted to company quartermaster sergeant, equivalent to colour sergeant. The job came with responsibility for supplies and stores. It was also an exalted rank that traced its history to the eagle-bearers of the Roman legions.

Despite his soldierly qualities in the firing line, Jack was often in trouble with superior officers out of the trenches. His diaries record several direct confrontations with officers, mostly the result of his independent spirit being bound to the cogs of the military machine. The most serious cases brought him before his commanding officer, Colonel Bertie

Stacy. The two seldom saw eye to eye. Jack once went over Stacy's head and demanded to appear before the brigadier over a perceived injustice regarding leave.[12] Jack's close friend and fellow original, Sergeant Archie Barwick, remembered a parade when Hayes was missing: 'Most of us knew he was down in a little quiet restaurant but no one else let on so the parade had to be dismissed.'[13] Jack wrote of the incident, 'Had a good night at Lilly's', and followed it with 'Lilly got her … smacked'.[14]

A favourite poem of his was 'Luck or Pluck', which ends with the lines, ''Tis pluck that attains not luck that gains / She gives to the man that dares'.[15] Jack Hayes lived in the moment; he labelled most of his adventures 'stunts' at the expense of the 'mindless supervision of the parade ground'.[16]

He had many adventures. One took him and some friends to Amiens; the trip began with cigarettes and six bottles of champagne and ended with seven weeks in a convalescent camp. Jack called it mumps, but his official file called it venereal disease. While recovering in a camp of AIF incorrigibles, he read letters from men in his battalion at the front. They told grim tales of the fighting at Demicourt, Boursies and Bullecourt. Jack told his diary:

21 April 1917: Tucker not too good down here.
Often wish I was back with the Battalion.

23 May 1917: Got a letter … asking me to come back [to the battalion] (toute suite).

24 May 1917: Am going to keep quiet and see if I can get out of here. Just beginning to get sick of it.

25 May 1917: Bn [Battalion] still getting a rough time. (Fate sent me here.)

26 May 1917: I wish I was out of here. Thinking of the good times we [the battalion] used to have.[17]

On 29 May he was declared fit for active service and left hospital. He was offered a relatively safe job as brigade quartermaster sergeant. He refused it in preference to returning to the battalion, his home. When he got there, he found 'a lot of new faces', but when he met up with old friends whom he called the 'remnant', he 'made up for lost time'.[18] Archie Barwick described Jack Hayes as 'a fine chap and a great cobber', 'seething with humour'.[19] Jack's wartime diaries are laced with examples of his wit and irreverence. The Prince of Wales, he wrote, 'cannot ride much'. He described shellfire as 'No Bon for Soldats', and wrote that the rats preying on corpses in the mud at Hill 60 'appeared to mobilise in our rear, but never launched an attack'.[20]

Perhaps the most penetrating study of Jack Hayes is a photograph taken in a French café behind the lines. In it, four Australian friends, including Jack, are raising a toast. Three are in uniform but Jack is dressed as a civilian and looks like a Frenchman. Impersonating a civilian was a punishable offence in a war zone in the British Army. Had the military police or his commanding officer seen him, Jack would have been in serious trouble. The cheeky look on his face indicates he was willing to take the risk.

Jack seems very much the Australian volunteer: a soldier in the line and in camp, but doing whatever he pleased when away from his responsibilities. When C Company went into the line during the battle of Menin Road in September 1917,

Hayes organised the parties carrying water and rations to the front. Despite the barrages, the rations got to the men, usually under his supervision. At the end of a tour at Zonnebeke, the battalion pulled out 'badly shaken by four days of shellfire'.[21] The men were so exhausted they 'could not have gone another twenty minutes' when Jackie Hayes met them with a stew, tea and rum.[22]

The diggers looked up to Hayes, and the officers respected him because he made the most of bad situations. He had learnt bookkeeping from his father and kept meticulous records so that all men got what was rightly provisioned to them. But he also 'salvaged' the things that made life comfortable and memorable. Jack Hayes did his best to make sure that C Company lived off the fat of the land. Ex-diggers at the Marrickville Anzac Memorial Club told his son John that his dad was a legendary souvenir-hunter and salvager. He would 'slip out' of a route march to shoot a few pheasants then hop a lift to the next town and hand over his quarry to the company cooks. After a trip to Amiens, he returned with a garter to decorate the company cooker. Even a piano for the sergeants' mess was not beyond his remit.

At Strazeele during the German spring offensive in April 1918, Jack showed the knack that separated the great quartermaster sergeants from the others. The German advance had been so swift that the locals abandoned their farmhouses. Their kettles were still hot when the Australians arrived. Salvaging parties made the most of it. Jack 'sniffed out' half a dozen cooked chickens hidden in a chimney. When the Australians arrived with 'nonchalant reassurance': '*Fini retreat madame, beaucoup Australians ici.*'[23] Many fleeing Frenchwomen, their children and old people (the younger men were away at the war) returned quickly to their farms only to find their livestock and larders had been raided by the diggers – including the chickens.

Some diggers went to great lengths salvaging far and wide. A similar event is recounted in the diary of Lance Corporal George Godfrey. A group of diggers made themselves at home in a quaint Flemish farmhouse believing it had been abandoned. They set a tablecloth and cutlery for a three-course meal: 'Cabbage and carrots, mashed potatoes and pork with pancakes and jam to follow.' Everything was arranged 'as tastefully as we mere men could do' and the diggers were about to sit down for their meal when suddenly an old woman, the farm owner, arrived on the scene.

The diggers greeted her courteously, 'little dreaming that it was her own place'. They invited her to join them for dinner. Lance Corporal George Godfrey wrote:

> The old lady could speak good English and proved herself not without a sense of humour …
>
> I said, 'Madam we don't always live like this.'
> She replied, 'No. Only when you pinch it.'[24]

Jack Hayes possessed that blend of charisma and leadership that regular armies covet in their fighting ranks. He was far too independent to be constrained by parade-ground discipline or orders. A man who lived in the moment, and dwelt very little on the future beyond defeating the enemy. The first rule of a company quartermaster sergeant's responsibilities is 'get the job done'. If the men in the frontline needed equipment, water, food, ammunition, or leadership – there was no time to ask whose job it was. Hayes got the job done.

CHAPTER 2
HAROLD ANDREWS

Most of what we know about the capture of Chipilly Spur comes from an after-action report and maps made by Jack Hayes and his five mates, and a descriptive letter written by Harold Andrews to Charles Bean, which Bean used poorly in the *Official History*. Harold Andrews is remarkable among diggers' sources because besides his letter, which is a blow by blow account of the Six's adventure, written with a laconic turn of phrase, he also kept a wartime diary (1916–17) and collected numerous war souvenirs, artefacts and photos. After the war he continued to write about his war experiences well into his old age – sometimes in the margins of a dog-eared copy of the 1st Battalion history, and also for the Hastings River Historical Society. His writing is completely free of ego: honest, humorous at times, and sometimes sensitive and full of pathos.

Harold Dudley Andrews was the son of dairy farmers William and Elizabeth Andrews, who owned the property Coleraine on the Hastings River in New South Wales. Harold came from a long line of staunch Ulster Presbyterians on his father's side. His mother, born Elizabeth White but known as Bessie, was the granddaughter of a convict transported to

New South Wales for stealing a pair of shoes when he was only a boy.

When Harold signed up in July 1915, aged eighteen, he needed his father's permission. The sum of his material possessions was a horse, a saddle and a bridle, one heifer and £46 in the bank. He went to Liverpool training camp in Sydney with his cousin Norm Way of Beechwood, and his mate Austin Edwards of the Upper Hastings River. They called themselves 'the boys from the bush'. Harold reckoned he took to army life 'like a duck to water'. The strict, sober discipline of his Presbyterian upbringing prepared him for the rigour of army life and respect for authority. He accepted orders and later he would give them. Dairy farming had interrupted his schooling, but the church and his teacher, Mr Hooper, encouraged in him a love of books. As a schoolboy he read biographies of Ulysses S Grant, Gordon of Khartoum and Robert the Bruce, King of the Scots. In the army, he sought to emulate his martial heroes. He excelled in shooting and consistently scored 'the possible' on the rifle range. Unlike some diggers, he enjoyed the spit and polish of the parade ground. In Egypt, his commanding officer made him an orderly, a privileged position that meant Harold got to ride around the camp with the officers on well-kept, well-fed Arab horses and the finest Walers – the colloquial name for the legendary Australian-bred warhorse – while his mates slogged it out digging trenches and latrines.

Harold kept a war diary in 1916 and 1917, but stopped writing in 1918. His early entries are full of observations of the world and youthful wonder at 'how the other half lived'.[1] Sailing through the Suez Canal in February 1916 to join the 1st Division in Egypt, he laughed at the dark-skinned local boys who dived under the ship to collect pennies wrapped in silver foil tossed by Australian soldiers. He and Norm flirted with Aussie nurses at the top of the Pyramid of Cheops and enjoyed the kisses of French peasant girls at train stations as the Australians travelled through the Rhône Valley in 'box compartments' – ten men in full marching order to a compartment, marked for the Western Front.

In the frontline, Harold became a sniper and scout. He and Billy Kane took part in the battalion's first raid on the Western Front. Harold had the job of laying the fluorescent tapes to guide the raiding party to and from the objective. He was in no man's land for two hours, tangled in barbed wire under terrific machine-gun and shellfire before he finally got out by 'liberal use of wire clippers'. Afterwards he counted seven bullet holes in the tape reel he was carrying. Harold described the raid as 'fairly successful'. He did his fair share of patrols and listening posts in no man's land.

The attack on Pozières began at 12.28 a.m., Monday 23 July 1916. That night and the following day, Harold crossed no man's land nine times. He described carrying

> … Mills Bombs by the box-full, water in petrol cans (1-gallon size) two soldiers to 'the carry' in battle order to the forward line and then back again through that inferno – having to IGNORE the piteous call for the stretchers that were non-existent … the victims were weltering in their own gore. 'Get me in, Cobber?' … begging – 'a drink' … all had to be ignored.

Harold was shot in the chest but 'did not notice'. He carried on until around 9 a.m. when 'a huge "coal-box" … struck down sixteen of us in one burst'. A 'coal-box' was soldier slang for a 5.9-inch (14.5-centimetre) shell. The shell blast broke his leg and riddled his lower body with shrapnel. 'There I stayed, with others, until 3 p.m. on the Tuesday.'[2] Tommy stretcher-bearers carried Harold and his mates through a heavy barrage; the concussion of the shell blasts rendered Harold unconscious. He learned later that both of his bearers were wounded during the carry. The bearers on the stretcher in front of his were killed, and 'their patient had his leg blown off'.

> I was unconscious for nearly an hour & was brought
> round by the liberal use of water & brandy. Good old
> 'Mac' [William McKenzie MC – the famous fighting
> chaplain of the 1st Australian Brigade and hero of
> Gallipoli] – was doctoring me, after bringing me to
> he pulled out my pipe, filled it and lit it and then
> helped me into the motor in which I was taken to the
> [casualty] collecting station.[3]

At Stoke-on-Trent War Hospital, Staffordshire, he spent 'a lonely feverish night'. His temperature soared to 40 degrees Celsius. His mate Bob Abel, a London-born labourer of Galong, a pretty farming village between Harden and Boorowa in New South Wales, lay dying in the cot next to him. Bob's mother and two sisters raced from London to be at his bedside. All night they sobbed while Bob suffered.

Harold thought of his mother at Coleraine and worried 'Is it my turn too?' When morning came, Bob had died, but a nursing sister leant over Harold and 'nearly kissed me'.

'You've made it, boy!' she whispered. Harold wept. In the hospital in 'Blighty', the nurses called him boy or babe.[4]

Then came the telegram from Coleraine and an anxious mother's enquiry through the Red Cross: 'How are you?' It was reply-paid. 'Convalescent. Love to all,' Harold responded.[5]

Harold spent the summer in brilliant sunshine at Weymouth Convalescent Camp. His best mate and cousin, Norm Way, now a corporal, wrote from France with news that their cousins Colin and Bill Graham had been reported killed in action. Norm was still with 12 Platoon, C Company, under Platoon Sergeant Jack Hayes. 'I hope and pray the rumour may be false,' Norm wrote, 'but er [sic] have been a good many tight corners to get out of, since coming to France.'[6] The rumours were true. The Graham brothers fell within a week of each other. Colin died in the disastrous 5th Division attack at Fromelles – the bloodiest day in Australian history – and Bill in the Light Horse charge at Romani in Palestine. The 'furrows of pain' are with the Andrews family to this day. Harold's grandson, Peter, sobbed at the 'memory' of the tragic end of Colin and Bill Graham. Peter never knew them. The trauma had been handed down through the generations.

Harold's wounds were severe and he hoped to be sent home to Australia, but it was not to be. Some sixteen months later he returned to the frontline. C Company was at Anzac Ridge, Passchendaele, in a sea of mud. Harold wrote in his diary, 'The guns roared all around us … I am not quite as nervy as expected after my long spell.' He quickly earned promotion to corporal. Lieutenant Albert 'Eddie' Edwards, Harold's platoon commander, reckoned he could not have had a better NCO: 'for there is a vast difference between giving and taking orders, particularly in the frontline'.[7]

Harold represented C Company in rugby union. He played as a flanker (also known as a breakaway) on the edge of the scrum. Just before the Chipilly stunt, he scored the winning try in a tough match against A Company to decide the holder of the Silver Bugle, the coveted 1st Battalion sports trophy. Lieutenant Bob Traill described Harold's try as 'a beautiful run'. The match ended 3–nil (in those days a try was worth three points). Traill reckoned most of Harold's mates blew 'every brass razoo' celebrating C Company's win.[8] The Australian War Memorial in Canberra holds the Silver Bugle in its collection.

In the spring and early summer of 1918, the war was fought in fields of crops and woods, crossed by ditches, streams and sunken roads, which were old roads that over the years had become so worn down they sat much lower than the land on either side of them, offering useful cover to soldiers. The German offensives had swept through the forlorn cratered landscapes of 1916–17. Stimulated by the opportunities the landscape presented for cover and camouflage, a few Australian infantrymen went into the crop fields alone or in small teams of trusted mates to surprise, kill or capture Germans, often without orders and in broad daylight. Lieutenant Bob Traill regarded Harold as one of these unique and daring men, having watched him stalk and bayonet a German sniper in a cornfield who had infiltrated between the Australian outposts.[9] Harold recalled that German bullets twice dented his helmet during his daring raids.

On the morning of 11 July 1918, a handful of men from the Chipilly Six's 1st Battalion captured 120 Germans, including three officers and eleven machine guns, before their own headquarters or the German headquarters were aware of it, for the loss of three men. Bob Traill wrote, 'Today is a great day in the history of the battalion … one quite unprecedented in the war.' The war diary of the British XV Corps artillery stated that artillery fire was suspended because 'no one knew where the Australian infantry had gone on their marauding expeditions'. A digger wrote:

The Tommies next door just sat and watched. They had no orders to go out – our boys had no orders not to go out, just the difference.[10]

The British Second Army infantry training school invited Harold to give a talk on the tactics the Aussie stealth raiders were using. Years after the war, Harold wrote that his lesson was 'well received' by the officers and men of three famous English and Scottish divisions.[11]

The action at Chipilly Spur would be the supreme stealth raid of the war.

By 1918, Harold was a highly skilled professional digger: intelligent, conscientious and brave, with demonstrated leadership qualities and tactical skill. Seven days before the action at Chipilly Spur, he was promoted and held the distinction of being the youngest sergeant in the history of the battalion. His grandson keeps two photographs of Harold that tell a story of his big war. One, a portrait postcard taken in late 1916 or early 1917 in Wareham, Dorsetshire, shows Harold after his stint in hospital following his wounding at Pozières. He wears the familiar slouch hat and ill-fitting AIF uniform. He has dark brown hair and bright brown eyes and looks purposeful, but not rigid like a parade-ground soldier. His face has the softness of youth but his eyes seem sorrowful. Then there is the photo of Harold and his cousin Norm on Paris leave in March 1918. Harold strikes a cold figure, straight and lean, square jawed. His purposefulness matured as resolve. One still senses sadness in his eyes. He is twenty years old in the latter photograph. Harold wrote that he had learnt that war was about killing – 'You or me. As simple as that'.[12]

CHAPTER 3
GEORGE STEVENS

George Stevens was born in Young, New South Wales, on 19 March 1891. His father, Henry Stevens, was one of twelve children born into a successful settler family in the Oaks area near Camden, New South Wales.[1] The Oaks (named after the native casuarina) had been prime farming country ever since the first colonisers crossed the highlands south of Sydney in search of rich pastures. By the time Henry Stevens was a young man, there were fewer opportunities to take up land around the Oaks, but plenty of jobs in railway construction as the railways extended to keep pace with settlement and to satisfy the booming Sydney market's demand for fresh produce.

Henry took a job as a fettler and bought a small cherry farm at Pitstone, near Young – a town that has become famous for its cherry festival. At the turn of the last century, Pitstone was thriving because of its closeness to the railway siding at Young. In 1889, the Borough of Young installed the first electricity supply to homes in the Southern Hemisphere. It might have seemed to Henry that he was destined for a prosperous future. He met Emeline Sheather, daughter of a sheep farmer of Rye Park in the southern tablelands, and they married in December 1889. Emeline was a slight woman of average height with brown hair and blue eyes that George inherited. She had little formal education, but was an able bushwoman, practical and active. When George was born in March 1891, Emeline kept her newborn son in clothes she had sewn herself. The little fellow had not been around long when Henry died suddenly, aged twenty-nine. The coroner's report found that he died of natural causes. He left three horses worth £35, four sets of harness (£10), one sulky (£8), cash in a savings bank (£30), and land at Penrith (£160): a total of £243 to cover debts and support his wife and eighteen-month-old son.[2] Emeline went into domestic service in Young to keep herself and baby George.

Emeline remarried, to Charles Johnson, a farmer from Campbelltown. George went to school at Burrangong Heights Public School outside Young, later renamed Boara School. His favourite subject was maths. His daughter Dorothy remembered George being very good at arithmetic:

> Although he only attended a small school he could
> always do our homework problems in his head and
> say if we were right – even to intermediate standard.[3]

When George was eight, his half-brother Cameron, known to the family as Cam, arrived. Charlie Johnson took up the property Fairview, and the story goes that it was purchased with the proceeds of Henry Stevens' Pitstone property, or that the Stevens' property was inherited by George's stepbrother Cam.[4] Stevens family lore has it that George was 'stiffed' of his father's inheritance. Whatever the case, George left the farm at eighteen and got work as a fettler on the railways at Greenthorpe. When the war began, he was working as a carter for JWT Chant & Co. in Young. 'Chants' was a big general merchant serving the central western district. The company sold everything from bread, groceries and clothes to washing machines and other 'modern household luxuries', to farm machinery and spare parts. George drove a horse-drawn wagon and picked up stock from the railway siding and delivered it to the store, or carted it direct to homes and businesses around Young, sometimes covering thirty miles in a day. The work involved heavy lifting, horse driving, harnessing, a good manner towards customers (and horses) and a fair degree of independence.

On weekends he found time for sport, especially rugby league and cricket. His cricketing hero was Victor Trumper, a gifted Australian batsman of the original 'Golden Era' of Australian cricket. George played for Back Creek, Wambanumbah, and in the local lodge competition for the Odd Fellows.

In the summer of 1915, a cricket writer in the local *Young Chronicle* described George as a 'big gun' with bat and ball. As a batsman, he had a reputation for scoring freely and quickly, mostly 'by good cricket' shots. If he had a flaw in his game, the writer hinted, it was 'opening his shoulders' to chase a ball he meant to hit for six, only to be caught on the boundary. He opened the bowling and took wickets too.[5] There are two striking photos of George at this time, both probably taken on a cricket tour to Sydney where he represented Young. George leans on his bat in a classic cricket pose. Short and nuggetty, he calls to mind many great batsmen blessed with a low centre of gravity, powerful hips and strong shoulders. His face is round, still with a hint of the boy rather than the man. His hair is a soft light brown turning golden in the summer. He looks the paragon of Edwardian cricketing style in his cricket whites: a shirt 'made to fit easily at the shoulders, but not too loosely'. And a scarf around the waist, instead of a belt, 'because it looks better and will grip quite as firmly, and you will not run the risk of being caught at the wickets through the handle of the bat coming into contact with the buckle of the belt'.[6] The second portrait hints that trips to Sydney were not just about cricket: George and a friend recline in a flash sports car for the studio shot. George looks dapper: he wears a single-breasted three-piece serge suit, its coat and vest possibly lined with taffeta or a similar lightweight material; a white panama or cane boater hat; a white turtleneck; a necktie; and a fitted waistcoat with pocket watch and chain. George had style. The two mates are clearly having fun and a bit of a laugh.

It was through cricket that he met his best friend Ernest Hinton. Ernie's sister, Caroline, known as Carrie, became his sweetheart. Most of what we know about George's war comes from the letters he wrote to Carrie during his three years of service overseas.

In 1915, George had a steady job, a girlfriend and a place in the Young First Eleven. He was not too bothered about the war. Then on Saturday 11 December 1915, the 'Kangaroos' recruitment march came to Young. A contingent of thirty volunteers marched through the streets. They had started in Wagga and picked up others in Harden, and a 'great crowd' thronged the town centre to meet them and cheer them on. The streets were 'gaily decorated with flags and bunting'. The marching Kangaroos (who actually arrived by rail) exhorted the spectators:

Coo-ee! Coo-ee! Here come the Kangaroos,
Coo-ee! Coo-ee! And we never get the blues.

And when we're marching home again we'll bring
    the best of news.
Coo-ee my boys, for dear Australia.[7]

In the afternoon, the women of the Red Cross Society entertained the Kangaroos with lunch at the Odd Fellows Hall. Then the little army marched on, its stomach full. Local boys and men rushed out from the packed sidewalks to join them. At the corner of Lynch and Burrows streets, the mayor and several local notables made speeches. The *Young Witness* reported:

> The Kangaroos grouped round the speakers and their
> cry at intervals was 'What do we want?'
> > The answer would be 'More men!'
> > 'Will we get them?'
> > 'Yes!' And so the afternoon passed.[8]

Businesses were closed, which allowed the crowd to swell to 'several thousands'. 'The band struck up a spirited march, and immediately the whole of Burrows Street was one moving mass.' More speeches followed. The mayor presented the Kangaroos with a bugle. The same old men reiterated what had been said 'over and over again as to the need for men'. At midnight the crowd followed the 'marchers' to the station where they boarded a train for Galong and continued on their way, to the cock-a-doodle-do of the steam engine's whistle.[9]

A few days later, the local paper reported an appeal 'To the Boys of Young' written by a soldier in a recruitment camp in nearby Cootamundra:

If there are any fit men around Young, enlist at once, for
we are hard up against it and if the girls of Young have
any boy who is sound and fit, try and get him to come
and help us, tell him to think of Belgium and Servia,
and Nurse Cavell, and if he don't come then cast him
off, and get one in khaki, for that is where the MAN
is found.[10]

George and Ernie enlisted, both aged twenty-four. Carrie saw
her beau and her brother off on the Sydney train. The town
band organised by the Recruiting Association had stopped
playing due to a timetabling problem, so there was no farewell
serenade. Eleven months later, the two friends were in France,
in C Company, 1st Battalion, under Sergeant Jack Hayes.

*

When George and Ernie joined the battalion in November
1916 in the icy, sodden trenches near Flers, the frontline
soldiers met them with callous indifference. It must have felt
a far cry from the excitement of the Kangaroos march and its
promise of greatness. That week, the battalion had suffered
defeat at Flers on the Somme front, and George and Ernie
were replacing dead men. Those heroes of the Dardanelles and
Pozières were still lying out in the barbed wire or submerged
in a slurry of mud at a place called Bayonet Trench.

Bayonet Trench was the severest defeat the 1st Australian
Division suffered during the war. C and D Companies of
the 1st Battalion were practically annihilated. Survivors of
Bayonet Trench struggled to find words to describe it. Bean
called it 'the hardest trial that ever came to them'.[11] Sergeant
Archie Barwick wrote on the anniversary of the battle in

1917: 'I never saw the like of that night neither before nor since & as for mud & rain well don't mention it.'[12] Jack Hayes fought at Bayonet Trench but could not find words for it. The pages of his diary are blank.

The winter that followed was the worst in living memory. C Company struggled to regain its morale and physical strength. New reinforcements were particularly prone to sickness. The shock of trench work took its toll. In December 1916, George was hospitalised with pleurisy. He recovered in time to take part in the bloodiest year the AIF endured on the Western Front. George and Ernie fought in all the battalion's major battles – at Hermies, Demicourt, Boursies, Bullecourt and Le Transloy. George wrote home often, sending postcards of historical places and memorable landscapes: Table Mountain, Cape Town; the Houses of Parliament, London; Paris Quay and Saint Catherine Hill, Rouen; and Le Havre.

George's postcards to his little brother Cam are full of encouragement and boyish interest: 'How is the cricket going over there, I suppose you will be a gun before long?' and 'Knock up a good score.' When he wrote to his mother it was generally 'Just a line to let you know [I'm] all right' or 'I'm doing pretty well, but I will be glad when the winter is over'. He wrote of the usual things that concerned frontline soldiers: food, the weather, interesting places, and the mindless numbing routine of parades and route marches. Sometimes his dry humour colours his writing, as when an officer ordered George to be a marker on a rifle range: 'About 200 rifles shooting about 2 feet over your head all day and dirt and sand getting blown on to your head it seems a bit off at times.' He saved his longest letters for Carrie. He sent her colourful postcards, portraits – 'not very good' but 'might remind you of me' – souvenirs and war trophies taken from the battlefield.[13] In Young, Carrie visited Emeline often and passed on George's news. Carrie once found Emeline at Fairview with an unopened letter from AIF Base Records Office, Melbourne. Emeline could not bring herself to open it. She feared it was an official notice of the death of her son.[14] Many Young mothers had received such a letter since the Kangaroo March. 'The soldier died once but his mother died many times. She lived in agony from casualty list to casualty list without an hour's respite from fear and dread.'[15]

Emeline was spared that awful letter – but Carrie's mother got 'the death notice' in October 1917. Ernie Hinton was killed on Broodseinde Ridge, near Passchendaele. He was carrying ammunition to the frontline when the Germans 'slung over' a few shells. The diggers scattered and made for their dugouts. Ernie was the only man who did not make it.[16] Only the ploughshares of Flanders know where his body lies. After the Battle of Broodseinde Ridge, Jack Hayes wrote in his diary: 'Up to … eyes in mud. Many of the old boys gone.'[17] Ernie Hinton is named on the Menin Gate at Ypres.

George Stevens bore the burden of writing about Ernie's death to Carrie and the Hinton family. His health suffered again, and he spent the winter of 1917 as he had the previous one, sick in hospital in France, this time suffering from scabies and a septic wound in his leg. He did not return to the fighting line until June 1918 – just in time to witness, or perhaps take part in, the epic unauthorised stealth raids by men of the 1st Battalion near Merris that had so much in common with the extraordinary stunt at Chipilly Spur.

When the 1st Battalion marched back to the Somme to join Monash's Australian Corps and take part in the Battle of Amiens on 8 August 1918, George was serving as a stretcher-bearer.

CHAPTER 4
JERRY FULLER

His army mates knew Albert Hessel Gordon Fuller as 'Jerry', probably because Hessel sounded German.[1] Private Jerry Fuller, regimental number 7082, did not keep a diary that we know of, nor did he write a memoir of his war. What we know about him comes from the battalion war diary, attestation papers held by the National Archives of Australia, and stories passed down to John Hayes by his father Jack. The war photos of Jerry in this book come from Jack Hayes' collection. John grew up listening to the stories of his dad and Jerry and the old diggers at the Marrickville Anzac Memorial Club in Sydney. He learnt that before the Chipilly stunt, the veteran Hayes and the youthful Jerry were not particularly close, but afterwards became 'great mates for life'.[2] Jack's photo collection includes a studio portrait of Jerry after his return to Australia in 1919, aged about twenty, in AIF uniform, the Military Medal earned at Chipilly pinned to his chest.

Jerry enlisted in Cootamundra, New South Wales, on 17 May 1916 – which he claimed was his eighteenth birthday – after a previous failed attempt to enlist in Sydney. Of medium complexion, with brown hair and brown eyes, at five feet two and half inches (158.75 centimetres) he was well short of the official height requirement. According to the doctor who examined him, Jerry's eyesight was good but less than perfect, although it never seemed to bother him – he was a gun cricketer. His profession was tailor. When he enlisted he had five years' experience in the trade, including an apprenticeship with Evans & Colin of Alexandria, Sydney.

Tailoring was in Jerry's blood. His mother, Emily Fuller (nee Dive), was a dressmaker. Emily Dive was born in Newtown in working-class inner Sydney, the third generation of her family to grow up and work in the neighbourhood. She had a tough upbringing. Her father, who could never hold down a job, would come home 'speechless drunk' and hold an axe to Emily's mother's head. He died in an infirmary when Emily was young. Emily and her mother and sisters survived the depression of the 1890s because of their skill with needle and thread, and by selling garments to the 'Calico Jimmies' who owned the factories and warehouses.

Jerry's father, William 'Sonny' Fuller, was a hairdresser from Woolloomooloo. He and Emily married in Sydney on 30 January 1896. Their first-born son, William Roy, also served in the AIF; Jerry was their second child, born in Woolloomooloo in 1898. Shortly after Jerry arrived, the family moved to Dubbo, possibly because Emily's mother had moved there. It was a move beset with tragedy. In 1900, just days after giving birth to a daughter named Leonie, Emily died from 'acute capillary bronchitis' and 'failure of the heart'.[3] Sonny, with Roy aged three, Albert aged eighteen months and newborn Leonie, returned to Sydney by train to his parents' home at 25 Pitt Street, Waterloo. Emily's body was probably on the same train. William laid her to rest at Rookwood Cemetery, Sydney. A month after Emily's death, little Leonie died too.

Jerry and his brother were raised by their grandmother, Matilda Fuller. She was a tough old woman who'd grown up in Waterloo and seen the area change from billabongs and rich alluvial flood plains bursting with gum trees, banksias and flowering shrubs, waterbirds and kangaroos, to a hive of industry – 'the Birmingham of the south'. Natural springs that once fed wetlands ran like sewers and the toxic fumes of industry fouled the air. Boot factories, tanneries, fellmongers, bone mills, tallow refineries, a smelting works, wool washing and scouring companies, chemical works, and soap and oil factories belched noise and pollution into the air, leaving a thick smog smeared across Sydney's otherwise brilliant blue skies. Hundreds of smaller industries also moved in: foundries, bakeries, dairies, market gardens, brickworks and more than 200 shops and businesses, including Sonny's barber shop.

The Pitt Street home was a crowded two-storey terrace house that was the hub of the large Fuller clan. The boys slept in the attic on iron cots or on the slim veranda in summer. The toilet was outside. Another aunt and uncle lived next door, separated by a large cobblestoned area connected to the horse stables of the family omnibus business. The stables were entered through a back lane of cobbled brick, which was always slippery because the family washed their horse-drawn cabs there regularly. The horses and stables were a place of joy and fascination for Jerry and Roy and generations of Fuller kids.[4]

In 1904 Sonny married Louisa Catherine Swift. He took his sons and his new wife to Cora Lynn, a small brick rental cottage in Belmont Street, Alexandria. Jerry's first half-brother, Mervyn, was born in 1907, when Jerry was nine. A second half-brother, Harold, was born in 1912 and a half-sister, Louisa, in 1915. With three extra mouths to feed, Roy and Jerry had to pay for their keep. Roy got a job as a clerk. Jerry took up his apprenticeship as a tailor with Evans & Colin. When the war began, the boys were still in their teens and anxious to join the AIF.

*

Roy signed up on 5 January 1916, aged nineteen. He fought with the 13th Battalion until wounded on the Somme in August 1916 (shrapnel in his back). In hospital in England, he suffered fits of 'depression', 'maniacal excitement', 'epilepsy' and 'mania'. He went absent without leave and was court-martialled. In September 1917, a medical board recommended he return to Australia and be discharged from the army as 'medically unfit'.[5] In November 1917, Roy returned to Sydney and was admitted to Broughton Hall, a convalescent hospital for shell-shocked soldiers. That same week, Jerry joined C Company, 1st Battalion, in the ruined village of Ypres as it prepared for the battle of Passchendaele.

C Company commander Burt Withy, a merchant of Mosman, Sydney, was looking for a new batman. Fuller, a tailor who knew a bit about hairdressing and grooming horses, was ideal. The diggers had a way of looking after lightweight boys who had just arrived in France. Being an officer's batman could potentially spare the young boy the rigours of trench warfare until his body adapted and he learnt a few things that might help him survive – for a while, anyway. Withy was a dependable frontline officer and a demanding company commander. Under Withy's command in 1917–1918, C Company became the most competitive and motivated company in the battalion. It repeatedly won the Silver Bugle – the fiercely contested intra-battalion trophy for sports, musketry and drill competitions. In the frontline, Withy pushed his officers hard to maintain discipline, vigilance and the killing edge. Such drive was the mark of a good commanding officer, but it often led to resentment among the platoon officers and NCOs charged with seeing his orders through. The Chipilly Six's platoon commander, Lieutenant Bob Traill, complained in his diary:

> I don't know whether Bert Withy thinks we are an Army Corps or not, but last night (and the working hours these nights are only from 10.30 to 3.15) he wanted 2 men put on a listening post on the railway line, and have them changed every hour, complete digging the trench for the platoon post; send out a patrol of 4; send 2 fatigue parties up to C.H.Q. for food; and send 3 parties up for wiring and working materials, wire the platoon front, start digging sleeping possies and keep sentries in the trench all the while, with men to relieve them. As he told me I didn't quite realise [the difficulty of finding men for the jobs], afterwards it struck me all of a heap. I'll have a bit of his ear tonight, the dirty dog.[6]

But the battalion commander Bertie Stacy liked Withy's 'energy and administrative drive' and 'devotion to duty in and out of the line'. Stacy recommended Withy for the Military Cross, citing the 'splendid example' he set 'to all ranks by his coolness and disregard of danger'. Traill commented that the 'Old man must have been in a generous mood'.[7] A busy company commander like Withy meant that his new batman Jerry Fuller was destined to see a lot of action.

At Passchendaele, Withy placed his headquarters behind the crest of a position known as Anzac Ridge. Harold Andrews, then a corporal, wrote in his diary that the ridge 'simply trembled & rocked with the concussion' of bursting shells. The 'scream and crash' was 'enough to wake the dead … it cannot be described in words'.[8]

When the battalion was relieved from the frontlines on 10 November 1917, Jerry had been a digger in France for twenty-one days, nineteen of them beside Withy in one of the greatest battles of the twentieth century.

CHAPTER 5
BILLY KANE

Billy Kane faced danger and adversity from the day he was born. Like many working-class men of the 1890s generation, the war was just another of the struggles and hardships of life. He was born three months premature in a wagon accident beside a muddy goldfields road in Victoria in 1893. His mother, Ellen Kane, was being taken to the Castlemaine Benevolent Asylum at the time. In a small town like Muckleford on the goldfields of central Victoria, she was a perplexing and disturbing woman. The local papers delighted in describing her as 'simple', 'weak-minded' and 'a lunatic'.[1] She was frequently arrested for vagrancy and wandering, and often physically and sexually abused by men who took advantage of her being destitute and vulnerable. Ellen lived much of her short life in asylums and prisons, giving birth to two further 'illegitimate children' before her untimely death in 1922.

Billy spent his first years in the care of his widowed grandmother. The Kanes were Irish Catholics who had come to Victoria during the gold rushes. Billy's grandparents, David and Ellen Kane (nee Smith) married in Rutherglen in 1862. They had three children, though only Billy's mother (Ellen) survived. In the 1870s, David Kane took up a selection in South Muckleford, near Castlemaine. The local newspaper described them as a 'respectable and well-known' family.[2]

But in 1880 things took a turn for the worse. David killed a man in a savage bar fight, beating him over the head with the butt end of his whip. (A few old stones beside the Muckleford creek are all that remain of the old pub today.) A court found David Kane guilty of manslaughter but recommended mercy on the grounds of provocation.[3] Thereafter, bad blood followed David Kane and his wife in the tight-knit community, and the local paper reported on their feuds and misdemeanours in detail. The behaviour of their daughter Ellen unsettled their neighbours. When David died suddenly in 1889, aged fifty-eight, both his wife and daughter fell into poverty. David's widow sold their two-roomed weatherboard house with its new iron roof, together with one bay mare, one steer, two calves, about two tons of hay and two small sacks of oats. The old grandmother with her dependent daughter and little grandson pleaded for help. The Castlemaine Benevolent Society took in her daughter and the weary grandmother took in the premature baby boy. Billy's grandmother said of baby Billy, 'the child was not as big as your boot'.[4]

Billy Kane attended the Muckleford School (now the South Muckleford Hall – Kane's name is mentioned on the First World War Honour Roll) and was taken under the wing of a local philanthropist and teacher, Miss Rose McDonald of Campbell's Creek. Miss McDonald was a member of the Benevolent Asylum Board. She gave Billy additional tuition and introduced him to other children in the district. But there was not much prospect of further schooling for a poor Irish Catholic lad. It was probably Miss McDonald or her connections in Castlemaine that found Billy a job as a roustabout on a surveying team working on the east coast. Billy worked his way north, first through the forests of Gippsland, then up into the red cedar country of the Macleay River, before settling in Congarinni, a small timber and farming town on the Nambucca River on the mid north coast of New South Wales.

Billy found work as a teamster and sleeper-cutter in the ironbark forests of the Nambucca. Timber-getting gave men with no capital a chance at an independent life. He worked for piece rates for 'the timber king', Allen Taylor & Company Limited. Taylor, a prominent Sydney businessman and politician, had shipping and timber interests along the eastern seaboard. In the years before the war, the New South Wales government began a major railway construction project on the north coast, and Allen Taylor & Company were contracted to supply 250000 railway sleepers. Taylor paid hundreds of bushmen like Billy Kane 3 shillings and 9 pence to 5 shillings and 4 pence per sleeper.[5] The timber-getters worked alone, or in teams in isolated bush camps. The forests rang with the sound of their broadaxes and crosscut saws and the cries of the teamsters hauling logs. Billy loved the timber-getter's life. It prepared him for the rigours of army life, but the independence, skill and speed that were the virtues of the timber-getter often placed him at odds with the machine-like drudgery of parade-ground drill.

When the war began, Billy Kane was in work, on a contract that was not likely to end soon. He was also enjoying the life of a young man involved in competitive sports such as rugby league (he was known as a 'fine forward') and wood-chopping – the highest calling among bushmen of the Nambucca. It took the reports of casualties from Gallipoli to convince Billy and his mates to enlist. On 13 August 1915 the *Nambucca and*

Nambucca wood-chopping competition, c. 1913.
Billy 'Cobber' Kane, bare-chested, stands on the block nearest the
camera. Second from right, also bare-chested, is Kane's mate, Silas
Cook, who enlisted and served in the 1st Machine Gun Battalion.

(Courtesy of Trevor Lynch)

Bellingen News reported that the Friendly Societies Hall in
Macksville was 'packed to the doors by friends and admirers'
bidding the boys farewell.[6] There was a supper followed by
speeches in their honour, and songs like 'We don't want to lose
you but we think you ought to go'.

In the crowd was a beautiful young woman with bright
almond eyes and dark red hair, Emma Provost. Emma was the
daughter of a prominent local selector – one of the first farmers

Emma Provost, aged nineteen.
(Courtesy of Robyn Franks)

to take up land when the New South Wales government opened up the country to closer settlement with the legislation of the Crown land acts (the so-called 'Robertson Land Acts') in 1861. Emma's father did not approve of her interest in Billy. Kane owned no property and had few prospects beyond what he could hew with his hands. Emma's family were Protestants; Billy was an Irish-Australian Catholic in an age when the distinction mattered. If it were not for Billy's letters to Emma, kept by the Kane family for more than a hundred years, we would have few insights into his character and experiences on the Western Front.

*

Billy and his mates probably imagined that they would fight the war side by side. That fantasy ended abruptly at Liverpool Camp in Sydney. The huge army camps were unhealthy places. Billy became ill with pneumonia. His mates sailed for the war while he was stuck in an army hospital. Eventually, Billy joined C Company, 1st Battalion, near the French village of Armentieres in the early summer of 1916. (The village was made famous in the wartime song 'Mademoiselle from Armentieres'.) At that time, the Australians were fresh from Gallipoli, but many of the men were new recruits with no battle experience. The only other members of the Chipilly Six serving with the battalion were Jack Hayes, then a corporal, and Harold Andrews.

Billy had about two weeks' experience in trench warfare before he volunteered for the battalion's first raid on the Western Front. It was a night attack supported by a 'hurricane bombardment' of artillery fire. The objective was a German strongpoint near Fleurbaix known as the Water Fort. Five officers and about ninety volunteers, including Billy and Harold Andrews, trained for the raid for several days. The job was to get into the German trench, kill what they could, collect information of intelligence value and return with two prisoners. The raiders dressed in British Army uniforms to prevent the Germans from identifying them, and blackened their faces 'so that they would not show up at night'. Private Thomas Wilkinson, a clerk of Chatswood, New South Wales, went over the top with Billy:

> [We] crept up under a thunderous roar of guns of all calibre, which attempted to cut the barbed wire to let us through. The terrific hurricane of shells burst only a few yards in front of us, the earth shook and trembled, and it was like Hades broke loose.

The raiders found four lines of barbed wire, untouched by the shellfire.

> After kicking and struggling and cutting our clothes and hands to pieces, jumping into three ditches up to the armpits, and struggling out, we eventually reached the German parapet.[7]

One of the leaders, a Gallipoli veteran, was shot as he leapt into the enemy trench. Men used bayonets and bombs freely. Billy captured a German. Afterwards he wrote to Emma, telling her his prisoner 'was very much frightened of me and well he might as I would have fixed him lively'. The German spoke good English and told Billy 'He was going on leave to Berlin the next night' – rotten luck.[8]

As Billy and his prisoner made their way across no man's

land to the Australian lines, all hell broke loose. 'Fritz run amok' with a 'hate' of his own, Jack Hayes wrote in his diary.[9] More Australians were killed and wounded returning through the German counter-bombardment than there were casualties in the raid. Billy told Emma it was 'a pretty rough time ... hell while it lasted'.[10]

On 19 July 1916, Billy and his mates marched to Warloy on the Somme front. Booming guns, shattered villages and blackened bodies told them they had entered the mainstage of the war. This was the battle of Pozières.

For two and half days he dug trenches and carried ammunition under constant bombardment and gas attack. Billy wrote a brief note to Emma: 'Drop me a line whenever you can ... I cherish a letter from you.'[11] He went over the top at 12.30 a.m. on Sunday 23 July. C Company's objective was a second line of German trenches in the village. Jack Hayes and Harold Andrews also went over that night.

The capture of the village cost the Australians 5000 casualties. In the confusion, Kane was reported dead. In Castlemaine and Congarinni the papers wrote that 'many friends ... mourned the loss of a good fellow'.[12] We can only imagine Emma's feelings. Then, in September, she received a letter from Billy reassuring her that he was alive. From his hospital bed in Etaples, France, he described his 'dreadful experience' trench fighting at Pozières:

> Our orders were 'no prisoners and no retreat, do or die' ... A German shot my section corporal, but did not kill him. I measured him and gave him a dose of cold steel. As I was attacking him he shot me in the knee with his revolver.

An officer yelled 'dig for your lives'. Billy threw the dead German out of the trench and picked up a shovel. The diggers expected a counter-attack at any moment. His heart raced because he'd swallowed mouthfuls of phosgene gas and was pumped up on adrenalin. He dug until his wounded knee seized up:

> I fell to pieces … I hopped along as best I could towards the first line of trenches and helped a comrade who was seriously wounded … I got a helmet, a watch, and some money off the German swine who shot me … I am lucky to be alive. It will be some time before I can move about again.[13]

At the First Northern General Hospital, Durham University, he slept in soft linen sheets, took walks in the university gardens and hobbled into town in his hospital-issue blue flannel suit and red tie to meet the locals. Five months later he returned to a joyless battalion in the trenches near Flers and a dreadful winter. He suffered from scabies and persistent ill health resulting from his wounds and the pneumonia at Liverpool Camp. He wrote to Emma less often and with less optimism: 'Don't think it hard when you write so reauglery [sic] that I don't answer … There is very little news here, except war news'.[14] He was beginning to feel like so many other frontline diggers, like 'a race apart'.[15]

A bout of venereal disease saw Billy hospitalised again. It meant he missed the fighting at Bullecourt and Boursies where hundreds of his battalion fell. When he was fit again, he scored a job as a groom, tending to the officers' chargers at 1st Australian Division Headquarters. In the ironbark forests of the Nambucca Valley, he'd worked a team of horses to pull his sleepers from the forest. It was Billy's good fortune that someone in authority knew his skill as a teamster and horseman. The 1st Division received 200 horses in June 1917, many in poor condition.[16] Billy fed them on nosebags, washed and scrubbed them and pegged them out on picket lines or hobbles by night. Most of the work was second nature to him. But the army had some stiff regulations: grooms worked with jackets off, sleeves rolled to the elbows and braces down: 'Quick hard grooming is what is required. A man must put his will and weight into it.'[17] It was a thrilling job, too. He rode big Arab horses and Australian-bred Walers at full gallop, often acting as orderly or messenger for officers. Billy's daughter Phyllis cherishes a striking portrait of her father in his groom's uniform. The portrait is touched in colour; we see the young man as Emma saw him in the letters she opened. He has auburn hair and blue eyes – like his mother. He looks determined and proud. He is tall, five feet ten inches (178 centimetres), and wiry from work in the bush and two years of trench warfare. His uniform is the familiar pea green of the Australian infantryman, with the addition of spurs on his heels and an epaulet on his shoulder to mark him as a man with 'special duties'. He wears his slouch hat, folded at the side, with a sprig of emu feathers, emulating the 'gentlemen of the Light Horse'.

The German spring offensive of 1918 marked the end of Billy's time as a groom. The attack threatened to cut a wedge between the British army north of the Somme and the French army to the south, and turn the British army back towards the channel coast. With their 'backs to the wall', the AIF needed every man who could hold a rifle in the frontline, so Billy returned to C Company as a rifleman and company headquarters runner. In June, he became an early victim of a new, pathogenic and highly transmittable strain of flu. Billy was fortunate that his symptoms were only mild. This was the first wave of what would become the deadly pandemic known as the Spanish influenza.

CHAPTER 6
DICK TURPIN

John Richard 'Dick' Turpin was the oldest of the Chipilly Six, joining up at about twenty-seven years of age – though it is difficult to know for sure as he often changed the date and place of his birth on official papers. The son of a sheep farmer, he enlisted at Cootamundra on 25 October 1916, in the same draft as Jerry Fuller. He stated on attestation that he'd served eight years and three months in the 6th and 12th Light Horse militia regiments, active in the Tamworth/New England area, before being dismissed for drunkenness. He gave his trade as 'labourer', and his next of kin as his mother Annie in Tamworth. Tall, at just under two metres, with dark hair and blue eyes, he was a square-shouldered bushman with a face furrowed by the Australian sun.

However, if he left letters and diaries from the war years, they have not survived, so we know much less of his life before the war than we do of the other five Chipilly men.

On arrival in the UK in January 1917, he was hospitalised with laryngitis and venereal disease. He finally made it to France in August 1917, where he was made a Lewis gunner. He took up stretcher-bearing during the Third Battle of Ypres.

He went absent without leave for six weeks after the fighting at Westhoek Ridge, near Passchendaele, in October 1917, and on Christmas Eve that year he was court-martialled and given a suspended prison sentence of one year's hard labour that would hang over his head for the rest of the war.

At the Battle of Amiens on 8 August 1918, Dick was serving with C Company as a stretcher-bearer. His mate on the other end of the stretcher was Private George Stevens. Perhaps the two men knew each other before the war? Cootamundra is only a stone's throw from Young as far as a bushman was concerned.

PART TWO
CHIPILLY SPUR

MAP OF TROOP POSITIONS AT CHIPILLY SPUR

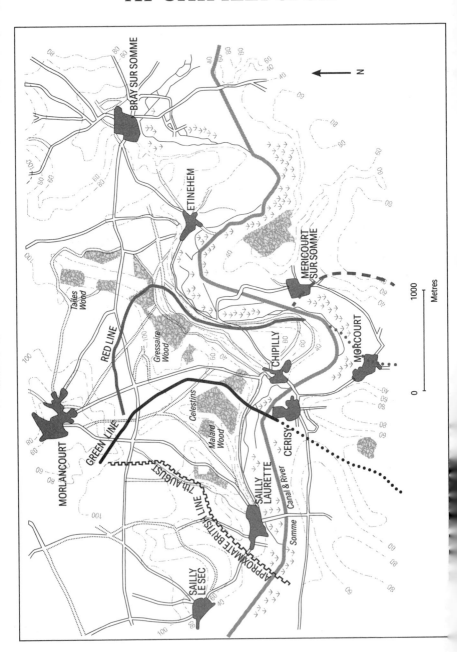

9 August 1918: The Australian Corps had captured its objectives south of the Somme River (marked by the dotted lines). However, the English III Corps, north of the Somme, was still fighting on the so-called 'Green Line'. The 'Red Line', Chipilly Spur, was held by the Germans who fired into the flank and rear of the Australian Corps' advance.

CHAPTER 7
'SOME WORTHWHILE SOUVENIRS'

East of Amiens on 8 August 1918, a huge Allied army comprising French, Canadian, Australian and English soldiers launched a massive offensive aimed at shattering the German army on the Somme. On the first day of the offensive, five Australian divisions advanced eleven kilometres and captured all of their objectives as well as 7925 prisoners and 173 guns.[1] The Canadian Corps on their right made similar gains. Despite this 'brilliant success'[2] marking a 'black day' for the German Army,[3] the Australians, with their left flank pressed against the south bank of the Somme River five kilometres east of Hamel, finished the day under duress. In the English III Corps sector north of the river, the 58th London Division failed to reach its objective: the prominent high ground known as Chipilly Spur, a ridge that rose over the surrounding country running north to south from the Morlancourt plateau to form a peninsula looming over a bend of the Somme. Chipilly Spur was the key to the German defences on the Somme; German artillery and machine-gunners were posted right around its crest. The western terrace was thick with German machine guns that overlooked the 58th London Division assembly area in the gullies and woods.

For two days the English Corps Commander, Lieutenant-General Richard Butler, sent his infantrymen against Chipilly Spur in a series of costly frontal attacks. A British tank battalion was nowhere to be seen, bottomed-out in the treacherous gullies and re-entrants, or lost in the morning fog. Several kilometres ahead of the Tommy infantry, the guns of British III Corps fired a creeping barrage, a tactic that sought to protect advancing infantry by pounding the ground just ahead of them – it required precision on the part of both the artillery and the advancing troops.[4] But the Tommy infantry would never reach the protection the falling shells offered. German machine-gunners on the spur swept them with bullets while artillerymen in the woods poured canister shot over open sights into the massed ranks of Tommy infantry in a scene reminiscent of the Napoleonic Wars. Over two thousand men of the 58th London Division were lost in these futile attacks on a front not much bigger than a few footy ovals.

The Tommies went to ground, allowing the German machine-gunners and artillery on Chipilly Spur to turn their fire onto the flank and rear of the Australian advance south of the Somme River, inflicting casualties, destroying gun batteries and harassing supply lines. A German source from the battle described 'targets in bewildering numbers'.[5] A digger officer in the frontline sent a runner to headquarters with a message that read 'all our tanks ... received direct hits from 77 m.m. Guns firing from Chipilly Spur and were in flames in no man's land'.[6] Another wrote:

The Huns are shelling our batteries from the rear ...
and got 1½ batteries ... he had perfect observation

over our dumps and wagon routes … damn those
tommies.[7]

The battle of Amiens had reached a crucial moment. The
Germans owned the high ground. The diggers feared 'Fritz'
might try to cross the Somme River and 'cut in behind'
the Australian advance.[8] As the light faded on the evening
of 8 August, Lieutenant-General John Monash sought
permission from his commanding officer, General Henry
Rawlinson, Fourth Army, to send an Australian brigade
(nominally 3000 men) across the river to capture Chipilly
Spur the following day.

*

Friday 9 August 1918 was a warm clear day. At around
10 a.m. Company Quartermaster Sergeant Jack Hayes and
his friend Sergeant Harold Andrews left their battalion lines
near the village of Cerisy and went exploring the villages
along the Somme. They were absent without leave from their
battalion. Hayes was expecting to be granted 'Anzac leave',
a newly instituted form of two-month furlough to Australia
(plus travel time) for men who had enlisted in 1914. Harold
Andrews recalled that Hayes 'suggested a stroll' because he
was looking 'to obtain some worthwhile souvenirs' to take
back to Australia. Many diggers were inveterate souvenir-
hunters. German pickelhaube helmets, watches, medals –
particularly the Iron Cross – as well as daggers, Luger self-
loading pistols and everyday items, including alcohol and
cigarettes, were all highly sought as trophies. Smaller articles
like German postcards were sometimes sent home with letters

from the front. But in the fighting along the Somme in 1918 the diggers found several chateaus that were brimming with luxury goods. It is likely that Jack was on the hunt for things of great value.

As they strolled along the Somme they saw rolling cornfields bursting with clumps of bright red poppies and blue cornflowers. Here and there, smashed wagons and dead horses littered the sunken roads. A knocked-out British Mark V tank, its yellow flag hanging listlessly, signalled that the German gunners on Chipilly Spur were good at their work. Dead men, mostly Germans, lay about in lonely stiffened poses or in groups of shattered torsos ripped apart by bursts of shrapnel. Clouds of flies rose from the mutilated corpses. Many of the dead had been prisoners, blasted by their own guns firing from the opposite bank of the river in Celestin Wood and the crest of Chipilly Spur.

Harold Andrews continued:

Hayes and self unarmed, in our stroll discovered a footbridge well to the west of Chipilly, as we were satisfied this village was empty, we crossed at a point about ½ mile from the enemy.[9]

Hayes and Andrews moved cautiously under the shade of the shell-torn poplars – swallows skimmed across the surface of the river in glints of lustrous blue, snapping insects. No shots were fired, so

… we decided to have a close look at the village as it was rumoured that our battalion was to make a crossing at night to capture the village and Chipilly Spur.

Hayes and Andrews had kept their hands free to carry souvenirs, but now they armed themselves with abandoned German rifles and ammunition and 'stalked' a chalkpit north of the village. They heard yelling, turned and saw a group of British soldiers waving at them from the frontline, almost a kilometre behind them. Casually, the two Australians walked back to 'pay their respects'.[10] The soldiers were from the 2/10th London Battalion, which had failed to capture Chipilly, despite several attempts the previous day, and had suffered heavy casualties. That morning they had been reinforced by a hundred conscripts, eighteen- and nineteen-year-olds with no battle experience.[11]

The two veteran Australian sergeants yarned with them for a while then took the footbridge back to their battalion. At C Company, 1st Battalion Headquarters, the atmosphere was tense. The failure of the English III Corps to capture Chipilly Spur was holding up the general advance. Hayes, having just come from the area, volunteered to take a patrol across the river after dinner and occupy the village.[12] The battalion's commanding officer, Colonel Bertie Stacy, was away at a school and Major Alexander Mackenzie was commanding. Mackenzie relayed Hayes' suggestion to the Brigade Commander, Iven Mackay.[13] A quartermaster sergeant was suggesting tactics to a brigadier! But Mackay had word from III Corps Headquarters that the 58th London Division would be attacking Chipilly Spur again at 5.30 p.m., reinforced by the inexperienced United States 131st Regiment. He rejected Hayes' suggestion.[14]

At 4 p.m. the British commenced an artillery barrage as a prelude to their attack, and at 5.30 p.m. the Australians, watching from south of the river, saw American troops 'sweep along the upper part of the [Chipilly] ridge ... and enter

Gressaire Wood'.[15] But nearest to the Australians, the 58th London Division attack aimed at Chipilly Spur and the village did not go well. The German defenders fired into the London infantry as they attempted to advance across the gully between Malard Wood and the slopes of the spur. The objective was almost two kilometres further east, where the high ground of the spur falls sharply to the marshlands of the Somme. But few of the infantry involved in the attack had any idea that this was the objective. Nineteen-year-old conscript Private Bill Gillman, 2/2nd London Battalion, a boilermaker's mate of Stratford, London, recalled, 'We were just told to take the ridge and establish ourselves there because the Somme was on the other side and that was the ... objective':

> Unknown to us there were from ten to twenty heavy German machine guns in emplacements. My God, he really opened up! He let us have it ... He just swept us. I looked round as I was advancing and you could see the numbers of our people melting away, just dropping all around you. Those that fell were shot over again ... There was nothing you could do. It was getting so bad, as I took my steps I thought, 'The next one will be it!' ... I jumped for this big shell hole ... I knew there was no hope of getting any orders because there was nobody to give any. The bullets were hitting the back of the shell hole; it was raining bullets.[16]

The watching Australians quickly realised that the British attack was faltering. It took Mackay only twenty minutes to send a written message to Mackenzie authorising Hayes and Andrews to take a 'strong patrol' across the river to 'see what the position was'.[17] Usually, a strong patrol meant a platoon or platoons (44 to 100 men), and at a bare minimum eighteen men with a Lewis gun under an officer. But Hayes and Andrews had something else in mind, and took just four volunteers.

George Stevens and his fellow stretcher-bearer Dick Turpin knew their NCOs were keen to look for souvenirs in the village, and George was also keen to settle 'a few of my old pals' accounts with the Huns' – no doubt thinking of Ernie Hinton.[18]

Jerry Fuller was in awe of Hayes and Andrews. Although they were only a few years apart in age, there was a vast gap between them in combat experience. Jerry's best mate in the battalion was Billy Kane.

Billy had just returned from hospital after a bout of Spanish influenza. He carried a distinctive limp from his wounding at Pozières, and would celebrate his twenty-sixth birthday souveniring in Chipilly with his mates.

The diggers were ready to go within ten minutes of hearing their sergeant's instructions. They tucked empty sandbags in their webbing to carry souvenirs, threw bandoliers of ammunition over their shoulders – 200 rounds per man – and stuffed their pockets with bombs.

CHAPTER 8
THE SIX 'CUT LOOSE'

At 6 p.m. Hayes led the Chipilly Six over the footbridge under scattered fire from Chipilly Spur. The first British troops they found were remnants of two platoons of D Company, 2/10th Londons, under Captain Jack Berrell, a former carpenter of Glenariffe, County Antrim, Ireland.[1] Berrell told Hayes that his men were held up by heavy machine-gun fire from the high ground along the western terrace of the spur. Berrell was an experienced frontline soldier. He had enlisted in Potchefstroom, South Africa, and served as a private in the South African Brigade during the first battle of the Somme in 1916 before taking a commission in the Royal Fusiliers.

Berrell's orders were to attack the German machine-gun posts on the western terrace of the spur by clearing the village of Chipilly and outflanking them from the south. His battalion commander had arranged for a barrage of smoke, high explosives and Vickers machine guns at 7.30 p.m., under which Berrell was expected to attack.[2] Hayes volunteered the six Australians to act as Berrell's scouts and reconnoitre Chipilly for them.[3] Berrell tried to discourage him because the 2/10th London Battalion had not been able to get a foothold in Chipilly in over thirty hours of fighting. But according to Harold Andrews, 'the village looked good for souvenirs'.[4]

Before Berrell could object, the Six 'tore for the village, through a veritable hail of machine-gun and rifle fire' from the spur above. They spaced their run – each man twelve yards (eleven metres) apart – so that a burst of fire would not wipe them all out.[5] They reached a chateau winded but unhurt, with Berrell's men running after them. They 'souvenired to our hearts' content'.

Then Hayes sent Billy Kane to bring up a British Lewis gun crew. George Stevens and Dick Turpin, who had volunteered as riflemen for the patrol, were sent through the village to look for Germans. Andrews and Jerry Fuller went almost two kilometres north-east 'across country' and reconnoitred the spur to a sunken road that plunged down to the river and the town of Etinehem. While they did that, Hayes watched the German machine-gunners on the western terrace as they fired on the British infantry. When he was satisfied with this reconnaissance, he took Berrell's men plus the Lewis gunners north up the spur to a position near the quarry he had explored that morning. It was an excellent position to fire into the flank of the German machine guns.

It was just before 7.30 p.m. and still daylight; the time is known because it was then, 'promptly and effectively', that the British barrage in support of Berrell's advance commenced, landing practically on top of the six Australians and Berrell's men.[6] The fire was intense. Smoke shells shrouded the spur in a veil and rounds from the Vickers guns cracked overhead, so close it was obvious the British machine-gunners had mistaken them for the enemy.[7]

The Tommies began to withdraw, but the battle discipline of the Australians held. Hayes and Andrews decided to use the smoke as cover to creep around the southern crest of the spur and outflank the German posts on the high ground, effectively isolating the German machine-gunners on the western terrace by cutting them off from their flank and rear.

They slipped through the long grass into dead ground. Jerry Fuller and Billy Kane followed, leaving Dick Turpin and George Stevens near the village. Along the crest of Chipilly Spur, German machine-gunners peered into the smoke, waiting for the English to attempt another frontal assault, unaware that the six Australians were creeping around their southern flank. About one and half kilometres ahead of the nearest friendly troops, Hayes and Andrews saw a German post above the sunken road leading to Etinehem. They shouldered their rifles. Both were first class shots.[8] Andrews 'often thought' his 'initiation in ... sniping' came from boyhood on the family farm at Wauchope and that military training turned his skill to what he called 'deadly purpose!'.[9]

Both men 'cut loose' with their rifles, then got into position to rush the post. Fuller and Kane yelled like madmen and stamped their feet to make it sound like a whole army was coming. Andrews fired down the length of the German post, while Hayes crept down the sunken road. Then Hayes attacked, firing and yelling as he charged up the embankment. He practically fell into a small post he had not seen. A German fired at him point blank. The bullet singed Hayes' tunic but he was not hit; he killed the man and captured two others. He dragged his prisoners back to Andrews, Kane and Fuller, and together they 'fled for the chalk pit' two kilometres to the west on the other side of the spur, where Turpin and Stevens had brought up Captain Berrell and the Londoners.[10]

They found Berrell and the two platoons of D Company 2/10th Londons talking about what to do. Andrews told them to advance 'before [the] smoke lifted'.[11] The Australians opened the breeches of their rifles to allow them to cool. Then the Six took off again on the run across the spur. The III Corps and Australian Corps artillery were pounding the area. Some Australians watching the battle from the southern side of the river acted on their own initiative. Infantry in Cerisy turned around a battery of German 5.9-inch (14.5-centimetre) field guns and were firing them at the German positions on the spur, adding to the firepower of the guns.[12] Lance Corporal Charles Deitz, 1st Battalion, watching from the south bank of the Somme, called the outcome 'a wonderful and appalling sight'.[13] He did not know that six Australians were pressing close to the barrage, outflanking the Germans on the high ground. Andrews recalled how he and Turpin were 'hurled down like straws' several times by the concussion of their own shell bursts.[14] But they had experienced the worst of shellfire in 1916 and 1917 and become skilful at reading it: 'an experienced man can tell when a shell is going to fall very close by the sound it makes in the last few seconds of approach'. At Hazebrouck in 1918, Hayes had laughed (and cursed) at shellfire and had actually gone into a barrage to guide less experienced men to safety.[15] He had also bandaged his wounded mate Archie Barwick and carried him to a service wagon bound for a field hospital, then returned through the shellfire to recover Barwick's diaries. That was a fine thing too, because Barwick's diaries are the most quoted source in Australian films and literature related to the First World War.[16]

On Chipilly Spur they pushed close to their own barrage because it had a force and momentum of its own. The concealing smoke was their greatest ally and they knew the Germans would be dead, cowering or retreating from the force of the explosions. The six pushed further down the sunken road, collecting German 'potato masher' or stick grenades from posts that had been annihilated by the shellfire. They bombed several 'German dugouts and posts into silence' as they passed.[17]

They saw some Germans running into a heavily armed post about twenty metres above the sunken road. Hayes decided to attack.[18] He skilfully divided the patrol. Two men approached the post from a flank and two from the rear, then 'rushed in for bayonet work'.[19] The Germans were utterly surprised. They expected a frontal assault from the British who were still the best part of two kilometres away. They did not expect to be assailed by four men apparently coming out of the ground. The result was panic. The German garrison fled for a dugout, leaving seven machine guns. Hayes persuaded them to surrender by detonating a German stick grenade at the dugout entrance. A German officer and 31 soldiers came out with their hands up, crying for mercy.[20] Turpin and Stevens rushed in with their bayonets to dissuade the Germans from changing their minds.

The prisoners were handed to a 2/10th London party, which had followed the six Australians on Andrews' instructions.[21] The prisoners were 'marshalled' into the sunken road 'just as the smokescreen rolled away', leaving clear visibility for hundreds of yards.[22] Some Germans could be seen retreating towards the village of Etinehem and across the Somme marshes.[23] Fuller and Kane pursued them while Andrews brought a captured machine gun into action and opened fire. Fuller and Kane took off down the slope and got behind the Germans, shooting down some and bringing in nine more prisoners. Just then, Andrews' machine gun jammed. He brought another gun into action and kept firing while his mates cleared out more German stragglers and captured a further two machine guns.[24]

Andrews' fire also encouraged the rest of Berrell's men to advance in the wake of the Australian patrol. A 2/10th London sergeant, Herbert Darby of Ipswich, Suffolk, led a party and mopped up some machine-gun posts completely cut off on the western terrace by the Australian outflanking manoeuvre.[25] Simultaneously, American troops began to advance out of Gressaire Wood to the north. The Americans 'tore into' the Londoners, the Australians and their prisoners with Lewis guns.[26] All dived for cover. Hayes reported that when the Americans finally caught up they were 'greatly surprised to see them as they did not know anyone except the enemy was ahead of them'.[27]

This marked the moment when the Allied high command's objectives in the Battle of Amiens were completed. Hayes' six-man patrol had completed Berrell's job of capturing Chipilly and outflanking the hostile machine-gun posts from the south, and the entire III Corps objective of capturing Chipilly Spur (the Red Line). The six Australians captured a further twenty-eight prisoners during mopping up and consolidation. Then, according to Andrews, they

> … rested up awhile, smoking Hun cigarettes, kindly offered by a onetime Hun waiter in a London hotel, who wanted to know what was his chance of getting to England. He also informed us that the ridge [Chipilly Spur] was at 2 p.m. that afternoon manned by about 360 men with about 30 guns, most of which were collected afterwards. The enemy at this point had held out for about 30 hours against repeated attempts to dislodge them.

The Chipilly Six were in action 'or had the enemy in view close up for about 4 hours and did not receive one injury'.[28] At 9.30 p.m. Captain Jack Berrell handed Andrews a note, 'glowing in terms', which recommended the six Australians 'for their conspicuous work and magnificent bravery with me to-day'.[29] Andrews remembered that Berrell 'distinctly said' that the spur was taken by the six Australians before D Company 2/10th London Battalion came up.[30]

The six then strolled back to their battalion on the other side of the river, taking 28 prisoners with them and leaving the rest for the 2/10th London Battalion and the Americans.[31]

That evening (9/10 August), British III Corps belatedly agreed to Monash's proposal for the Australian Corps to cross the river. At around midnight, Monash's orders reached the frontline. The 50th Battalion crossed the Somme at 3 a.m. under a heavy mist to find Chipilly Spur captured.[32]

Afterwards there would be investigations and recriminations as to how Fourth Army headquarters could agree to the boundary of the Australian and III Corps being a river dominated by the Germans on the spur. Lieutenant-General Butler of III Corps was relieved of his command.[33] For all the advances in Allied command and control in 1918, the generals and staff still had a capacity to make appalling decisions that cost men's lives. The Chipilly Six saved lives. Harold Andrews remembered the German positions on Chipilly Spur were 'heaped' with empty shell cases 'indicative of the terrible fire that crumbled all frontal attacks for over a day'.[34]

The following morning, 10 August 1918, Private Bill Gillman, the nineteen-year-old conscript of the 2/2nd London Battalion who had survived the costly headlong charges of his battalion on 8 and 9 August, climbed Chipilly Spur with the remnant. Only fifty-one men in Gillman's battalion answered the roll call out of an ordinary strength of around 1100 men. Gillman recalled:

> We knew we'd just been slaughtered … we had just been made up to strength … [with] a lot of kids, it was their first action and they never knew any more. They never had a chance to see what the war was like …

> … [The German machine-gun posts] were about ten or twelve yards [11 metres] apart, dotted right along the length of the top of the ridge. You could see them, you know, squares, dugouts, cut right out of the top of the ridge … and when you were up there you could look right down on the Somme flowing down below … I remember the first gun pit I looked at … they were all heavy machine guns … They never stopped firing at us – belt after belt because the bloody cartridge cases were piled up in a heap.[35]

There were bodies lying about. In a machine-gun post overlooking the Somme, Gillman saw

> … a Jerry down there, still sitting up … and a red handkerchief over his head and I pulled the handkerchief away … it was just as if a butcher's knife had cut him clean from the centre of his head right down to the neck … I put the handkerchief back just out of respect for the man although it didn't matter … Action over.

Shortly after the fighting at Chipilly Spur and the battle at Froissy Valley less than two weeks later, George Stevens wrote to a mate in Young:

I have been having rather an exciting time lately, only a bit risky … I had the best day's shooting I ever had in my life, and don't forget I settled a few of my old pal's [sic] accounts with the Huns. I shot something like a dozen straight out, besides a lot more we got between us and were not certain who got them. I was fairly mad when I got mixed up with them, and run in to bayonet a Hun straight off the reel, but the yell he gave and the hands went up, I couldn't do it. It was 'some stunt'. I have been mentioned in dispatches twice now in the last two stunts [Chipilly and Froissy Valley] but I don't know if anything is going to come of it … I am satisfied I can go through after last time. A Hun fired point blank at me and missed. What do you think of that? He didn't get a second shot, though.[36]

Besides two mentions in dispatches, George would be awarded the Military Medal for his 'daring and valuable' work in the capture of Chipilly Spur and at Froissy on 23 August 1918.[37]

Platoon commander Lieutenant Bob Traill spoke to the Chipilly Six a few days after the capture of Chipilly Spur, 'in the blazing heat of the day':

It's good to see them all again and have a crack. My Sergeant Andrews, Q.M. Jack Hayes, Fuller and a couple of stretcher bearers distinguished themselves in capturing 47 Huns and 27 M.G.'s on their own. It is quite an epic. The Tommies were to have a second attempt at Chipilly and these 5 [sic] went over, whilst they were talking about it, went round the flanks and did the trick. The way they worked it was very clever and the Tommy Captain nearly fell on their necks and kissed them. Undoubtedly they took the position for them and the Captain admitted it. But in the papers there was no mention of the Aussies' work, but plenty about the dash of the blasted Tommies! The Captain was good enough to take their names … Hayes deserves the V.C. and Andrews the D.C.M. and Jerrie Fuller.[38]

But Jack Hayes did not get a Victoria Cross, nor the accolades he was entitled to.

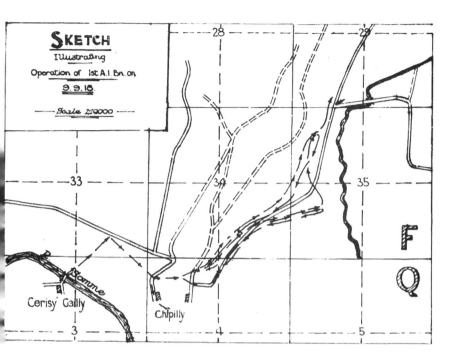

Hand-drawn map made by the Chipilly Six showing
the route taken on repeated trips across the spur.
(Note the cartographer has incorrectly dated the action.)

PART THREE
FROISSY VALLEY

CHAPTER 9
THE CHIPILLY SIX'S LAST BATTLE

After the Battle of Amiens and the capture of Chipilly Spur, the Allies chased the withdrawing German army eastward. On 23 August 1918, Jack Hayes, Billy Kane and Jerry Fuller were wounded when the battalion attacked in the Froissy Valley. Jack Hayes was expecting to go home on Anzac leave any day, yet had volunteered to lead his old 12 Platoon in the attack.

Harold Andrews remembered 23 August 1918 as a 'sad day'. Some of the heaviest fighting in the dawn attack occurred on the extreme left flank, close to the Somme River, where C Company, and in particular Jack Hayes' 12 Platoon, lost some of its finest soldiers. As well as Jack, two other Gallipoli veterans, Lieutenant Vic Fowler and Sergeant Jimmy Lynch were severely wounded. Corporal Norm Way – Harold Andrews' cousin and best mate – took command. Harold wrote that Norm was killed 'rallying the remnant of his platoon only twenty yards from their objective behind a tank which missed the MG position'. George Stevens, who had distinguished himself at Chipilly Spur with Hayes, ran to Captain Burt Withy's company headquarters in a sunken road behind the battlefront with a message that 12 Platoon had been decimated. Withy turned to Harold Andrews and said, 'Go forward and see what you can do.'[1]

The objective was a line of ridges, intersecting spurs and small woods on the opposite side of the Froissy Valley. The valley ran from the sheer-sided slopes of the Froissy plateau immediately south of the Somme River in a generally southerly direction through the villages of Chuignolles and Chuignes. Harold led the remnant toward its objective in rushes while Lewis gunners gave covering fire. As they moved from cover to cover, a German anti-tank gun on Froissy Beacon at the northern end of the valley hammered away at them. To add to Harold's problems, German machine-gunners and field guns in the woods to his left, and enemy snipers hidden in railway yard buildings in the valley, caught C Company in a wicked crossfire.

The diggers took cover behind fallen logs and began a sniping duel. Then some British Mark V tanks intervened, firing their cannons into the German machine-gun posts in the woods and grinding enemy dugouts with their churning tracks. The 1st Battalion war diary noted that 'Those resisting were killed; others attempting to escape were shot down, and this had the effect of reducing many to submission and surrender'.[2]

Harold and a handful of men entered a small wood and captured an enormous 15-inch (38-centimetre) naval gun and about 70 prisoners. The enemy anti-tank crew on Froissy Beacon saw the large group of prisoners and took them for Australians. Harold said many of the prisoners were 'blasted down' by their own guns, 'mistaken in the dust and smoke for us! Such is war!' But fortunes turned against the Australians. Allied artillery shells began to land on them, causing casualties.

The survivors of C Company withdrew across the valley to the forward slope of a hill in front of the village of Chuignolles to avoid the friendly fire.[3] When the ground was retaken later, the 3rd Battalion (AIF) were credited with capturing the naval gun, which had been firing on Amiens. But Harold always insisted it was he and a group from the 1st Battalion who were the first to capture the gun and take the prisoners.[4]

At midday, Hubert Wilkins MC, the Australian official photographer who carried his camera into infantry fighting in 1918, took a picture of Burt Withy's C Company shortly after the action as they rested in a sunken road.

It is a rare portrait of the Australian in battle. Harold Andrews sits with his elbows resting on his knees and his back to the embankment. His sergeant stripes are clearly visible and he looks lean and athletic. Captain Burt Withy is two places to his left. Around them sit riflemen, stretcher-bearers, and other headquarters details. Several wounded men lie under blankets. Are the other members of the Chipilly Six in this photograph? The men look grim. They had just been told they would be going over the top again in a few minutes.

The orders for the second attack arrived so late that there was no time for detailed orders or preparation, and no tanks. At 1 p.m. an Allied creeping barrage in support of the attack commenced. Harold and the men in the photograph leapt to their feet and raced after the barrage. They retraced their advance of the morning, through the railway lines and buildings in the valley floor, and climbed the slopes of the ridgeline to the east. The German anti-tank gun on Froissy Beacon caused many casualties. By 3.30 p.m. Harold and the remnant were on the heights of the spurs east of Chuignolles. From the ridge, Harold watched fresh men of the 9th and 11th Australian infantry battalions leapfrog his weary men.

The Queenslanders and Western Australians scaled the steep slopes to the plateau and finally captured the anti-tank gun that had caused C Company so much trouble. By 5 p.m. the high ground belonged to the Australians. The outcome of the fighting was a brilliant success for the Australians. Bean called it 'the hardest blow ever struck by the AIF in France'.[5]

The fighting on 23 August was yet another example of the initiative and skill of the Australian Infantryman in 1918, and how fortunate Monash was to command them.

Harold wrote:

> [The dead] were buried in one temporary grave …
> under fire as so many others were. No burial service,
> with only their handkerchiefs for covering – no time
> to scrounge a blanket, as relief was pending and the job
> must go on.[6]

Among those Harold buried was his cousin Norm Way, and his old school friend Private Alf Perrett. Norm's death affected Harold deeply. Blood and mateship bound them together. They had seen so much together since climbing the pyramids with Aussie nurses in Egypt and enduring the hellfire of Pozières and Passchendaele. Years after the war, Harold would still be trying to come to terms with Norm's death. He told his son Graham that his final act before burying Norm was picking up what was left of him.[7] Back in 1915, Alf Perrett and Harold planned to enlist together when both turned eighteen. At that time in the war, the Australian government required parental consent before a young man under twenty-one could enlist. Harold's father consented; Alf's did not. Alf waited and signed up on his twenty-first birthday. The battle on 23 August 1918 was his first. Harold thought Alf might have lived had he been around long enough to learn the ropes: 'He may have been too eager to dispel his own "fear of fear"'.[8]

For the wounded members of the Chipilly Six – Jack Hayes, Billy Kane and Jerry Fuller – the war was over. Dick Turpin was in hospital recovering from the effects of gas. Only Harold Andrews and George Stevens remained in the fighting line.

CHAPTER 10
JACK HAYES' WOUNDING

Billy Kane and Jerry Fuller's wounds at Froissy Valley were 'Blighties' of the best kind – not life-threatening but war-ending, ensuring their return to Australia. For Jack Hayes, survival would depend on how quickly he could get from the battlefield to the surgeons in an army base hospital on the Channel coast, and ultimately England.

Hayes was shot in the chest at point-blank range while trying to rush a German post. The bullet that hit him went through the box respirator (gas mask) hanging around his neck and covering his chest, and penetrated about two and a half inches into his abdomen and liver behind the lower ribs on his right side. The bullet bore particles of dirt, fibre from his uniform and metal from his gas mask deep into the wound.

Jack told his son that Jerry Fuller saved his life. Fuller and a German prisoner pulled Jack to cover in a nameless wood and propped him up against a fallen tree in a semi-supine position with his legs tucked up so that the blood and fluids would collect in his pelvis rather than in his chest. Then they bandaged his wound. His son John remembers his father saying that Jerry Fuller then went on and captured the man who fired the shot. Fuller reportedly dragged the prisoner back to Hayes and said, 'I've got the bastard that shot you and I'm going to shoot him down for you,' but Hayes told him, 'No. Sit him down next to me.' The wounded Australian and the prisoner shared photographs of family and home.[1]

Harold Andrews said a 'good Samaritan', a bearded German prisoner, arrived and 'asked my permission then proceeded to dress all of our wounded men'.[2]

When Australian stretcher-bearers and their captured German helper saw Jack, they did not expect him to live. The bearers were under orders only to remove wounded men who had a chance to live and fight another day. The worst cases were to be left and recovered post battle – if they survived. The bearers told Jack's mates not to give him anything to eat or drink, fearing the bullet had entered his stomach. Jack stayed in that wood for a day and night, one of the last of the Australian wounded to be carried from the battlefield. Meanwhile 'Fritz … bombed like the devil'.[3] The heat was oppressive. It had not rained in weeks. A chalky white layer of dust settled on the blanket that covered him and choked him when he moved. His tongue and throat would have been parched and painful from want of water. An agony for him and a different type of agony for those watching their leader and talisman, unable to help.

Eventually, stretcher-bearers from the Third Brigade, the men of the outer states who had relieved C Company on the captured ridgeline, carried Jack to a tented field ambulance station behind the new frontline. A doctor treated Jack's wounds and re-dressed them. Then army medical corps staff loaded him onto a Sunbeam motor ambulance bound for the 53rd North Midland Casualty Clearing Station. The clearing station – a type of forward medical base – was next to a large graveyard, a relic of the First Battle of the Somme in 1916. (It is now the Daours Commonwealth War Graves Commission Cemetery.)

Jack was given morphine for the pain, a subcutaneous infusion of saline 'to buck him up' and hydrate him, and an injection of anti-tetanus serum to protect him from tetanus and sepsis, known as gas gangrene, from the dirt and metal fibres in his wound. Gas gangrene was a common cause of infection and death among soldiers suffering from penetrating wounds.

The speed with which a man suffering from a gunshot wound to the abdomen could get from the battlefield to an operating table made a great difference in saving his life. The doctors swiftly transferred Jack to the 12th United States Army Base Hospital at Rouen on the Channel coast in less than a day. The only diagnostic evaluations of abdominal trauma available to the American doctors were Jack's symptoms, the physical signs on examination of his wound, and x-rays to establish the location of metal fragments and shattered bones. The doctors operated on Jack on 6 September 1918, nine days after he was shot. The surgeons removed some metal fragments and debris from his chest but the bullet and several small metallic 'foreign bodies', probably from his respirator, were not removed.[4]

Jack was transferred to a British Army hospital in Cardiff, Wales. The Welsh doctors debated whether to operate again and remove the bullet. The medical history of abdominal wounds stretched back hundreds of years. Poor surgical outcomes in penetrating abdomen cases from the American Civil War, the Franco-Prussian War and the Boer War influenced British surgeons throughout the First World War. In those late nineteenth-century conflicts, many soldiers died from infections caused by hands, surgical equipment and other forms of cross-contamination of the wound that led to strep and staph infection, blood poisoning or gangrene. During the First World War, intrepid surgeons made breakthroughs using strict antiseptic principles. At the end of the war, abdominal surgery was firmly established, though the abdomen was considered 'still more or less an unknown region in surgery'.[5] But the Welsh surgeons who treated Jack remained conservative. His son John explained, 'The doctors would not take the bullet out, it was considered it would kill him to try and get it out.' Centuries of experience had it that the mortality rate for penetrating abdominal wounds was 80 per cent. In other words, Jack had a one in five chance of living if the surgeons simply left him alone. Physicians called this the 'expectant approach'. In layman's terms, Jack was left to die, but if he survived, good luck to him.

The Welsh hospital board decided the best thing for Jack was for him to return to Australia, where he might die in the arms of his mother. On Christmas Day 1918, Jack embarked on the hospital ship HMT *Takada* with 400 Australian wounded. It was four years and one month since he had last smelt the gum leaves of home.

*

Jerry Fuller and Billy Kane were also going home. It is not known whether they were hit in the dawn attack on 23 August or in the second attack after midday. According to Jack's account, Fuller was prominent in the fighting at dawn, rushing posts with Jack and taking prisoners. Sometime after Jack was wounded, Fuller went on and was shot in the left shoulder.

Billy Kane suffered a wound described in his service record as 'gunshot wound right side – slight'. It would, however, dog him for the rest of his life. But it did have a silver lining: Billy's war was over. He was going home to Emma.

The battalion's field ambulance treated Kane and Fuller, suggesting they walked off the battlefield, unlike Jack. Whatever happened in the chaos of battle that day, Jack always credited Jerry with saving his life.

CHAPTER 11
DICK TURPIN'S REDEMPTION

With Jackie Hayes, Jerry Fuller and Billy Kane out of the war in hospitals in 'Blighty', by 18 September 1918 their mates in the 1st Battalion were up against the formidable Hindenburg 'Outpost' Line near the village of Hargicourt.

Brigadier Iven Mackay and Colonel Bertie Stacy pulled Harold Andrews aside and offered him a commission in the field as a second lieutenant. The job meant commanding a platoon of men – something Harold had already accomplished as a sergeant. Instead of footslogging on the hard cobblestone roads of Picardy, he would get his own horse and groom. It also meant higher wages, a batman to look after his needs, and numerous other small mercies and incentives. But Harold said no. He told Mackay and Colonel Stacy that he had 'no wish to be an officer' and 'just wanted to be with the boys'.[1] Instead, he took over Jack Hayes' job as company quartermaster sergeant.

One of Harold's first jobs as a senior sergeant was to disarm and detain 127 men who refused to take part in an attack near Hargicourt on 21 September 1918. The incident has sometimes been falsely described as a 'mutiny'. After months of almost constant frontline action, the diggers had been told they would be pulled out for a rest. But they were suddenly ordered to attack part of the Hindenburg 'Outpost' Line because an English Division had failed to show up on time. At this stage of the war the aggression and ambition of Monash did not match the condition of his troops. As brilliant and as willing as the diggers had been, the men were exhausted, but Monash agreed to a British request to throw the 1st Battalion into the attack.[2]

The battalion had been over the top on 18 September and spent two days in the frontline before it was relieved on the night of 20 September. Most of the battalion were resting in a sunken road when the orders arrived at 1 a.m. warning them to prepare to go over the top again. Some men walked out, led by a few NCOs, saying they had done their bit and it was time for others to do theirs. Others woke up, hollow-eyed, cold, wet and exhausted and followed their mates out, not knowing orders to attack had been issued nor understanding the consequences of their actions.[3]

By 3.00 a.m. on 21 September it was becoming clear that more than half the battalion had walked out. Nevertheless, Colonel Stacy insisted that the remnant go over the top according to orders. Zero hour was 5.40 a.m. Of a nominal strength of 1034, only 110 men 'hopped the bags'. The battlefield was devoid of cover besides the folds of rolling hills. The air was choked by mist and gas. The diggers ran into barbed wire entanglements that channelled the attackers into killing zones where they could be mown down by German machine-gunners.

The small band of diggers rushed the German trenches aided by a hurricane bombardment of shells. Most of the German garrison cowered in their dugouts and surrendered.

A few fired wildly over the Australians' heads. The diggers took the ground. The big stretcher-bearer, Dick Turpin, was mentioned in despatches for his gallantry in the advance. He had just come back from leave. With Captain Hayward Moffatt MC, an original soldier of the battalion, and one of its most popular officers, Turpin raced to the frontline to take part in the attack. Dick was awarded the Meritorious Service Medal for his repeated acts of gallantry and devotion to duty in 1918. His citation, signed by Colonel Stacy, mentioned his 'cheerful nature and untiring zeal' that were 'an incentive to all those associated with him'.[4] It was redemption for the big man who had gone into the stunt at Chipilly Spur with a suspended sentence of a year's hard labour hanging over his head.

After Turpin's outstanding efforts in all the campaigns of 1918, Brigadier Mackay dropped the suspended sentence. It was fitting that when the Armistice was declared he was with his battalion in France, and widely considered by officers and men to be one of its finest soldiers.[5] When he was finally discharged from the AIF in early 1920, he had been promoted from private to lance corporal.

However, the victory at Hargicourt on 21 September came at a tragic cost. Captain Moffatt died of wounds in the attack. One of Moffatt's men wrote that although Moffatt was severely hit in the shoulder by a piece of shrapnel

> … he refused the aid of a stretcher and walked back to the dressing station. Here it was seen his wound was serious, but he refused to go back to the main dressing station until he had reported the position of affairs at the frontline as he had left it.

As news of Moffatt's death spread, hardened soldiers wept 'unashamedly'.[6] After hearing of Moffatt's death, a sergeant who was a leader of the walkout said, 'If General Mackay is prepared to have us in the line, we'll go back with him.' The message was sent. Mackay replied, 'It's too late now.'[7]

The walkout would have been a major political and military embarrassment had it not been for the Armistice. Monash, earlier an advocate of the death penalty for serious offenders, argued that the joyful reception of the Armistice should be reason to forget it. But Mackay and Stacy insisted that the severest punishment should be meted out to the men who had taken part in the walkout. All 127 of them were court-martialled.

Harold Andrews was called as a witness. Among the men were several from C Company whom he knew and liked, men he'd been over the top with and shared numerous dangers on patrols and raids, fatigues and lonely listening posts in no man's land. 'Most of them had excellent combat records, many over a long period. Quite a few wore Military Medals.'[8]

The Field General Court Martial found the defendants not guilty of mutiny but guilty of desertion. Their sentences ranged from three to ten years imprisonment. Most of the harsher sentences were reserved for corporals and sergeants.

Hargicourt was the last time Harold Andrews, George Stevens and Dick Turpin went over the top. It was also the last battle for the 1st Battalion. It was a bitter end for a proud and storied unit – the 'Premier Battalion' – the first Australian infantry battalion to be raised in New South Wales in 1914, with a distinguished list of battle honours, beginning with the landing at Gallipoli.

CHAPTER 12
THE WAR IS OVER

With the war ended, the Australian Imperial Force and the Australian government faced the massive administrative and logistical task of returning 167 000 Australian servicemen, nurses, and their spouses. The wounded Jack Hayes, Billy Kane and Jerry Fuller would be among the first to go home. George Stevens, then Harold Andrews and Dick Turpin would follow.

The men convicted of desertion at Hargicourt were among the last Australian soldiers to return from the war. Their commanding officers seemed determined to see them rot in prison cells. But when the commanding officers who wanted to punish them had themselves gone home, Major-General Talbot-Hobbs, the highest-ranking Australian officer remaining in Britain, remitted the convicted men's sentences. At least two of them, Private Richard Stafford, a twenty-two-year-old labourer of Wollongong, a lad known to the Chipilly Six as a member of C Company, and Private Charles John Johnstone, a twenty-two-year-old box-maker of Gladesville, Sydney, died in prison of Spanish influenza.

Just before the Armistice, Harold Andrews decided to take up an officer's commission after all. He wrote that he was 'sad to leave the boys' but 'thankful for the respite'. He attended an officer's training course at Trinity College and played 'breakaway' for the famous double blue guernsey of the Cambridge University first fifteen. He was in Cambridge when the church bells pealed proclaiming the Armistice on 11 November 1918. Harold described the feeling as 'electrifying, the city of bells went wild and let off a full head of steam after four long years of ... blood, sweat and tears'.

Harold's officer's course was wrapped up quickly. His report card read that his 'power of command' was 'very fair indeed'.[1] It was about this time that Harold also learned he'd been awarded the Distinguished Conduct Medal for his 'daring patrol work in front of [the] lines' at Chipilly Spur.[2] Second Lieutenant Harold Dudley Andrews was proud of his achievement, but more excited by the prospect of going home to Coleraine on the Hastings River.

*

The Chipilly Six had survived the war. Their leader, Jack Hayes, was twenty-three and so badly wounded that he was not expected to live. Second Lieutenant Harold Andrews was the youngest sergeant and the youngest officer in the history of the 1st Battalion. His recovery from serious chest wounds and a broken femur at Pozières was nothing short of remarkable. At the time of the Armistice, Harold was twenty-two. Privates Billy Kane and George Stevens were in their late twenties. Kane had been shot in the leg at Pozières and in the chest at Froissy Valley. He'd also been racked by pneumonia and the Spanish flu. George Stevens avoided German bullets and shrapnel, but his war years were beset with illness. The youngest, Jerry Fuller, was barely twenty. The eldest, Dick

Turpin, was around thirty, and had been wounded three times and gassed.

They were infantrymen like so many thousands of others in the war. The shock troops of the Empire, as Jack Hayes called them. The infantry of all combatant nations were the men who

> … endured day after day, hour after hour, the enemy's fiercest barrages … who, at last, put all to the test through the merciless clatter of machine guns and through the high explosive barrages to drive the enemy from his fortified places and to hold them when he had gone.[3]

What made Jack Hayes, Harold Andrews, Billy Kane, George Stevens, Dick Turpin and Jerry Fuller exceptional was that at Chipilly Spur on 9 August 1918, they did it all by themselves. In the most decisive moment of the battle north of the Somme River, when the battle was on the line and the dead were piling up, the Chipilly Six got the job done.

In 1918 the AIF was a special force. While its battalions were diminished by attrition and with no hope of being brought up to strength, its professionalism and experience grew. The Chipilly Six epitomise the confidence and competence of the best of these young soldiers. At Chipilly they recognised the problem north of the river and quickly assessed that they had the skill, tactics and weapons to deal with it. They knew they were good at it. They knew what needed to be done and they achieved it. Many diggers believed Jack and his mates deserved Victoria Crosses. But others claimed the credit for what they did. Now more than one hundred years later, surely it is time to recognise that the Chipilly Six stand high in the pantheon of men who in 1918 won the war by acts of monumental motivation and skill.

Along with their wounds and medals, the Chipilly Six returned home with memories, experiences and bonds of mateship that would define the rest of their lives. The war had changed them. The world around them was in a state of change too. The Allies were victorious. The values of the white British race they had fought for were upheld. But the Six felt more distinctly Australian in ethos and in outlook. The Spanish flu and the Bolshevik revolution in Russia were obliterating the old order of things in Europe. When they got home they realised that Australia had changed, too. The familiarity of home was comforting but the differences in Australian society seemed irreconcilable. They were working-class boys who knew no other job as well as they knew soldiering. What bound these six young men together more than any other quality was their attachment to the AIF and its ethos of resourcefulness and battle discipline, where men in the ranks were ready to lead.

But would that matter in the struggle of the daily grind, where there was no bugler's reveille to stir them to the cause as Horatius did in the brave old days of Rome, and no killing that needed to be done?

PART FOUR
HOME

CHAPTER 13
A CHANGED AUSTRALIA

As the transport ship *Boorara* crossed the Equator, Lieutenant Harold Andrews DCM watched as some 'victims' were 'provided for Father Neptune' for a ceremonial dunking. The seafaring tradition of 'crossing the line' also featured boxing, rope-climbing and fancy dress. To add to the thrill, a heavy swell was running and one 'monkey' nearly went over the side. Harold remembered:

> … no one turned in until the clear night gave the Southern Cross a perfect setting. That was the first tangible sight – and the real sense of 'belonging' to the 'down under' that was home … Europe was forever behind us. But thoughts were not absent for those who had been denied this privilege … as one could witness to by the subdued 'yarns' which took place over the ship's rails.[1]

Australia was a country of less than 5 million people; 340 000 had gone to the war, 59 330 were killed and 152 171 were wounded.[2] The returning AIF were met with a public outpouring of patriotism, relief, joy and sorrow. At the Anzac

Buffet in Sydney's Domain, on wharves in all the capital cities, and in countless railway stations and halls throughout the country, volunteers and Red Cross staff, mayors and dignitaries joined with family and friends to greet the returning diggers with salutations and martial music, followed by sandwiches, jellies, cakes and scones.

But behind the hugs and handshakes, there was apprehension – even distrust – among many Australians towards returned soldiers. The rise of Bolshevism in Russia and the Spanish influenza pandemic had unleashed forces beyond the control of Australians. Many worried that the diggers would bring these infections home too. The turbulence of the war years fuelled further fear, distrust and misapprehension. The Australia the diggers returned to was bitterly divided. Class and religious divisions over conscription lingered.

During the war years, Australians had been divided over whether the AIF should be a volunteer force. Almost half the men eligible to enlist did so – meaning that slightly more than half did not. Most Australians were pro war and pro Empire, but politicians, newspapermen and some clergy appealed to sectarian and class differences. The ruling class and the protestant British majority painted themselves as loyalists. Irish Catholics, who were widely seen to be anti-conscription, were deemed seditious, despite the fact that Catholic Australians – mostly of Irish background – enlisted at a rate proportionate to their numbers in the general population. Many in the middle class accused striking workers and unionists of disloyalty and derided men not in uniform as shirkers. In 1916 and 1917, domestic politics was consumed by bitter fights over conscription. In two referendums, volunteerism prevailed by a slender majority.

In 1919, William Morris 'Billy' Hughes was prime

minister. The diminutive Welshman was an aggressive politician. He possessed the explosiveness of the first punch in a pub fight and a cutting wit. At the beginning of the war, Hughes was a Labor Party hero. But his pro-conscription stance saw him thrown out of the party. In 1917 he formed the Nationalist Party with some of his former Labor Party colleagues and some maverick conservatives who supported conscription. The Nationalists won the 1917 election and would dominate federal politics in a coalition with the conservative Country Party for most of the 1920s. As a wartime leader, Hughes proved to be 'the greatest Imperialist, the greatest nationalist and the greatest militarist in the country'.[3] The split in the Labor Party over conscription condemned it to a decade in the political wilderness federally and extinguished the radical nationalist tradition that once had many in the labour movement boasting that Australia was the world's leading social democracy and a 'workingman's paradise'. Instead, those inside and outside the party believed it had 'blown its brains out'.

In 1919, strikes and industrial disputes smouldered throughout the country, flaring up like stumps that refuse to burn out after a bushfire. During the war, the price of milk, bread, butter and essentials like shoes and clothing nearly doubled.[4] Wages rose, but they did not keep pace with inflation. It was clear in working-class neighbourhoods that profiteers in business, industry and on the land were 'killing the pig' while working families with a son or two at the front were struggling. Things came to a head in 1917: workers, unions and housewives protested. They accused the 'profiteers' of starving the families of soldiers at the front. Tempers were already running red hot over the question of conscription when a massive general strike broke out. It began in Sydney with workers at the Randwick tramway and Eveleigh railway workshops walking out over the introduction of a new card system that monitored the hours of work each man put in ('clocking on'). The strike spread from the NSW Government Railways (NSWGR) to the Melbourne waterfront and the coal lumpers in Newcastle, embroiling 173 000 workers and resulting in nearly 5 million lost working days.[5] Jack Hayes' old Bathurst neighbour, Ben Chifley, was one of the leaders of the strike.

Returned soldiers could be found on either side of the picket lines. Striking unionists in Broken Hill in 1919 and 1920 – many of them returned soldiers – closed mines for eighteen months. At the port of Fremantle, returned men were prominent on both sides of a clash that became known as the 'Battle of the Barricades' when the Western Australian government tried to use non-union labour ('scabs') to unload a ship that had not been fumigated against Spanish influenza. Unionists fought scabs in hand-to-hand combat and one man was killed.

In Brisbane in 1919, a mob of returned soldiers sacked a small eastern European neighbourhood in an outrage aimed at supposed Bolshevik elements. Similar riots targeting 'red-raggers' and the 'Wobblies' – members of the Industrial Workers of the World (a global 'one big union' movement), broke out throughout the country.

The spectre of militant diggers – whether self-described loyalists or Bolshevik 'red-raggers' or militant right-wingers – was an unsettling sideline in most people's lives. More pressing was the *presence* of returned men on the streets: gambling, drinking, carousing – hedonistic, chauvinistic and often disrespectful of civilian authority. The legend of the rootless, restless digger is captured in classic literature like George

Johnston's novel *My Brother Jack*, and in the testimonies of returned men such as A. Tiveychoc's *There and Back: The story of an Australian soldier 1915–1935* – the true story of Corporal Rowland Edward Lording, the boy digger who returned with horrible wounds and underwent more than fifty operations before dying prematurely in 1944. Lording recorded in graphic detail his heroin-addled experiences in a repat hospital, and the poverty and desperation of the homeless, workless digger.

The diggers sang on street corners, in 'two up' circles down cobbled back streets, in hospitals and clubs and in groups in their parents' homes:

> Here's to the good old beer, mop it down, mop it down
> [Repeated]
> Here's to the good old beer, it's all that's left to cheer
> Mop it down

The diggers loved to sing:

> No more estaminets to sing in,
> No ma'moiselles to make me gay;
> Civvie life's a bleedin' failure,
> I was happy yesterday.

Binge drinking was not just a digger problem. Drinking was practically a popular sport among Australian males despite legislation in most states that banned drinking in pubs and hotels after 6 p.m. In 1920 Australians were drinking 55 litres per head of population each year, an estimated 90 per cent of it between five and six in the evening. Legislation banning drinking after six had come in during the war in most states, largely because of the misbehaviour of diggers breaking camp.

The fear of moral decay caused by the shameless drinking and debauchery of returned men unsettled the Calvinist sensibilities of the ruling class and led to endless nights of anguish for mothers.[6] Their purgatory of worry during the war years was replaced by a desert of unknowing. The returned man knew he had changed. The abyss between his life experiences and those of his family, friends and community was enormous.

Statesmen and official memory-makers fashioned heroic tributes to the digger. Every town built its own memorial. But the hapless, homeless digger on street corners was unsettling.

Being a survivor carried the burden of memory. The bushman Bill Harney 'rode 800 miles to Borroloola on a horse, to forget about it all'.[7] Others believed it was their obligation to remember. Harold Andrews called this the privilege of coming home. And even Harney and the unsettled diggers in Alistair Thomson's classic book, *Anzac Memories: Living with the Legend*, learned to live with it. Nevertheless, there is some evidence that returned soldiers were more prone to suicide than civilian men.[8]

Many returned men believed the diggers deserved unique rights and services because they had been volunteers in the Great War for civilisation. They had faith that the politicians would make good on their promises of compensation for their effort and sacrifice. They expected to be returned to their jobs, or given preference in jobs. They were hungry for the land, service homes – and pensions to cover the cost of their wounds and to support widows and orphans – which had been promised to them. They formed leagues and clubs as places to gather but also to campaign for what they argued was their entitlement. The returned soldiers' movement became a powerful political pressure group in the years between the wars. This increased the force of their argument that they were owed a moral debt by Australians because they had given so much as volunteers. Returned soldiers became the primary recipients of funding and services of the welfare state, and it was an enormous cost on the public purse. The war cost Australia £376 993 052 from 1914 to 1918 and £831 280 947 by the mid-1930s.[9] The cost of repatriation and post-war charges were a financial burden many working families could ill-afford to pay after their own sacrifices during the war. The diggers demanded all of these things in a society that had not healed either its grief or its divisions.

Yet the end of the war also marked the beginning of what many remembered as the 'confident years'. As Harold Andrews put it, the returned diggers had seen 'how the other half live'. They came home with a renewed confidence in the Australian ethos and the knowledge that, in comparison to what they had seen in Egypt, England and France, Australians enjoyed a higher standard of living, less rigid class distinctions, more space and greater opportunities for economic mobility. The insecurities of the public and the legend of the unsettled digger should not belie the many thousands – perhaps the silent majority of returned men – who sought jobs, wives, relationships and meaning in their lives. Many returned men expressed great relief at being home and embraced responsibility. Some made the transition seemingly without much difficulty; others struggled, beset by physical wounds or war trauma.

Australians became 'consumers', epitomised in the rise of the department store and entrepreneurs like the irrepressible Hugh D MacIntosh – the boxing promoter and owner of the Tivoli Theatre – who marketed himself as a 'friend of the diggers'. People lined up to see the latest Hollywood stars on the big screen, leading to a shift in musical tastes and fashion among the young.

Women enjoyed more rights and freedoms too. Before the war, Australian women had won the right to vote. During the war women replaced men in clerical roles in offices and in some factory jobs. The historian Marilyn Lake describes the interwar years as 'a golden age of the woman citizen' in many ways. The feminists of the time championed economic independence for married women rather than notions of equality. It was a period of mass mobilisations. In 1923 women across all classes and creeds met in the nation's capital, Melbourne, to defend the £5 maternity allowance from a cost-cutting federal government, arguing it was a basic right. Women instigated Australia's first Council of Action for Equal Pay in 1937 and won an important victory when governments agreed that child endowment should be paid to mothers rather than fathers. Nevertheless, marriage, economic dependence and mothers' continuing responsibility for children rendered women vulnerable to male power.[10]

The idea of the family comprising a male breadwinner and *his* female homemaker and their children survived the war and became more entrenched. Marriage rates soared in 1919 and the early 1920s, with a corresponding increase in the rate of divorce.

With money and mobility some single women became freer than their mothers' generation. The most daring were the 'flappers', who danced to jazz, smoked cigarettes and wore short panties (known as scanties) under their bright dresses. But there were not a lot of flappers around in 1919 and the roaring twenties, and the Jazz Age never really took off in Australia. The older generation was puzzled by the worldliness of its returning sons and often ashamed of the freedoms of their daughters. Most people conformed to an insular society focussed on appearances and respectability.

In the country the social world revolved around the pub, church, sport (tennis and cricket in summer, the football codes in winter) and the various friendly societies, lodges and tradesmen's institutes. Women formed their own groups or auxiliaries of the men's clubs. The horse and railway connected communities and livelihoods; only a few wealthy farmers owned cars. Roads were mainly dirt or gravel. Few towns had sewage, paved streets or electric lights.[11] Aboriginal people were more visible in the towns than the growing cities. They had been pushed to the fringes and camped in humpies along the creeks or lived in government reserves and Christian missions, out of sight and out of mind to the rest of Australia. Several hundred Aboriginal men had served in the war, from the Gallipoli landings to the last battles in Damascus and on the Hindenburg Line. Several hundreds more had volunteered and were turned away. When conscription was defeated and the AIF was being bled dry by its victories on the battlefield, the recruiting agents relaxed the racial barriers to enlistment and Aboriginal men found it easier to enlist. When these men came home, most were excluded from the rights available to their white brothers in arms. Racism, whether directed against the original inhabitants of the country or the perceived threat of cheap Asian labour, was common and as openly expressed as a yarn about the weather or the weekend's football results.

In the city, remote Australia was fading like Lawson, Paterson and the writers of the *Bulletin*.

In 1919, Australians were united in their patriotism and relief at the end of the war, and in their grief over those lost, but they remained divided on the old battle lines of religion, conscription, industrial labour, politics and the meaning of loyalty. But almost universally they believed that the future would be brighter than the last half decade, as long as Australia was tied to the White Australia Policy and the British Empire.

This was the Australia to which the Chipilly Six returned.

CHAPTER 14

THE RETURN OF
PRIVATE JERRY FULLER MM

Jerry Fuller was the first of the Chipilly Six to come home. When his hospital ship *Nestor* sailed from Liverpool in December 1918, Britain was in the grip of the Spanish influenza pandemic. In the AIF depots at Salisbury and Weymouth, the soldiers were inoculated, made to gargle Condy's crystals (dissolved in saltwater twice a day, because the potassium permanganate was believed to be a disinfectant) and spread out in huts in sections or 'divisions' with windows and doors open – in mid-winter – to prevent infection. The cramped living conditions of army huts and hospitals were poor protection against the ravaging disease, but leave taken in the big cities of London and Paris could be a death sentence. Despite the army's best efforts, grave diggers and chaplains were busy in the northern winter of 1918–19.

The Spanish influenza killed at least 50 million people worldwide, most in a brief period between mid-September and early December 1918.[1] The timing was unlucky for Australians returning from the war, and the prospect of the diggers introducing the disease to their homeland was terrifying.

For a time, Australia avoided the pandemic, thanks mostly to its natural defence as an island continent at the far end of the world, and stringent quarantine measures run by the Commonwealth government. But as the diggers began to return in greater numbers, cracks began to appear in Australia's defence against the virus.

Jerry Fuller was one of the unfortunates whose ship entered Australian waters just as pandemics were declared in Melbourne and Sydney, almost certainly due to returning soldiers breaking quarantine at Melbourne's Broadmeadows camp and travelling to Sydney by train. Patriotic welcomes of returning soldiers at Port Melbourne and the Woolloomooloo wharves were cancelled and replaced by severe quarantine measures, police guards and unprecedented emergency laws. The state governments mandated a series of public health measures aimed at stopping transmission of the virus: crowds were banned, businesses, schools and other public meeting places were closed and masks had to be worn. The police issued fines to people breaking the emergency laws.

Jerry and the other wounded men aboard the *Nestor* were quarantined on arrival in Melbourne. Local state and army authorities did not want a mass of potentially infectious diggers let loose in the city. Local returned men were eventually allowed to go home, but trains taking the New South Wales diggers to Sydney were cancelled. Jerry and 1200 men were hastily transferred to the hospital ship *Argyllshire* bound for Sydney. When the ship entered Sydney Heads in early February 1919, quarantine officials found a case of Spanish influenza on board.[2] Jerry and the others were abandoned by their officers and dumped at the quarantine station at North Head without adequate food or shelter from strong winds and pelting rain. The wounded diggers endured three days of this before they started to riot. Hundreds of men pushed up against a police guard at the entrance to the quarantine station and threatened to break down the barriers and make their own way to Sydney.

The state commandant of Australian military forces in New South Wales, Major-General George Lee CSM, DSO, MiD, intervened and arranged for the men to be taken by steamship to the city, but a mutiny broke out when the diggers learnt they faced further quarantine inside the Sydney Cricket Ground. About fifty men lowered the steamship's boats, rowed to shore and disappeared into the suburbs, but the majority remained disciplined. Under the leadership of two fine young NCOs, Sergeant Major Frank Morgan, 36th Battalion, whose face was heavily scarred by shrapnel, and Sergeant Jack Emanuel, MM and Bar, 17th Battalion, they disembarked, donned face masks and marched through the streets of Sydney to the gates of the cricket ground. There, they sat down and refused to enter quarantine until each man had undergone a medical inspection. The NCOs argued that if the doctors found them fit, they should be demobilised immediately.

A police guard had followed the diggers and good naturedly bantered with them. Now some of the police and soldiers cooperated to keep a lane about two metres wide between the civilians and the *Argyllshire* men. Across this intangible barrier Jerry Fuller greeted his father, stepmother and his little half-brothers and sisters for the first time in years. Some of the diggers were seeing their children or relatives for the first time.

A reporter from the *Sydney Morning Herald* captured some of the moments when the diggers saw their family in the crowd. A woman called out to her husband – a corporal, with two wound stripes, three years' service stripes on his sleeve, and the dark blue and crimson ribbon of the Distinguished Conduct Medal on his chest:

'Can't you come home, Dick?'
'Don't look like it,' he replied.[3]

A mother rushed towards her son. She was restrained by family members and pushed back a 'safe distance'. She demanded loudly that he be allowed to come home straightaway, just across the park.[4]

General Lee arrived and admonished Morgan and the leading NCOs for being 'quite wrong and unsoldierly' for refusing to enter the quarantine grounds. Lee, a fifty-nine-year-old career soldier, had served as an officer with the NSW Lancers in the Boer War. He had no experience of fighting on the Western Front and had spent the war in Australia running the school of instruction at Victoria Barracks and perfecting his polo skills.[5] He told Morgan and Emanuel that their demands would not be met unless all of the men entered the cricket ground. Sergeant Emanuel responded that the diggers had not been 'disorderly' and brought no 'disgrace on the AIF'.[6]

Morgan returned to the men and told them that Lee refused to 'lower' himself to speak to them.[7] The diggers met this with cries of 'Oh! Oh!' and 'We don't want him!'.

Morgan continued: 'General Lee's statement is this: "There is the gate open there over in the [Cricket] Ground." His orders are for you to go in there.'

The men called out, 'For how long?' and Morgan answered, 'There is no definite period stated, and if you don't go in there, well, you are left on this piece of ground for the Government of New South Wales to deal with.'

Men from the *Argyllshire* wearing masks march into
quarantine at the Sydney Cricket Ground.
*(*Sydney Mail, *19 February 1919)*

A digger replied, 'We don't want to be in there for the
remainder of our lives.'

The men were willing to accept further quarantine but
not indefinitely. The diggers had a remarkable capacity to
organise and think for themselves. A lance corporal suggested
that if they agreed to enter the cricket ground they should
group themselves in 'divisions' of fifty, each allotted a separate
hut. That way, if a man did catch the Spanish flu, only his
close contacts would undergo further quarantine. The rest of
the men would remain free to go home. 'If I catch the flu …
I don't want to keep the majority of you in isolation with me,'
the lance corporal said.[8]

Then the diggers saw the inspector general of police
in the crowd. The NCOs approached him and asked for a
meeting with the deputy premier. In 1918, the diggers had

a saying: 'Those that can, get on; those that can't, get around.'
The Chipilly Six used it at Chipilly to outflank the German
machine-gun nests on the spur. Now Morgan used it to get
around General Lee. The police inspector listened to the
NCOs then dispatched a messenger to Parliament House.

A few hours later, the *Argyllshire* men were lying on
their kit bags on the hard ground outside the cricket ground
when a government car pulled up under a gas light. The driver
ushered the NCOs into the plush interior and drove them
to the premier's office where they met the acting premier,
George Fuller, and his cabinet.

Morgan made an impression on the politicians. His
dignity was above reproach and totally absent of self-interest.
The battle scars on his face and jaw probably had an effect
on the politicians too. Fuller assured the NCOs that 'Your
grievances will be remedied'.[9] He also guaranteed them if
there was no infection in the next three days they would be
demobilised and released. But if infection did occur within a
'section', then those men would be detained until the risk to
the public had passed. The cabinet also made a promise to visit
the men and speak to them.

It was dark when Morgan and the NCOs returned to the
cricket ground. A late southerly change and a thunderstorm
had driven off most of the crowd. But some families remained,
and a few urchins who delivered food and drink to the diggers
for a few copper coins. When Morgan told the men about
Fuller's promise, it was met with cheers of approval.

The *Sydney Morning Herald* reporter wrote:

That settled it. The men rose to their feet in a body,
formed themselves into probably half a dozen sections
and, at the instance of Sergeant-Major Morgan, gave

three cheers for the police and the press, and then moved in double columns into the cricket ground.[10]

The following three days passed without incident or infection, so on 14 February the men were released. To mark the occasion, the diggers raised a pair of army-issue trousers on a flagpole. Someone called out from over the fence, 'Are you fellows all Bolsheviks now?' A digger replied, 'No fear … we're not going under any flag. We're just going on our own.'[11] It had been more than six weeks since Jerry Fuller had left Liverpool on the *Nestor*, and he had spent almost half that time in strict quarantine in Melbourne and Sydney without adequate food, shelter or medical treatment.

The *Argyllshire* incident caused great anxiety to the public. The fact that the press reported that one of the diggers was in hospital in a serious condition with Spanish influenza had hardened public opinion and justified their fears. Most people sympathised with the returned soldiers' predicament, but the so-called 'mutineers' or 'deserters' who left the steamship as it stood off North Head were widely criticised as being a menace to public health. Some of the absconders handed themselves in, but many had to be rounded up. They were court-martialled and sentenced to jail. Those found assisting them were also arrested and charged. George Fuller was widely praised for his firmness in handling the 'unpleasant duty' of taking steps to protect the public from a potential threat of mass infection.[12]

On the day the *Argyllshire* men walked out of the Sydney Cricket Ground, the Sydney papers reported the first death from Spanish influenza in Sydney outside of quarantine facilities. By the spring of 1919, the disease had caused the death of more than 6000 people in New South Wales, and a further 3500 in Victoria. In all, about 13 000 Australians died from the disease. Then it suddenly disappeared, as quickly as it had emerged.

*

Jerry's shoulder wound had gone untreated since the *Nestor* arrived in Melbourne at the start of February. When the other diggers went home from the Sydney Cricket Ground, he was taken to the No. 21 Auxiliary Hospital, Georges Heights, overlooking Sydney harbour. Judging from the doctor's notes in his army records, Jerry viewed an army hospital as another form of detention that he needed to escape. On 14 April, his exasperated doctor wrote that Jerry frequently missed treatment because he was 'away pleasuring without leave'. He told his doctors that he felt 'well in himself' and insisted there was 'no trouble' with his shoulder. He continued to go absent so his doctor had no choice but to discharge him. Four months after sailing from England Jerry finally went home. He did not bother to apply for a wound pension or make a fuss.

Eighteen months later, in 1921, Jerry married Olive Myrtle Martin at the Methodist church, Newtown. Olive, known as 'Tot', was a singer and organist at the church where they married. They lived at 79 Station Street, Arncliffe. Their first child, Norma Rae, was born in 1922, followed by Molly in 1924, Kenneth (known as Tom) in 1928, and Ruth during the Great Depression. Jerry's descendants know little of Jerry and Olive's life at this time. But a few old photos of Jerry carousing with his army mates while absent without leave from the hospital amplify the brotherhood of the AIF. Jerry returned a restless young man and never found the words to describe his wartime experiences to his family.

CHAPTER 15
PRIVATE BILLY KANE MM RETURNS TO CONGARINNI

HMT *Mamari*, carrying Billy Kane and about 800 wounded men, docked at Port Melbourne a few days after Jerry Fuller arrived on the *Nestor* in January 1919. Unlike the *Nestor*, however, the *Mamari* was considered a clean ship. Disembarking diggers told the waiting reporters it was 'a splendid trip'. The weather had been fine, the troops healthy, and the meals, entertainment and educational lectures organised by the officers, excellent. A reporter covering the return of troopships informed readers that the happy state of affairs aboard the *Mamari* was 'a somewhat unusual experience in the recent history of troopships', including the *Nestor* and the *Argyllshire*.[1]

Billy underwent a medical examination and signed his discharge papers, then went to Castlemaine, probably by train, to see his mother and his benefactor Rose McDonald. Billy had a half-sister, Ada, and a half-brother, Daniel, both wards of the state born while his mum was doing time in the infamous Coburg prison. He found Rose McDonald at Our Lady of Perpetual Help Catholic Church in Campbell's Creek. We can only imagine these emotional reunions. Billy's daughters say he seldom spoke about his past. But he did tell of an epic bicycle ride 1300 kilometres north from Castlemaine to Congarinni to see his sweetheart Emma Provost, a feat he pulled off in a few weeks. He knew the route well enough, having travelled through the bush with surveyors as a boy.

Emma Provost and Billy Kane married at the Anglican Vicarage, Macksville, on 30 July 1919. Billy renounced his Catholic faith to marry Emma in the Protestant church. He had faith but he cast aside religion during the war. Billy and Emma's daughters have a photograph of the couple on their wedding day: Billy wears his AIF uniform and a boutonnière in his top pocket. Emma wears a white silk (or sateen) dress. The neckline is high and the dress falls softly from the shoulder to the ankles. Her headdress is a beautiful arrangement of flowers and foliage, and her embroidered veil trails to the floor. She wears white shoes and stockings and holds a bouquet of ferns and flowers.[2]

Not long after the couple married, 'a large and happy crowd' gathered at the Friendly Society Hall in Macksville to welcome home Billy and other newly returned men. Mr M Wallace, a local councillor, recounted the story of the capture of Chipilly Spur. The crowd heard how Billy and three other volunteers joined their sergeants to stamp out numerous German machine-gun posts that had held up the British attack. As the Aussie boys surged across the high ground, Billy captured 84 prisoners and killed and wounded many more (the numbers seemed to change with every retelling of the story), then when his mate turned a captured machine gun on the fleeing enemy, Billy and the others pressed on, advancing several miles and 'winning the position'.

This 'boys own adventure' retelling of the story was just what the patriotic crowd wanted to hear. Billy was met with rapturous applause and handshakes. Emma's mother, Sarah, was present too and received a medallion in recognition of the war service of her son Edward 'Ted' Provost, of the 2nd Pioneer Battalion, who had survived the war and been discharged in Brisbane. Mr Wallace told the mothers that the purpose of the event was 'to show appreciation of these gallant heroes, whose glorious deeds would never be forgotten, and which had done more to advertise Australia than anything that ever occurred'. Wallace said that the town's sympathy 'went especially to the unfortunate ones who lost their lives'. He wanted the bereaved mothers to know that 'the people would never forget the losses sustained'. Wallace spoke about the importance of finding jobs for returned men, including meaningful work for the wounded and disabled. He argued that while it was the Repatriation Department's job to assist those men and families for whom the effects of war meant financial loss, it was also the 'duty' of the community to fundraise on behalf of returned men and their families and to employ them whenever possible. Turning to Billy and the returned men, he said:

> It [is to be] hoped those who fought so well on the other side of the world would have the pluck enough to do the same for their country [in peace] and try to make this grand land of Australia what it ought to be.[3]

The speech captured the concerns of the public at the time. Pride in the initiative and skill of the fighting men of the AIF, anxiety at the scale of the loss of the nation's manhood, and also the underlying responsibility of those who had stayed behind to mould the returned warriors into responsible citizens.

Kane was a man determined to do his bit in war and peace and ask no favours. Like his mate Jerry Fuller, he did not apply to the Repat Department for a wound pension or welfare assistance. He had a harder edge about him – around town he became Bill or 'Cobber' Kane, not Billy. He would work away in the bush and come home for the weekends. He joined the Macksville RSSILA, but seldom had time to attend meetings. He played a bit of rugby league, swung his Kelly axe in local woodchopping competitions, and enjoyed a beer and a bet at the pub with his mates.[4] Two sons, Arthur James and William Charles, were born in quick succession. In all, Emma and Billy had ten children. In an era when jobs were scarce and costs high, Bill and Emma were destined for a life full of love and the laughter of children, but also honest toil and worry. There was grief too when William Charles died in infancy. Each year thereafter Bill and Emma Kane inserted a small memorial note in the local paper:

> In this world of care and pain,
> Lord, Thou wouldst no longer leave him;
> To the sunny heavenly plain
> Dost Thou now with joy receive him.
> Clothed in robes of spotless white,
> Now he dwells with Thee in Light.[5]

Bill's daughters say their dad never went to church but he always respected Emma's faith.

CHAPTER 16
THE RETURN OF COMPANY QUARTERMASTER SERGEANT JACK HAYES DCM

It's amazing the difference a week can make in a pandemic. Jack Hayes arrived home on 15 February 1919, one day after Jerry Fuller and the *Argyllshire* men were released from quarantine in the Sydney Cricket Ground and just as Billy Kane was beginning his epic bike ride. The *Takada* was a 'clean ship', and the welcome the men received at Woolloomooloo Wharf and the Anzac Buffet in the Domain was in stark contrast to the reception of the *Argyllshire*. The whole messy affair surrounding the *Argyllshire* became a 'catalyst for urgent change'. The *Takada* was allowed to proceed to Sydney without disembarking the New South Wales and Queensland diggers in Melbourne, where the virus was spreading unchecked.[1]

A special ambulance car took Jack from the Anzac Buffet to the Prince of Wales Hospital, Randwick. Built as an asylum for children in the mid-nineteenth century, the facility had been converted into a hospital for seriously wounded diggers and renamed the Fourth Australian Repatriation Hospital. Jack's granddaughter has a photo of Jack taken at the time. An Australian army doctor, with a characteristic medical bag,

Jack, and a young lady, probably Isabel, Jack's sister, link arms as they walk. All look happily at the camera. Jack looks old beyond his years but the irrepressible grin and laughter lines radiating from his eyes belie the seriousness of his wound. This photo, held by the Hayes family for more than one hundred years, is a national treasure.

The doctors at Randwick decided to remove the bullet straight away, advising him that if he didn't undergo surgery 'he would die in any case'.[2]

Jack asked that the operation be done on Anzac Day, 1919. Having been at the dawn of Anzac, he was content to make the day his last. If the surgery was unsuccessful he would go where all good soldiers go. That morning, 'an impressive service' attended by Governor and Lady Davidson was held in the grounds of the hospital to mark the first Anzac Day since the Armistice. Officiating clergymen representing the various branches of Protestants and Catholics led the gathering in the hymns 'God of Our Fatherland', 'Onward Christian Soldiers' and Rudyard Kipling's 'Recessional'. The service concluded with 'The Last Post'. Then the VIPs lunched with the walking wounded before visiting the 600 bedridden men, tactfully avoiding the isolation ward where a few dozen patients with Spanish influenza lingered in abject misery – their treating doctor had died from the disease the week before.

Jack's surgeon was the renowned First World War physician Colonel Alexander MacCormick. MacCormick operated at 5 p.m. He removed the bullet, but some small metallic 'foreign bodies' were difficult to extract and did damage to surrounding tissue. Jack's temperature soared to almost 40 degrees Celsius, and he was in and out of a feverish coma. The anxious doctors and nursing staff watched on for a week. Slowly, he began to stabilise, and his mother Blanche was allowed to visit. But he remained in hospital for almost a year. On 16 November 1919 – fifteen months after being shot in the Froissy Valley – he went home to his parents' terrace house at 24 Margaret Street, Enmore. A week later he walked into the running sheds at Eveleigh and rejoined the world of the railwaymen.

Sadly, there was none of the camaraderie of an infantry battalion in the once-familiar sheds. This was the legacy of the Great Strike, which left 'bitterness and a trail of hate'.[3]

The railwaymen were divided into hostile groups: the 'Lily Whites' were strikers who had returned to work stripped of their seniority and job prospects by proclamation of the chief railway inspector and the government, and they detested the so-called 'Loyalists' – those who rushed to replace the strikers alongside country men and public-school boys. Their railway cards were stamped 'stayed loyal' and Fuller's conservative government promised them seniority and promotion. Returned soldiers like Jack were deemed 'loyal', but they didn't really have much choice. At enlistment in August 1914, the NSWGR commissioners instituted a generous system whereby railway employees were not required to resign in order to enlist. Railwaymen joined the AIF on the promise that their pay would be maintained at its pre-enlistment level by the NSWGR, supplementing their military pay if necessary. This 'generous' system was instituted in 1914 when most believed the war would be over by Christmas. The NSWGR also guaranteed returned men promotion to the highest position that had been obtained by any man who was his junior at his time of enlistment. The returned soldier would retain seniority, provided he achieved a sufficient qualification within three months.

After the 1917 strike, this 'favouritism' of returned soldiers caused resentment, particularly among the Lily Whites. Not only could a striker find himself junior to a Loyalist scab but also to a returned soldier. The conservative state governments punished the strikers by sweeping away years of service, pay rates and seniority. When Jack Lang's Labor government was elected in 1925 and 1930, the Lily Whites were reinstated. And so it went, the interests of the Lily White or Loyalist being satisfied by successive conservative and Labor governments, leading to many railwaymen referring to it as 'the strike that never ended'.[4]

Jack's wound meant his Loyalist status gave him no real advantages. Railway historian Bill Phippen said that in terms of his job prospects after the war, 'Jack's injury came against him.' The standard career path – cleaner to fireman to driver – was no longer available to Jack. The fireman's place was on the footplate, where he was expected to shovel four and a half kilograms of coal into the firebox every ten seconds. On a decent hill, even more than that. Jack was physically incapable of doing it.[5] But his employers kept him on, first at 13 shillings and 10 pence a day as a tube cleaner, blasting soot and ash from the tubes that conducted the hot gases through an engine's boiler, and finally as a fitter's labourer, starting at 15 shillings and 6 pence. Bill reckons these were 'probably jobs given to Jack by the Railways out of obligation to a maimed digger'.[6]

Between Jack's wound pension and his railways wages he was on a relatively good wicket for a working-class lad. But pain and the loss of pride associated with being unable to do a prestigious physical job must have taken their toll. He lost numerous working hours due to medical treatment and found it difficult to get about without fits of coughing. He applied to the Deputy Commissioner, Repatriation Department, for a tram and rail pass:

> I wish to state that my war disabilities are gun shot
> wound, right chest, prohibiting me from walking to
> any great extent and where necessity compels me to on
> account of financial stringency it leaves me completely
> exhausted at the end of the day.[7]

He was unsuccessful.

Living in a terrace house with his parents and younger siblings was a world away from the 1st Battalion sergeants' mess he ran in France. The comforts of home versus the battle-lines in the Eveleigh running sheds did not compare to the blood and brotherhood Jack had experienced on the Western Front. He'd become used to hard living and hard drinking. In the army he drank almost every night. On 11 June 1917 he surprised himself, writing 'have not had a drink for 3 days'.[8] In the towns behind the lines, Amiens, Armentieres, and up around Morbecque, Sercus and Hazebrouck, he regularly 'promenaded' with the 'tabs' – digger slang for a prostitute or sweetheart (remember Lilly?). None of this sat easily with playing euchre in the living room with Mum and Dad. His brother Harry had also returned from the war and run into his own troubles. Harry was wanted by the police for failing to pay child maintenance to a girl up in the country. And he had an English war bride seeking a divorce.

Jack missed his army mates. Brotherhood was the one gift the war had given him.

*

In 1922, Jack bumped into some old mates from the 1st Battalion who lived in the district. Les Mudge, Jim Davidson and Reggie McKay were members of a 'loosely knit band of men' calling themselves the Marrickville Anzac Memorial Club. The club's headquarters were on Garners Avenue, Marrickville, in the heart of Sydney's inner west. It was only a couple of kilometres from Jack's home. Jack knew Les as a lance corporal in C Company; Jimmy Davidson, a clerk born in Newtown, had been a corporal, twice wounded in action at Doignies and Menin Road in 1917. Reggie McKay and Jack had been good mates in the army. Reggie was acting sergeant in C Company in 1918, and he was one of the men court-martialled after the walkout at Hargicourt. At his trial, Reggie argued that he'd been asleep in a dugout and when he awoke his platoon had moved out. A corporal told him they had been relieved. According to Reggie, no one heard the order to return to the frontline. Reggie followed a sunken road in the hope of catching up to his platoon. For this he was court-martialled, reduced to the ranks and sentenced to ten years in a military prison. Many 1st Battalion men, including Jack, thought this was hard on a good digger. Reggie had been over the top at Pozières, Mouquet Farm and Bullecourt and involved in all the fighting in 1918. But the battalion commander Bertie Stacy and the brigade and divisional commanders, Mackay and Glasgow, wanted the men punished severely. As John Hayes said, Jack and the CO 'never saw eye to eye'.[9]

Jack and his mates had no ill-feelings towards Reggie or the other men who were sentenced. They saw it as a failure of command, not the diggers' fault. Reggie was a good digger and a good bloke and that was it. It was this type of army tyranny that put Jack at odds with the officers in war and peace. It may well have also drawn him to the Marrickville Anzac Memorial Club. The interesting thing about the club was that it was formed of returned men, almost all of whom had served in the ranks. Its guiding ethos was inclusivity, volunteerism and maintenance of the wonderful spirit of comradeship so many diggers experienced during the war. Jack joined the club and threw himself into its busy social life and the voluntary work of caring for less fortunate diggers and their families. Les was the vice-president and Jimmy was the treasurer.

Jack's auspicious meeting with Jimmy, Les and Reg coincided with the opening of the new premises on Garners Avenue. Soon after, the diggers nominated Jack to be honorary secretary. He accepted and began what would become his life's work. As secretary, Jack attended all meetings of the club and conducted all its correspondence. It was also his responsibility to receive all monies and pay the same to the treasurer, and to carry out the decisions reached at executive meetings. Jack's life took on a routine and a purpose: he was the company quartermaster sergeant again.

Jack's day started with eight hours in the railway work-shops handing tools to fitters. Then he went home for tea. Then straight to the club – a couple of ten-ounce (284-millilitre) middies and a few laughs with the boys. Then some office work or a committee meeting. There was a regular round of Anzac smokos and gatherings, cricket, bridge and billiards competitions, a debating society, picnics and dances for the kids, and annual events that needed to be organised, plus letters to affiliates, hospital visits, the Christmas appeal, Poppy Day and Anzac Day. Finally, a dram of whisky and home to bed. The next day, he would do it all again. An invitation for Anzac Day 1923 is characteristic of Jack's organisational skills and erudite pen:

> The Marrickville Anzac Memorial Club will entertain
> at the club premises, in Garner's Avenue, the children
> of returned Marrickville soldiers, especially children of

deceased soldiers. There will be games and refreshments, and parents are cordially invited to bring their children along and make the function a success.[10]

The creativity of the club was wonderful. Faced with debt for building costs, in 1924 Jack and the committee decided on a Queen of Marrickville competition to clear the debt and contribute a stipend for young women graduating from secondary school whose fathers had died due to war service. Matron Alice Cashin, a local girl who had served as a nurse in the British Army, earning the Royal Red Cross and Bar (the first Australian to receive the honour), the French Croix de Guerre and two mentions in dispatches, represented the club. Alice Cashin was a huge favourite of the diggers. She was matron on the hospital ship *Gloucester Castle* when a German U-boat torpedoed it in the English Channel on 30 March 1917. Cashin organised the evacuation of her staff and the wounded into the ship's boats. For her coolness and devotion to duty she was credited with saving 377 lives. She then ran the 400-bed hospital at Whittington army barracks in Lichfield, England, where she was much loved by her patients. When she left England in July 1919, she was showered with daisies gathered by 'her boys'.[11] Alice Cashin was one of the first members of the Marrickville Anzac Memorial Club and a regular and popular attendee at social events. The Queen of Marrickville competition was a great success. Alice Cashin won with a resounding 75 346 votes to the 48 186 of her 'nearest rival'. In a happy ceremony at the Union De Luxe Picture Theatre she was crowned Queen of Marrickville.[12] The popular event became an annual feature on the local calendar.

On weekends Jack volunteered as a club welfare officer. He visited diggers in hospital, helped returned men seeking employment or a widow needing assistance with pension problems or a war service home loan and its cumbersome paperwork. Sometimes a down-and-out digger would show up at the club. John Hayes said his dad would give the burned-out digger a feed, a bath and some clean clothes, or just a place to have a good sleep at the club.

Joe Maxwell VC needed help frequently. Joe was a celebrity in the AIF. Journalists from the *Sunday Times* and *Smith's Weekly* sought him out for stories on the heroic diggers or for a quote on the 'bloody Repat Department' and its failures. Likewise, aldermen and mayors wanted Joe to cut the ribbon for their latest monument, or to say a few words on Anzac Day and Remembrance Day. The hungry public loved Joe, who epitomised the larrikin Anzac legend. But it came at a cost. He leaned on a lot of bars in the post-war years – everyone wanted a drink with Joe. His biographer, John Ramsland, tells an amusing story of a childhood encounter with his hero:

> Late one afternoon I was peddling my bike as usual
> on the pavement beside our house when I saw a man
> approaching … wobbling from side to side until he
> reached the dark shadowy block of flats. He then
> seemed to stumble and scraped his head against the wall
> of the flats. Blood started to pour down his face. He
> was well-dressed in a double-breasted pin-striped suit
> and hat. I immediately recognised him. It was Mr Joe
> Maxwell, VC, the only celebrity in our neighbourhood
> … Frantically I pedalled toward him. When I reached
> his staggering person, I reached up and grabbed him on
> the trouser leg. He stiffened, straightened up and looked
> down into my eyes for a long moment. His eyes were
> dark brown and bloodshot. And then he spoke: 'Never

let the grog get you, son.' Another pause and then he went down the dark stairwell of the block, unlocked his flat door and disappeared inside.[13]

Many of Joe's stunts ended in a heap outside the club on Garners Avenue, smelling of grog and piss and in need of some dinkum mates. There were hundreds of diggers like Joe. The club was a haven for some of them. The diggers had an ethos: in war you only judged a man's worth after you had been over the top with him, and the diggers knew that when you learned a bloke's weaknesses you appreciated his deeds all the more and condoned his 'little failings'.[14]

'Jack just loved those men,' John Hayes said. In the Marrickville Anzac Memorial Club, Jack had discovered 'the wonderful spirit of sacrifice' that 'meant all the difference between life and death'.[15] Jack had found a peacetime social organisation developed in the spirit of the AIF, the spirit of voluntary service. He was still a very young man at the time, only in his mid-twenties. John Hayes imagined his dad's life, and worried that his dad had 'found his life calling but he lacked a soul mate'.[16]

CHAPTER 17

THE RETURN OF PRIVATE GEORGE STEVENS MM

At the war's end, those diggers with the longest service, with family commitments, and those needing medical treatment were sent home first. This saw Jerry Fuller, Billy Kane and Jack Hayes swiftly return to Australia. Healthy men like George Stevens, Harold Andrews, Dick Turpin and thousands of others had to wait. General Monash, concerned that the diggers in camps in Britain and France would get bored and restless, came up with a vocational training scheme. Small groups of men were sent across Britain to study whatever they liked. Other men were picked in sporting teams.

In December 1918, the Department of Repatriation and Demobilisation issued a series of general instructions to all units outlining how to apply for non-military employment before demobilisation. George Stevens applied for farming work and was accepted by Lieutenant Cyril Benest MC, Royal Field Artillery, of St Aubin, Jersey, who organised a scheme run by the Royal Jersey Agricultural and Horticultural Society.

Jersey is the largest of the Channel Islands, lying in the Bay of Mont-Saint-Michel about twenty kilometres west of France, off the Cherbourg Peninsula. About 120 Australians joined the farming scheme and were stationed all over the island. Some were based in a hostel in St Helier, the island's main town, but it is likely George was billeted with other Australians (and New Zealanders) at Greve de Lecq Barracks on the north-west coast, or at Pearia House, Gorey, where several local accounts recall the diggers and 'their distinctive hats'.

George sailed to Jersey in March 1919 and would have been employed in dairying and harvesting the island's potato crop. The inhabitants of Jersey were pleased to have the diggers. War losses and deaths from Spanish influenza meant there was not enough local labour to lift the potato crop – the staple of the Jersey economy.

Over half the land area of Jersey is cultivated. The intensive lots, averaging five hectares each, and the ubiquitous Jersey cow, would have been familiar to George. He grew up around similar farms near Young. But the age-old Jersey custom of applying dried seaweed to the potato fields would have been novel to him.

The AIF and the Repat Department had to assure the labour unions in the United Kingdom that Australian soldiers assigned to industrial and agricultural placements would not be taking British jobs and that they would be paid trade union rates for any work undertaken. So George would have been paid 10 shillings and 6 pence a day – the award rate, plus a subsistence allowance of 6 shillings a day, considerably more than his army pay. In addition, he received railway vouchers to the value of £1/6/8 and was issued with a suit and overalls.

Jersey also offered George an opportunity to experience a unique way of life. He was able to live like a farmer and a tourist and not a soldier. When not farming, George and the other diggers took ferry rides to Guernsey, the second largest of the Channel Islands; explored Napoleonic-era forts and barracks; and mixed with the locals, whose mixture of English and French language, which dated back to the Norman invasion in the eleventh century, was still widely spoken on the islands.

George worked alongside local men and boys, and drank in the small stone taverns with them. The diggers made an impression on the small island community too. A local newspaper reported that 'Australia Day' was celebrated in great style on the island in 1919 – though it was probably Anzac Day that the diggers were commemorating.[1] Some of the Australians married local girls and brought them back to Australia.[2] Farming on Jersey must have been a fine way for George to see out his time before heading home to Australia. He was able to forget the drudgery of army barracks life and do meaningful and productive work. Did he hope to take over his stepfather's farm when he returned to Australia?

*

In July 1919, George returned to Australia with mixed feelings. His best mate Ern was dead, and he was still grieving that he had been unable to find and bury Ern's body. Also, any dream he'd had of taking over his stepfather's farm was dashed – Johnson wished to give it to young Cam. George went back to carting goods for Chant & Co., his employer honouring the promise made upon his enlistment in 1916.

George and Carrie married in St John's Anglican Church, Young, on 27 November 1919. The local paper reported that 'a large number of friends witnessed the ceremony'. Carrie was 'prettily dressed' in an ivory crêpe de Chine and georgette gown and a veil decorated with flowers. George gave her a pendant of rubies and pearls and a bouquet of water lilies, carnations and sweet peas tied in green and black thread – the colours of the First Battalion. Carrie carried a small silk handkerchief – 'a souvenir from France sent to her by her late brother', Ern. Arthur, Ern's brother, stepped in as George's best man. After a small reception at Carrie's parents' house, the newlyweds honeymooned in Sydney.[3]

George took up cricket again, opening the batting and bowling for the 'Traders'. By 1921 he was player and selector for the Young representative side, touring Sydney, Bathurst and Cootamundra – and may have come up against his old mate Jerry Fuller. He was a committeeman on the sub-branch of his local returned soldiers' league and helped organise a special annual test match – Soldiers versus Police. He also sang in the St John's church choir. The local paper described his 'sympathetic rendition' of 'Seek ye the Lord':

> When war and pain kill our dreams
> And life has taken our all
> He saves us from the miry clay
> And washes our sins away
> And makes us whole.[4]

George and Carrie's firstborn, Joyce Meryl, arrived in 1921. They named their first son, born in 1923, Ernest Albert. All told, the Stevens clan grew to comprise eight children, six of whom were girls. It must have been hard work raising a large family on a carter's wage, but the Stevens children never went hungry thanks to Carrie's practicality, a little help from her parents, and fresh milk and produce from the Johnstone farm.

CHAPTER 18

THE HOMECOMING OF LIEUTENANT HAROLD ANDREWS DCM

While George Stevens was working on Jersey for good pay and without any officers to bother him, Harold Andrews made the most of his footballing talent. Harold and his friend Lieutenant Herbert Martin, 2nd Battalion, were billeted with a family in Chatelet, on the frontier between Belgium and Germany, and represented the AIF in rugby test matches against the British Second Army and the Royal Air Force. The AIF team won 49 to 3 and 19 to 3 respectively.[1] The test matches were played in Cologne, Germany. Harold got to see his former enemies up close and found it all very interesting:

> Ex-officer types with scowling contemplation – the rest with varying degrees of tolerance and curiosity (no doubt because of the slouch hat) – we modestly assumed having gained some notoriety for boisterous high spirits since our arrival.[2]

Some of the diggers paid for the ticket to Cologne with their lives, as the Spanish influenza pandemic was still ravaging Europe. It was with great relief that Harold learned it was his turn to return to Australia on the *Boorara* in July 1919.

Writing in 1975 at the age of seventy-seven, Harold retained vivid memories of his return voyage. After the 'crossing of the line' off the west coast of Africa, the diggers enjoyed three days of shore leave in Cape Town. The men were given strict instructions not to fraternise with 'coloured South Africans'. Harold wrote:

> On the docks policemen were very active to prevent
> the natives scrounging from the fishermen their catch
> of crayfish. It made interesting watching from the deck
> during the evening hour. Several natives each with a
> crayfish in hand fleeing through the rail-trucks (over
> and under!) The natives were mostly too fleet of foot for
> the white policemen in this activity.[3]

The diggers backed the underdogs – leaning over the ship's rail and shouting and cheering as the crayfish 'thieves' evaded the policemen and their batons.

Alongside the precarious hand-to-mouth existence of the 'coloured' South Africans, Harold witnessed the opulence of the ruling class. Colonel Stacy invited him on an officers-only motor tour to the residence of General Smuts, the governor general, previously the mansion of Cecil Rhodes, the imperialist, diamond merchant and prime minister of Cape Colony. Harold signed the visitors' book and called it 'a highlight of that day'.

The *Boorara* continued its homeward journey via Durban. As it rounded Cape Leeuwin on the south-western coast of

Western Australia, the refrigerators broke down. This meant that scores of sheep carcasses had to be dumped overboard, attracting schools of sharks. Harold wrote:

> It was an awe-inspiring sight to see a sheep swallowed whole – or just chomped and torn to bits by these monsters. In the floodlight some of these sharks were seen to charge many feet out of the water in their frenzy to feed. No one wanted to have an experience of going overboard by any unforeseen circumstance!

But a cruel sea broke over the ship's deck as the *Boorara* neared Esperance, and a digger, Private William Bligh, was lost overboard. Unlike his namesake of the *Bounty*, he did not survive. Bligh left behind a wife and two children. Harold remembered his own shock as he and the other diggers strained their eyes looking for the hapless man in the heavy waters.

When the *Boorara* docked at Port Melbourne, the influenza restrictions had been lifted and the borders reopened. So for some reason that Harold could not understand, the New South Wales and Queensland troops were disembarked and told to continue home by train. Harold remembered it as a nightmare journey of some twenty-two hours. He arrived at Sydney's Central station just after noon, where a fleet of taxis took the diggers to the Domain. Harold heard the cry of 'Son! Son!' and saw his mother and father in the crowd. He fell into their arms – 'a survivor of the great adventure'.[4]

*

It was spring in Wauchope and Coleraine looked magnificent. The homestead faced north and sat on a bend in the Hastings River under the crest of a great bluff covered in eucalypts. Harold helped to build it as a sixteen-year-old. There were separate bedrooms, and luxuries including a living room, a bathroom with running water, and a modern kitchen fitted with a brick chimney. The floors and walls were made from beech slabs, the ceilings and beams from red cedar. Around the home was a wide veranda overlooking a garden exploding with wisteria, honeysuckle, lemon verbena, camphor laurels and roses. A flagpole boasting an Australian flag competed for height with a few gum trees in the adjacent paddock. The vegetable patch was stocked with beans, peas, lettuce, pumpkin, cauliflower, carrots and tomatoes. The heavy sweet perfume of sorghum rose from the paddocks. A row of pines separated the dairy from the homestead. All this and the muddy ruts made by the jersey cows trailing to and from the dairy filled Harold with memories and emotions 'stirring the soul'.

He went down to the river – the scene of many of his boyhood adventures – his eyes keenly searching for the flickering silver of schools of bream diving among the fallen branches close to the bank. Once, when playing there as a child, Harold had fallen in and been dragged down by the swirling current. As he descended, he could see the silhouettes of the branches overhanging the river, and ghostly rays of sunlight penetrating the cold dark water. Then, suddenly, a strange old man appeared and leapt into the river. He pulled Harold to safety and left him shivering beside his frightened cousins and sisters like 'a wet lamb'.[5]

On the property was a small worker's cottage named Llanfair, after a popular Welsh hymn, 'Christ the Lord is Risen Today', brought to the Hastings River by Presbyterian missionaries in the nineteenth century. Harold set himself up simply in the cottage with few material possessions besides his books and bible. He sat for meals with his family in the 'big house' but preferred to spend his nights alone on the veranda at Llanfair. He could not stand to be inside in the dark. Perhaps it reminded him of the dugouts in the trenches, or the thirty hours he spent lying with his leg broken and a bullet in his chest in the trenches at Pozières while the shells caved in the earth around him. Harold's son Graham, recalled:

'It took Harold years to overcome the horrors of the war and sleep inside, and even then he still had bad dreams of the war.'[6]

Harold thought about leaving the farm. He heard that the British Army was looking for officers on the North West Frontier. Up on the Khyber Pass, the Empire still employed its young men to kill. Would that be better than living with the memory of killing and the guilt of a survivor?

But each day he rose at 3.30 a.m. for the milking. Harold and his sister Bessie milked the herd of seventy Jersey cows by hand. After milking, they would clean the shed and equipment and separate the cream from the milk before Harold carted the cans of cream to the roadside, where it was collected by an employee of the butter factory and carted into town. Then Harold and Bessie would join their parents for breakfast (his younger brother Doug, who had worked the farm while Harold was at the war, had married and left the farm), usually home-raised bacon and poached eggs, with toast made from homemade bread, and a cup of tea.

Harold's father grew lucerne, corn, oats and 'cow cane' (a variety of sugar cane fed to cattle) on the farm. Father and son worked together, ploughing and harvesting by hand. Two

Harold harvesting sorghum with his draught horses
Prince and Kit, c. 1925.

(Courtesy of Roger Wilson)

docile draughthorses, Prince and Kit, pulled the plough while
Harold walked behind.

In the afternoon, he and Bessie would milk the cows
again. The whole process of separating, washing down and
cleaning would repeat itself before the family sat down for
dinner together.

Harold was in agony most nights because of his leg
wound. Pain and nightmares made it easy to wake at 3.30 a.m.
and begin the work again.

Sunday began like any other day with milking, but
otherwise was committed to the kirk. Presbyterianism was at
the centre of Harold's childhood and foundational in making
the man. Harold's grandfather built the first Presbyterian
church in the district, and when Harold was a boy his uncle
used to carry him on his shoulders to the church through the
paddocks.

During the war, Harold had stayed in Edinburgh with his cousin, the Reverend Isaac Graham. In 1918 Isaac returned to Australia and opened a new Free Presbyterian Church in Wauchope (now the Davis Memorial Church). Harold began to attend services there on Sundays at 11 a.m. and 7 p.m. Church services were simple, with few accoutrements and little outward display – all singing was done without accompaniment. Harold found solace in the message of the scriptures, the intellectual rigour in the theology, and the opportunity to talk about local issues and politics with the congregation, most of whom were farmers and relatives.

On 30 January 1922, Harold married his cousin Isabella 'Ivy' Graham of Koree Island at the Free Presbyterian Church. To marry one's cousin seems anathema to some people, but in rural Australia in those days it was not uncommon, particularly in small insular communities bound by codes of class, race and religion. Ivy and Harold made their home at Ennis, near Wauchope. For about two and a half years they lived in a modest home share-farming. In the mid-1920s, Harold and Ivy returned to Llanfair and Harold managed Coleraine for his father. There was much sadness surrounding Ivy and Harold at that time. The Hastings River was a close-knit community, still recovering from the war deaths of many local boys, including Ivy's brothers Colin and Bill Graham, and Norm Way and Alf Perrett. The young couple also lost their first two children, one at birth, the other from whooping cough when only a few months old. Harold became a 'reserved, taciturn man: he spoke when it was necessary and then usually only briefly. But he could produce a twinkle in his eye, a smile at the corner of his mouth and a chuckle.'[7] That twinkle shone brightly on 30 July 1927 with the birth of Harold and Ivy's only surviving child, William Graham Andrews. Harold planted a stand of bamboo alongside Llanfair to provide fishing rods for his son. The old love of nature and wide-eyed wonder and anticipation began to stir in him again.

CHAPTER 19
THE RETURN OF LANCE CORPORAL DICK TURPIN MSM

Dick Turpin married Lizzie Marie Barton, a forty-year-old widow and mother of two boys, in London's Lewisham Anglican Church on 28 October 1919. Like Billy Kane, Dick renounced his Catholic faith to marry outside his church. Dick, his 'English war-bride' Lizzie and her youngest son, Jack, migrated to Australia in June 1920, making Dick the last of the Chipilly Six to return. The family disembarked at Fremantle and boarded at the rectory of St John's Church on Cantonment Street, one of several places where new English migrants stayed before taking up work on the land.

What influenced Dick and Lizzie to choose Western Australia and not his home state of New South Wales? At the time, the English press regularly advertised land and opportunities in the dominions under appealing slogans such as 'ready-made farms' and 'Australia for the British'. The Western Australian premier, the conservative James Mitchell, visited Britain and spruiked the south-west and the Great Southern region of Western Australia for development as a vegetable and dairying area that would finally eliminate the state's dependence on produce from the eastern states. The jarrah, karri and redgum forests, the protected inlets and rivers draining into the Southern Ocean, were seen as signs of fertility. English families, particularly men who had returned from the war, were encouraged to migrate and take up the opportunity to open up the country.

Lizzie Turpin must have been a woman of drive and vision. She applied successfully to take over Springdale, a property on the Wilson Inlet fifty kilometres west of the port of Albany in the remote south of the state. The property had recently been vacated following the death of a pioneer of the Denmark district. Lizzie and Dick converted the homestead into a retreat for visitors (it is still in use today). An article in the local paper, the *Albany Dispatch*, welcomed the new couple to the area:

> The opening of Springdale House as a boarding house will be a boon to holiday-makers at Denmark, as this house is definitely the best and most spacious in the whole of the district, with a veranda 90 feet by 14 feet overlooking our beautiful [Wilson] inlet and within one minute's walk to the mineral springs and a lovely sandy beach for the children to play upon. The proprietress (Mrs L. Turpin) served with the British Army in France during the war as a nurse, and received the G.S.M. Mr Turpin was also on active service in France and received the M.S.M. Visitors to Denmark cannot do better than spend their holidays on the shores of the beautiful lake.[1]

These were confident years in Western Australia. According to Premier Mitchell, 'There was no such thing as bad land in Western Australia.' Before the war Mitchell opened up the wheatbelt by enticing gold miners in Kalgoorlie to put down their picks and shovels and take up superphosphate. 'Gold brought these men to Western Australia,' Mitchell was quoted as saying, 'and superphosphate will keep them here.'[2] He strongly supported moves to place the Agricultural Bank under a board of trustees that issued loans to would-be farmers. He built roads, waterworks and railway lines to far-flung settlements beyond the Darling escarpment. The sleepers were often cut from whatever stand of timber was close by, but that type of cost-cutting led to inefficiencies if the timber proved inadequate.[3]

After 1925, the price of gold and wheat exports fell on international markets and did not recover.[4] But Mitchell's ambition and optimism did not waver. He turned his attention to the south-west and the Great Southern and his long-held ambition to build a vibrant community of British dairy farmers and orchardists who could feed the growing Western Australian population. While the public began to call him Moo Cow Mitchell, the Commonwealth and Westminster governments and the London banks agreed to facilitate Mitchell's agricultural scheme through a migration project known as 'Group Settlement'.

Stanley Bruce, who had replaced Billy Hughes as Aust-ralian prime minister and leader of the Nationalists, described the policy as 'men, money, markets'. British migrants were encouraged to flood in and take up land. This would be financed by loans from London, and paid for by the productivity of the new Australian farms selling their produce to the growing Australian cities and throughout the Empire. The state government foresaw the need for experienced bushmen with farming experience to be employed as foremen or leading hands. Dick applied, and was successful. The foreman was

Group 114, English group settlers on the Styx River near Denmark,
Western Australia, c. 1920s. The 'groupies', many of them
ex-Tommies and their families, were totally unprepared for the
hardships they were about to face. The figure fifth from the right,
standing immediately behind the seated women and wearing
a shirt and tie, could be Dick Turpin.

(Courtesy of Ross McGuinness, Denmark Historical Society)

the most important job on a group settlement, if it were to
succeed.

The Group Settlement Scheme saw 15 000 immigrants
arrive in Western Australia in the first half of the 1920s.[5] The
British parliament was only too keen to get rid of its surplus
population, and former soldiers were particularly encouraged
to apply and take their place in a 'land fit for heroes'. Each
group consisted of twenty to thirty men and their families.
They usually came from the same region, town or community.
Each man was promised a block for his family on the proviso

that he worked cooperatively for the group – clearing and preparing all twenty to thirty settlements plus a school for the kids. The blocks were allocated among the group by means of a lottery. Titles would be given when all the blocks were prepared for settlement: twenty-five acres of cleared land ready for cropping. Each man received a sustenance allowance of up to 10 shillings a day for a forty-eight-hour week. There was no overtime pay, but the settlers were expected to put in extra hours improving their blocks. An enterprising 'groupie' – as the settlers became known – could acquire up to 160 acres of land for free, besides office and survey fees of £13/1. Interest on the outlay on each block would be capitalised, and when the settlers were released from group work to farm their own blocks, the Agricultural Bank would apportion a suitable debit to be charged against each block. The groupies were to repay the debt over thirty years, the last twenty interest-free. Plant and stock would be supplied by the bank on an advance repayable in eight years, the last five interest-free. As Western Australian historian Geoffrey Bolton put it, 'The details sounded fine on paper.'[6]

Dick and Lizzie Turpin witnessed dozens of families coming through Springdale and Denmark on their way to group settlements. Most of them had no farming experience, and those that did knew pastureland and hop fields that were used to the plough. Nothing could have prepared them for the landscape that confronted them. The foot-slogging settler's view was limited to a few metres by huge stands of native jarrah and tingle with trunks as wide as a London bus, and a thick understorey of devilish bracken fern that presaged hard work.

Dick was allocated to Group 114, comprising twenty families from Devon and Cornwall, whose settlement was to be in the Styx River valley, about thirty kilometres north-west of Denmark. Dick's first job was to ride through the bush on his fine mare, Black Bess, and survey a track to the staging camp. Then, with an advance party he erected temporary slab and iron huts, which in time would be replaced by more permanent cottages. The main party would then proceed to clear the blocks and, where necessary, provide fencing and a water supply.

The problems confronting the Devon and Cornwall families and their digger leader Dick Turpin were great. Roads would have to be cut before the land was cleared. High rainfall, poor soils, swamps and mosquitoes were other problems the settlers were utterly unprepared for. The settlers named the site Tealdale, a nostalgic name. Within a few years, Dick and the heroic remnant would call it Hell's Hole.

CHAPTER 20
SOLDIERS' CLUBS vs THE LEAGUE

In 1919 the New South Wales government initiated a fundraising drive with the aim of raising money to build a state war memorial in Sydney's Hyde Park. The various sub-branches of the Returned Sailors' and Soldiers' Imperial League (the RSSILA, the forerunner of the RSL) were given the choice of spending all or part of the money collected on the state war memorial or putting it towards memorials in their communities. At the time there was much public debate over appropriate forms of memorialisation. Some people preferred sacrosanct memorials built in marble and stone; others preferred utilitarian memorials such as parks, drinking fountains, halls and clubrooms.

Harry Seymour, a prominent local business owner and the president of the Marrickville sub-branch of the RSSILA, was passionate about the idea of a memorial club. In 1917, Seymour, then aged forty-four, left his booming business – Seymour's Emporium, on the corner of Victoria and Marrickville Roads – in the hands of a caretaker and enlisted in the AIF as a private. He fought with the 17th Battalion at Passchendaele and in the campaigns of 1918, rising to the rank of second lieutenant. Years later, in 1971, Jack Hayes, Les Mudge and Jimmy Davidson sat down together and recorded for posterity Seymour's vision for the Marrickville Anzac Memorial Club:

> Mr. Seymour had never forgotten a personal experience during the war when he was moving down to a rest camp to go on leave. He had walked some 15 kilometres in full marching order, was covered in mud, and just about 'all in'. With some distance to travel, he met up with a younger soldier who insisted on carrying his rifle and pack the remainder of the journey.
>
> He had seen so much of this happen, and the thought crossed his mind: 'I wonder if this spirit will always continue when we get back home?' He determined to make every effort to see that it did.[1]

In the 1920s, there was quite a bit of competition around memorial buildings. Almost every town in Australia built one. In Sydney, the central memorial in Hyde Park was going ahead, and the Marrickville municipal council had backed local artist and sculptor Gilbert Doble to build a winged Nike – the ancient Greek goddess of victory – outside the impressive council buildings at the top of Marrickville Road. This meant Seymour and his band of diggers would have to conduct their own fund-raising campaign to pull off their idea of a club supporting local diggers and their families. The committee decided to appeal for funds to be used on the ratio of 70 per cent for the soldiers' club, and 30 per cent for bursaries for local children whose fathers were killed in the war.

The people of the district gave their hard-earned money to the diggers. Seymour's aunt donated the first £10; the local Presbyterian minister, who had lost a son in the war, also contributed. The diggers organised a carnival at the Shrublands (now the site of St Brigid's Catholic Church and primary school) on Marrickville Road. Local children enjoyed puppet shows, pony rides, toffee apples, apple dunking and face painting, and gave small donations from their own pockets or handouts from their parents.

Many prominent community members did their bit too, including the mayor, Alderman Ben Richards, and the Honourable Carlo C Lazzarini, the local state Labor member, who seemed always to be in a hurry: 'He would pour his tea into the saucer so that it would cool quickly so to drink it, as there was usually a State car waiting outside to take him somewhere.'[2] Lazzarini had a long parliamentary career. A tailor by trade and a devout Catholic, Lazzarini was the first Italian–Australian to win a seat in the New South Wales parliament. During the war he was president of the Federated Clothing Trades Union, and a member of the Industrial Vigilance Committee, which took over the party machine and expelled Billy Hughes, William Holman and many others over conscription in 1916. After the war he became party whip, chief secretary in Jack Lang's first cabinet, and later one of Lang's most vocal critics. Lazzarini never forgot his constituents; he and his wife Myra were regulars at the Marrickville Anzac Memorial Club. 'Charlie' Lazzarini and Jack Hayes became great friends. When Lazzarini faced retirement after thirty-five years as the sitting member for Marrickville, he asked Jack to replace him. But Jack declined. 'He wasn't interested in politics in that sense,' John Hayes said.[3] Lazzarini was still in parliament when he died of heart disease on 26 November 1952.

Another key local personality was Father Frank Clune, a brave Passionist padre famous in the AIF. He won a Military

Cross for bandaging the wounded under intense shellfire at Menin Road in 1917, and exaggerated stories of him capturing prisoners or carrying grenades to the frontline persisted well after the war was over. Joe Maxwell VC knew Clune as a parish priest before the war, and in the trenches. In his book *Hell's Bells and Mademoiselles*, Maxwell described Clune as a 'wonderful old fellow, who wore a beard, and was always among the men'. Maxwell remembered Clune at Pozières in 1916:

> During the hectic days … our fellows were bombing
> the enemy from a trench. Dead and wounded lay
> everywhere. Still the tragic and bitter struggle went on.
> The supply of grenades was running short when the old
> priest arrived with two petrol tins filled with water.
>
> 'We don't want water, we want bombs,' yelled one
> excited digger.
>
> 'All right, boys, here is the water. The bombs are here
> also,' replied the old padre with a twinkle in his eyes.

Later that day he was seriously wounded while ministering to 'his lads'.[4]

Clune returned to Marrickville in September 1919. He'd been a parish priest there for twenty-eight years. A great crowd of parishioners welcomed him home – mostly Irish–Australians and Italian migrants who worked in the factories and woollen mills. Clune had known these people since they were children, and had baptised and married many of them. He told his flock:

> I went to the war because I felt it was my duty … and I
> saw a great opportunity to do missionary work. If Christ

were to visit this planet again during the past four years, I ask you today where would you find Him? You would find Him out there in the frontline, comforting the wounded and the dying, and that is the reason why I went. I felt it was my duty as a priest. You hear a lot of stories about me. They tell you about taking prisoners – and many other things. My work there was to do the work of a priest, and if I did that work well, it was far better for the men, the country, and the cause, than if I were to go looking for prisoners, or doing any active work in the soldier's life.[5]

These founders of the Marrickville Anzac Memorial Club raised £758. As promised, the diggers gave £200 to the kids and put the rest into establishing the club. Appeals for interest-free loans, repayable in three years, boosted the total collected for the club and the kids to £1330.

The scale of the effort is impressive. Working people (including families and housewives) raised the money and took pride in the honorary nature of the work. The movement depended on the generosity of people who spent most of their day as homemakers, or working in the local factories, railway yards and shops. The first committee of the Marrickville Anzac Memorial Club consisted of a master painter, an engine driver, an electrician, a butcher, water and sewerage employees, a lift attendant, mattress maker, bootmaker, horse-breaker and several labourers.[6] The people giving funds were neighbours, parishioners, wives, shopkeepers and schoolchildren. They were busy people with everyday concerns, and perhaps a son, brother, or father had been to the war, or died there. These families were the hardest hit by the economic strain of buying war bonds, patriotic fundraising and the rising cost of living.

From the beginning, the Marrickville Anzac Memorial Club was a people's organisation in which a private could be club president and a nurse could join the committee alongside a padre and a quartermaster sergeant. These were Jack's friends and associates.

It soon became clear to the founders of the club that the interests of their working-class community outweighed their allegiance to the head office of the Returned Sailors and Soldiers Imperial League in Sydney's CBD. Things came to a head in 1920 when the club broke away from the league. Woollen mills were issuing suit-lengths of tweed for ex-servicemen, which members could collect from the league's head office in Sydney during normal office hours. As most workers could not afford to take the time off, Seymour arranged for one of his storemen to collect the order by cart and deliver the tweed to members. But the league objected to this. The disgruntled Marrickville diggers severed ties with the league. The Marrickville Anzac Memorial Club became the first independent returned soldiers' club of its kind. Other returned soldiers' groups followed suit in Eastwood, Epping, the Eastern Suburbs and Lakemba, eventually forming their own Association of Returned Sailors and Soldiers Clubs of New South Wales.

An article in the *Labor Daily* with the headline 'Bally War is Over: Diggers at Play: No More Soldiering for Them', described the history and philosophy of the association:

> This association started out with ideals – to foster the spirit of camaraderie that existed on active service; to encourage and assist in the formation of returned soldiers' and sailors' clubs; to promote inter-club, social and recreational activities; to assist distressed comrades

and generally guard the interests of returned soldiers and sailors.[7]

Looking back, today's casual observer may see no difference between the soldiers' clubs and the RSSILA. Both organisations sought to guard the interests of returned men (mostly) by pressuring governments on a host of welfare entitlements including pensions, war service home loans, soldier settlement and job preference. At the local level, both groups spoke for and assisted returned diggers. But there were significant differences.

The RSSILA was a federated national body. Formed in 1916 as men began to return from Egypt and Gallipoli, it was originally known as the Returned Soldiers Association. During the war years, the league's powerbrokers in its central office strongly supported the Nationalist government of Prime Minister Billy Hughes. The league's first national president, William Bolton, became a senator on a Nationalist Party ticket.[8] Bolton was stridently pro conscription. He maintained a conservative policy and insisted returned soldiers approach the government through appropriate channels. As dissatisfaction grew with the government's treatment of returned soldiers, Bolton's law and order policy met with opposition from within the league. Captain Gilbert Dyett, a Victorian, campaigned to replace Bolton as national president and succeeded in July 1919. Dyett continued to covet close ties with the Nationalist government and strengthened the centralised bureaucracy of the league. By courting influence with the Nationalist government, the league's executive positioned itself within the old pro-conscription group. Yet the bitter conscription referenda of 1916 and 1917 demonstrated that many of the rank and file diggers favoured volunteerism.

To add further tension, those holding office were usually officers, which to many diggers replicated the old hierarchy of army life.

Jack Hayes told his son that the league was run by officers and annual membership fees were too expensive for the average digger. Bill Gammage noted similar responses from numerous diggers he surveyed while writing his classic book on Australians in the First World War, *The Broken Years*.[9] The clubs appealed to the rank and file diggers like Jack because they were affordable social places where working-class diggers could uphold the value of mateship and look after their less fortunate friends. Some remained members of both organisations. Others turned their back on the league.

By the end of 1919 the league boasted a membership of 150 000 returned men. This was mostly due to aggressive recruiting on troopships and in the demobilisation offices as the diggers prepared to come home. But by 1927, active membership had fallen to less than 30 000.[10] In contrast, membership of the returned soldiers' clubs had risen steadily.

'Introduce your cobber to the club' became the catch-phrase of a movement that began with the Marrickville Anzac Memorial Club and grew to fifty affiliated clubs and almost 5000 members by 1927.[11] In 1929 the Association of Returned Sailors and Soldiers Clubs changed its name to the Australian Legion of Ex-Service Clubs.[12] By the 1930s the clubs had an unofficial estimate of 40 000 members across New South Wales and Queensland, rivalling the league in size and popularity. Their numbers included affiliated clubs, the Diggers' Association and the NSW Railway and Tramway Returned Sailors and Soldiers Association. The competition between the league and the clubs was sometimes fierce.

The emergence of the clubs and the characteristics of the mostly working-class neighbourhoods where they became popular is a subject worthy of further study. The clubs distinguished themselves from the league by advertising that they were independent and highly democratic, and that all those elected to office – president, treasurer, secretary and the like – served in an honorary nature. One of the criticisms of the league at the time was that it was controlled by a centralised bureaucracy of paid officials with close ties to the conservative government. A digger writing on behalf of his returned soldiers' club in 1919 put it this way:

> I might state the returned men in this district ... and there are many, will not let Torydom influence them in any way in regard to their political opinions. Most of these men were workers before they enlisted, and they state that ... The R.S.S.I.L. [League] executive will not influence them ... One man speaking to me this morning stated, 'self-preservation is the first law of nature,' and we are sticking to the people whom we expect to stick to us, and that is the Labor Party.[13]

The clubs, while primarily social, also raised money for returned diggers' causes, did pension work, hospital visits, organised a Christmas appeal and argued for job preference. All money raised went directly to the needs of returned men and their families, not to administration costs or a centralised bureaucracy. At a meeting between delegates of the league and clubs aimed at finding common ground, the Country Party MHR for Richmond, Frederick Herbert Green, a former officer in the AIF (he lost a leg at Menin Road in 1917) and for many years a member of the New South Wales Council of the RSSILA, attacked the soldiers' clubs movement, calling it a 'fungus growth' and firing a broadside at the delegates. One of the clubs' delegates replied, 'You are not in parliament now, you are addressing a body of intelligent men.'

The following day Green abused his parliamentary privilege by repeating his criticisms in parliament; he was shouted down by the MPs opposite him. The stoush was widely reported in the *Labor Daily* and regional papers.[14] There was a sense of class snobbery about it too. This was an era before the ubiquitous RSL sub-branch with its cheap middies and counter meals that Australians became accustomed to after the Second World War. In the 1920s the league headquarters looked down its nose at such frivolity. But the clubs were a place to go and have a good time. A league official publicly denounced the clubs as being 'rude and degrading' and 'a waste of good time' because the men loudly sang wartime songs of the 'Madame Marcelle' [sic] type.[15] This was a reference to the popular soldiers' song 'Mademoiselle from Armentieres' and a snide crack at the way the average digger managed to 'mongrel' the French language. One gets the sense that Jack Hayes would not have minded that in the least.

All this was in the future when Harry Seymour and his mates were raising money for their club. Seymour owned a terrace house on Marrickville Road and fitted it out as a temporary meeting place for the diggers. Les Mudge recalled:

> We had a three-quarter billiard table and bought a few journals for reading material. No one ever thought of serving liquid refreshments while we were housed there. Apart from meetings, we would go down of a night to have a yarn, a read, or a game of cards with mates.[16]

The committee purchased an 1800-square metre block on Garners Avenue. Building commenced in late 1920. Sir Walter Davidson, KCMG, governor of New South Wales, opened the building on 30 July 1921. Jack's granddaughter Helen has vivid memories of the club. The original building centred on a very large hall able to accommodate over 300 people. They entered the hall through two large doors with glass panelling at the top. In the middle of the hall was a stage for musicians and concerts. Next to the stage was a door through to a big kitchen with a stove, fridge and lots of drawers and bench space for catering. Beyond the kitchen were several rooms for members only. There were billiard tables, a library, offices and a bar with tables and chairs where beer was sold and a very large trade was done after six o'clock closing.[17]

CHAPTER 21
JACK MEETS MAY

One day in 1922, Jack Hayes was walking down Sydney's Pitt Street and noticed a bright young woman in the crowd. When her blue eyes met his, they recognised each other immediately. It was his neighbour from Bathurst days before the war – Sarah Jane May Slocombe, the girl who used to teasingly call him 'Mick' or 'Mickey Dripping' because of his Irish heritage. Jack always fancied May but he went to war for the adventure and never got beyond talking blarney to her. While Jack was in the trenches, May Slocombe married another Bathurst railwayman, James Purdon.

Jack learnt that May had a five-year-old daughter, Thora, known as Megs. But her marriage had not been successful. May and James Purdon were in the midst of a divorce. Once the court was satisfied there had been twelve months of separation, and that May had the means to support her daughter, the case would be declared *decree absolute*. In other words, the judge would put the case to rest, and when that happened May planned to move back to Bathurst with her daughter.

Soon Jack was spending a little less time at the Marrickville Anzac Memorial Club and more time with May.

The couple went to the Tivoli in Castlereagh Street for each new show. They saw Ella Shields, Will Fyfe, Ada Reeve and all 'the top liners'. They enjoyed the nightclub scene too.[1] Jack noticed that May wore her skirt just below the knee, exposing her slender calves and ankles, which was daring for the times. May kept her hair a little shorter than most of the other young women of Sydney. A natural blonde, she had her hair done every week and 'was particular without being flashy'. She liked pink lipstick and pale pink nail polish, face powder and always Ponds face cream. She was petite and wore fashionable dresses with straight lines. Her skin was fair and tanned easily in summer. Jack kept a photo of May taken on a typical hot Sydney summer day at the beach. She wears a fashionable one-piece bathing suit. Her fine chin is tilted at the camera as she shields her eyes from the sun. This was the photo Jack kept in his wallet.

Jack loved fine clothes, and for shows at the Tivoli he wore a three-piece suit with a short suit jacket with a single button at the waist; a white shirt with a soft attached collar, and a dark tie. His trousers were slim with a cuff and his shoes were leather with a round toe, laced above the ankle. He had a Fedora hat, a fob in his waistcoat pocket and a striking white flower, known as a boutonniere, in his lapel.

May's daughter, Megs, took to Jack. He had a charisma that attracted all kinds of people, children and dogs included. Jack would lift Megs up in his arms or hoist her on his hip, ignoring the pain in his chest. She was a bonny child, 'calm and lovely'.[2]

On 28 April 1923, Jack and May married according to the rites of the Methodist Church in Newtown, Sydney. May was three months pregnant with their first and only son, John. She wore a light grey dress with lavender flowers and a wide-brimmed hat that framed her face. Their first home was a rental in a group of six terrace houses at 33 Trade Street, Newtown, not far from the train station. Terrace houses had gone up all over the inner west in the boom just before the crash of the 1890s. 'There was a saying that they were built by the mile and sold by the yard.' The trade described them as 'Queen Anne at the front and Mary Ann at the back.'[3] In other words, they looked good from the street but were slapdash on the inside, often damp, uncomfortable and unhygienic. They fitted Newtown's reputation of being rough as bags, or at least not very salubrious, but May remembered it as 'a nice area, always very clean, never any squabbles'.[4]

It is difficult to comprehend the inner emotional life of May and the thousands of women of her generation who married returned soldiers. History has ignored these women; their lives and feelings have gone undocumented. When the papers mentioned women, it was by their husband's name – May became Mrs JC Hayes. Most of what we know about women of the 1920s comes from the stories passed on by their children and grandchildren. May's mother, Amelia, is remembered as a mysterious woman of Spanish origin, with dark eyes and olive skin. In looks and outlook, May was said to be more like her father, Jack. Jack Slocombe was a Somerset-born railwayman. He wrote a weekly piece for the pro-Labor *National Advocate*, where he argued, often with an acerbic wit, against conscription and 'money power' in defence of volunteerism and trade unionism: 'If you are ineligible by age, infirmity or sex, don't vote away men's lives – place your cross opposite "No". Down with the profiteer and the capitalists.'[5] In an era when women were still the legal chattel of their husbands, Jack Slocombe was outspoken on the rights of women too – 'How much more appreciative would husbands

Jack Hayes (bottom right) next to a Lemnos local, 1915.

(Courtesy of Helen Thomson)

Above Dead Germans above a sunken road, Chipilly.
(IWM Q7291)

Top left The village of Chipilly on 10 August 1918, after a set-piece battle had raged in the area for over thirty hours. This photo gives a good indication of what the six Australians would have seen when they cleared the village while souvenir-hunting ahead of British troops on 9 August 1918.
(AWM H15934)

Below left View of the Somme River from Chipilly Spur, 17 August 1918. This is where the six stealth raiders advanced on 9 August 1918.
(AWM E02989A)

Jack Hayes (right), 31 August 1914.

(Courtesy of Helen Thomson and Nola Moore)

Jack Hayes (left) in 'French civvies' in France, raising a toast with mates, c. 1916–18. By February 1918 he was one of only sixty-nine original members remaining in the battalion.

(Courtesy of Nola Moore and Helen Thomson)

Above Private Harold Dudley Andrews on discharge from hospital in Wareham, late 1916 or early 1917, after treatment for wounds he received at Pozières. He sent this to his family and wrote on the back: 'As a token of Remembrance. With Love from Harold.'

(Courtesy of Graham and Peter Andrews)

Right Portrait of C Company, 1st Battalion, in the midst of battle, 23 August 1918, by Captain Hubert Wilkins MC. Harold Andrews, his sergeant's stripes just visible, sits with his back to the embankment mid-photo. The battalion had been over the top that morning and had just been told they would be going over again in a few minutes.

(AWME03004)

Above Harold (left) and Norm Way: cousins and best mates on Paris leave, March 1918. The diggers had a saying that if you were lucky enough to enjoy the pleasures of Paris, you didn't care which German got you afterwards.

(Courtesy of Peter Andrews)

Mates: unknown (left), Private Ernest Hinton (centre),
Private George Stevens (right), c. 1916.

(Courtesy of Rich Baker)

Billy Kane, in slouch hat, and mates at their send-off,
Macksville, New South Wales, 1915.

(Courtesy of Trevor Lynch)

Harold Andrews in his officer's uniform, c. 1919.

(Courtesy of Peter Andrews)

Jack Hayes (centre) on his return to Sydney, 15 February 1919.

(Courtesy of Nola Moore and Helen Thomson)

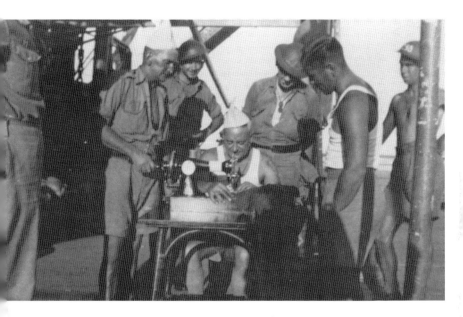

Above Jerry (seated) sewing, with mates from the 2/3rd Field Workshop, en route to Egypt, c. 1941. The scar from the bullet wound he received in the Froissy Valley in August 1918 is visible on his left shoulder.

(Photo courtesy of Rick Dollemore)

Top left Jack pouring drinks for his digger mates, c. 1920s. Jerry is at Jack's right. The other returned men are unknown. Note the returned soldier badges on their lapels.

(Courtesy of Helen Thomson)

Below left A Depression-era portrait of Carrie and George Stevens (front row, left and centre respectively). Behind George are his stepfather and his mother Emeline.

(Courtesy of Rich Baker)

Dick and Amy Turpin, c. 1960s.

(Courtesy of Richard Turpin)

May Hayes (left) and some of the Marrickville
Anzac Memorial Club Women's Auxiliary, c. 1950.

(Courtesy of Helen Thomson)

Three generations: Jack, his daughter Thora (Megs), and granddaughter Beverley. Jack outlived both his beloved girls.

(Courtesy of Helen Thomson)

Private 'Jerry' Fuller, c. 1919.
'The kid' was the youngest member of the Chipilly Six.

(Courtesy of Mark Deacon)

be,' he asked, 'if only they were wives for a while' – perhaps influenced by his daughter's unhappy first marriage.[6] May's granddaughter Helen remembers her as a stoic, capable, no-fuss woman who provided consistency and reliability. May viewed Jack's war experiences and the ongoing problems of his wound with respect and compassion.

In her book *Shattered Anzacs: Living with the scars of war*, historian Marina Larsson found that in the war years and the 1920s, young women were encouraged to desire soldiers who had given the 'great and glorious gift' of their health for the nation.[7] The tabloids and women's magazines emphasised the masculine appeal of wounded soldiers and suggested to young women that war injuries made men desirable. These commentators implied that if desire did not fire young women, then old-fashioned Edwardian maternalism should. *Everylady's Journal* suggested to its readers that the vulnerability of disabled and badly wounded soldiers 'awakened a spirit of "mothering" in young women and urged them to embrace feminine roles as nurturers and healers'.[8] And of course there was the simple act of hitting it off, love, affection and companionship.

When May married Jack, she entered a world that her civilian experience could not prepare her for. Her brothers did not go to the war and her first husband was one of the eligible men who chose not to enlist (bearing in mind that more than half of those eligible declined to do so). Little in her life could have prepared her for the routines of regular hospital treatment that Jack required or the unconditional mateship of the Marrickville Anzac Memorial Club. But she and Jack shared a love of people, sharp wit, and a set of working-class values and dignity closely attached to their family history, the railways and the Australian Labor Party.

Jack had a wife and two kids and a dead-end job. He wanted to get out of their rental and into a home of their own, but to change jobs in an era of high unemployment was a risk few responsible men were willing to take. Once again, his mates at the Marrickville Anzac Memorial Club helped him out. Les Mudge worked as an ironmonger at the Metropolitan Water, Sewerage and Drainage Board. And in those times of men, money and markets, opportunities were coming up in big infrastructure projects funded by loans from the London banks. Les got Jack a job as a chainman (a surveyor's offsider) building the Woronora Dam, an expansive state government project intended to secure Sydney's water supply in the years before construction of the Warragamba Dam in 1960. Very soon, Jack's talent for organising was recognised. He became a storeman, then a clerk, costing and relieving wages.

Jack also went to night school and studied to be a drafts-man. In 1925 he qualified with honours in House Drainage and received a prize at the annual awards at the East Sydney branch of the Technical College, Darlinghurst.[9] It was a measure of the man that he sought to develop new skills and improve his family's prospects. Jack became a draftsman with the Water, Sewerage and Drainage Board, beginning at Level D.[10]

May embraced change too. She joined the women's auxiliary of the Marrickville Anzac Memorial Club. Her granddaughter, Helen, remembered May explaining how it came about:

Nana joined because Poppy was always at the club
every night. [He] went to work at the Water Board,
came home for dinner and off to the club. Nana told
me when I was a lot older 'if you can't beat 'em, join 'em'

and that is what she did and became the president of
the Ladies Auxiliary. All the family had their wedding
supper at the club and the Ladies Auxiliary always did
the food, wow I could not even think about it.[11]

I discovered an audiocassette recording of an interview with
May done for a bicentennial project on Australian communities. The tape had been lying in a cupboard somewhere in the
Powerhouse Museum, Ultimo, and had probably not been
listened to since it found its way there in 1988. At the time of
the recording, May was ninety-two. She says:

> From the time he was a very, very, very young man,
> [Jack] was a member of that club ... They were very
> dedicated to one another. It took a lot of building up ...
> They had to work hard, anyone on a committee or even
> a member would give their services to the club [without
> charge] whether it was a side of beef, or a plumber to do
> a job as needed ...
>
> When I first went to the club, there was another
> lady there running a committee. She said to me, 'Why
> don't you join?'
>
> I said, 'Oh, no. I don't want to join.'
>
> My husband said, 'Why don't you join, May?'
>
> 'Oh', I said, 'all right.'
>
> My son was five years old at the time.
>
> [It was] more social than anything else ... There
> were twelve ladies on the committee and we did all the
> catering over the years. Oh, what the club put on in
> those days. There'd be chicken, sausage rolls, lobsters,
> prawns ... smoked kippers, salads of all kinds, savouries
> – Gosh! Savouries to burn. There would be anything

from two to 300 patrons in the early days of the club
… of course the club were all young people just starting
families and there were a lot of children … They were
good days really.[12]

That was the point of the club. Not everyone had been to the war. It was a community of people with common values, who had shared in the hardship of the war through sacrifices of many kinds and a commitment that their sons, brothers and husbands might fit back into the life of the community in their own time.

CHAPTER 22
THE FIRST ANZAC DAY DAWN SERVICE

John Hayes did not care to speak of his father as a hero of the Great War, though he was certainly proud that his father wore the Distinguished Conduct Medal. He'd often heard Jerry Fuller and the others repeat the story of Chipilly Spur. He knew old diggers reckoned Jack would have got the VC were it not for the fact that Chipilly was an embarrassment to the British given that so few diggers had captured what had been the objective of an entire corps. But it was what his father did in peacetime in support of ex-diggers and their families that John admired most. John remembered his childhood fondly and appreciated the love and care of his parents. He also grew up aware of the impact of the Great War on his father and his mates:

> There was my sister, Thora, then along came me.
> We were fortunate to have them as parents. Life was
> happy and pleasant, although at times Jack suffered
> pain from his wounds.

In the course of remembering his father through the eyes of his younger self, John recounted a remarkable story:

> It was the night before Anzac Day and with some of these friends they went to a dinner at the Gallipoli Club. Coming home in the early hours of Anzac Day they went to the cenotaph in Martin Place and saw an elderly lady placing flowers on the memorial. She was paying homage to her son who had been killed during the war.[1]

According to John, Jack and his mates paused with the old woman and prayed with her, even though Jack was never one to pray during the war. Afterwards, the friends continued their walk home to Marrickville. As the sun rose behind them, they spoke about the camaraderie and selflessness they experienced during the war years. Like the old woman, they grieved for their 'brothers' who were dead and the poor buggers locked away in hospital wards. There and then, as they rubbed shoulders on the streets of their old town, they decided they would go to the Cenotaph on Martin Place at dawn each Anzac Day, as the grieving mother had done, and pay homage in a silent ritual to the men who landed at Gallipoli and started the Anzac tradition, and all who had served in the war.

The dawn service is one of Australia's most poignant cultural rituals, repeated each year in countless towns and cities around the country, extending to New Zealand and around the world. It is memorably evoked in Brian Fitzpatrick's poem 'Cenotaph', with its passerby halted in the darkness by the sound of ghostly hoofbeats echoing through the stillness of Martin Place.

There are no first-hand records of the diggers' meeting with the old lady in Martin Place. The earliest account, told repeatedly by 2GB radio broadcaster Frank Grose, a former Salvation Army pastor and close friend of Jack Hayes, holds that eight carousing diggers were present at the dawn encounter with the old lady at the Cenotaph.[2] Grose began attending the dawn service in 1929 and started broadcasting it to a national audience in 1931. Was Jack one of the men in the origin story?

The most quoted second-hand account names five diggers linked to Jack by their membership of the Marrickville Anzac Memorial Club, the Gallipoli Club and the Association of Returned Sailors and Soldiers Clubs. This version of the story appears in a pamphlet written in 1981 to mark the sixtieth anniversary of the Marrickville Anzac Memorial Club, entitled 'The Dawn Service in Sydney: How it started'. While it does not name Jack, the importance of the Marrickville Anzac Memorial Club in the origin story is compelling:

> On returning from a function in the early hours of one morning in 1927, five members of the Association of Returned Sailors and Soldiers Clubs, (later to become known as the Australian Legion of Ex-Service Clubs) saw an old lady with a bunch of flowers proceed to the Cenotaph.
>
> Mr G Patterson spoke to her and asked if they could be of any help, and as the lady placed the flowers on the Cenotaph they bowed their heads and said a prayer. They then proceeded home. Those five men were Messrs Jim Davidson of the Marrickville Anzac Memorial Club, Ernie Rushbrook, G Patterson, LA Stickler and W Gamble.[3]

This account was written after all the men named (and Jack) were dead. This story is repeated on the website of the Sydney Dawn Service Trust and has been reprinted on countless pamphlets on Anzac Day in Sydney. The source is revealing but it is also flawed. There are inaccuracies in the spelling and identification of 'the five'. This underlines the fact that no serious historical work has been done to acknowledge the founders of the dawn service, which is a disservice to the men involved.[4]

The Jim Davidson mentioned was none other than Jack's mate Jimmy Davidson, with whom Jack had served in the trenches. Jimmy's father was a well-known identity in Marrickville and former president of the Marrickville Labor League. By 1927 Jimmy was a successful businessman, running a hardware store in the district. 'Ernie Rushbrook' – actually Ernest Alfred Rushbrooke – was a London-born thirty-one-year-old jeweller of Epping. Rushbrooke served as a private in the 37th Battalion and was twice wounded in action. He returned to Australia in March 1918. In 1927 he was the honorary president of the Epping returned soldiers' club and honorary state secretary of the Association of Returned Sailors and Soldiers Clubs.

'G Patterson' – actually George Watson Paterson – of Lakemba was the son of a Presbyterian minister. In 1927, Paterson, then aged forty, ran the Argent Manufacturing Company, producing and printing cardboard boxes. He had served in France with the 30th Battalion, finishing up, as he put it, 'just a blinking sergeant'.[5] Paterson had grown up in a prominent western suburbs family. One of his brothers took the cloth. Two other brothers enlisted in the AIF, including George's younger brother, Malcolm, a well-known rugby league footballer with the Western Suburbs team. Malcolm Paterson served at Gallipoli as a private in the 2nd Battalion and remained there until the evacuation, being among the last of the covering party to leave.[6] He was commissioned in France in 1917 and killed shortly afterwards near Hermes on Easter Monday, felled by a sniper's bullet to the head. George Paterson was the president of the Association of Returned Sailors and Soldiers Clubs.

'LA Stickler' – Lawrence Alfred 'Len' Stickley MM – a thirty-one-year-old carpenter living in Epping, served with the 18th Battalion in Gallipoli and France. He earned his Military Medal for 'coolness and presence of mind' in a successful raid in the Armentieres sector in June 1916. Stickley was twice wounded in action and finished the war as a company sergeant major.[7] He was honorary treasurer of the Epping club.

The last man named, W (Bill) Gamble, remains a mystery. AIF enlistment records and nominal rolls held by the Australian War Memorial and the National Archives of Australia point to two likely candidates: William Gamble, regimental number 6625, a twenty-three-year-old despatch clerk of Zetland, Sydney; and William Gamble, regimental number 6440, a twenty-four-year-old iron moulder of Rozelle. The latter was discharged in 1916 suffering from shell shock and stammering. In the 1920s he was married and living in Lakemba and may well have been a mate of Paterson's and a fellow member of the Lakemba Soldiers Club.

What bound these men (and Jack Hayes) was their membership of the soldiers' clubs that sprang up in the suburbs of Sydney, starting in Marrickville in the years immediately after the war. After the poignant meeting with the old lady in 1927, Ernie Rushbrooke introduced a motion at a delegates meeting of the Association of Returned Sailors and Soldiers Clubs in March 1928 'That a wreath be placed on the Cenotaph at dawn, 4.30 a.m. on 25th April 1928'.[8] The diggers endorsed the proposal.

What happened next has been passed down in the Hayes family for over nine decades. Jack and May Hayes, with Jimmy Davidson and a group of Marrickville diggers, their wives and a knot of widows and grieving parents, met at the Garners Avenue club rooms in the predawn of 25 April 1928. From there the group made their way to Martin Place and joined their friends and associates from the other clubs.

'No attempt was made to attract the attendance of the general public', but about thirty women and children and more than a hundred men gathered silently.[9]

At the time, the Cenotaph was only partly built. In 1927, the premier – the 'big fella' Jack Lang – had thrown in £10000 to add the bronze sculptures of the sailor and soldier at the eastern and western ends of the plain sarcophagus. But the noble figures had not yet been added. That first dawn service was a small, solemn and little-publicised event. But it was charged with emotion. The reporter for the *Sydney Morning Herald* was one of the few to witness it:

> The significance of the hour, corresponding with that when the first fruits of the sacrifice of Gallipoli were gathered in, was very real to the knot of 150 persons who gathered round the simple eloquent stone. The eerie silence of the night was intensified when those bareheaded men and bowed women and children gave their feeling token of two minutes' mute respect and remembrance. There was not even a trumpet call nor a spoken prayer. The silence was all.[10]

George Paterson led a small party in laying wreaths, including an invitee from Western Australia, representing the Third Brigade – the first men ashore at Gallipoli in 1915:

> In more than one place there was a repressed sob of pity, and handkerchiefs stole quietly to eyes that were misty as the early morning light.
>
> As the people moved away one old lady, partly crippled with age and obvious long distress, haltingly walked to the foot of the Cenotaph, where among the array of beautiful and expensive wreaths she hid modestly her token of long remembering – a tiny bunch of white daisies, picked from some suburban garden, and held together with a piece of cord. She could not have given more, for coupled with the posy was the pathos of her coming at so early an hour.[11]

The small group of diggers 'expressed their satisfaction with the unexpected success of their innovation'. Ernie Rushbrooke said, '[It] shows that the public are still very far from forgetting what the occasion means.'[12]

Then, as now, Anzac Day was a public holiday. The RSSILA laid their own wreaths at 9 a.m. and concluded the day with a sunset ceremony. But the solemn act of remembrance at dawn captured the public imagination. The blank unfinished symbol of the Cenotaph made it 'A fitting memorial to all, without class or creed'.[13] It was 'unconstrained by any prescription of meaning beyond the words TO OUR GLORIOUS DEAD and LEST WE FORGET'.[14]

John finished his story:

It was from this that the 'dawn service' was born.
Starting from a small group of people, over the years
it became a ceremony of thousands and a significant
event. The dawn service extended throughout Australia
and is a very prominent part of Australia, paying respect
to those that died for freedom and beliefs.

John Hayes' account of his father's involvement is not
sufficient historical evidence of itself to prove that Jack Hayes
was among that small band of diggers who met the old lady
in Martin Place. But it seems entirely characteristic of Jack
that he would be there. Jack was a larrikin and a talisman in
war and peace. We can see him coming home through Martin
Place shoulder to shoulder with his mates. By 1927, when
the idea of the dawn service is said to have taken hold, few
original diggers like Jack remained. He was among the first
young men recruited in Martin Place in 1914, and unlike the
other men linked to the origin story, he had landed at dawn
on Gallipoli on 25 April 1915. Jack was a custodian of the
Anzac tradition. If the origin story lies somewhere between
truth and myth, surely it is big enough to remember a man
like Jack Hayes.

PART FIVE
THE 1930s

CHAPTER 23
THE GREAT DEPRESSION

On a sultry late summer night in 1930, Jack Hayes and a group of mates were driving home from a cricket match through McGraths Hill on the outskirts of western Sydney. As their Chevrolet Tourer rounded a bend at high speed, it hit the back of a stationary lorry. The quiet lamp-lit street was transformed into carnage. The impact was so severe that witnesses said the lorry was thrown into the air. Jack and his two mates were flung through the windscreen of the Chevy and lay prostrate among the shards of glass and debris strewn across the road. The lorry was carrying greyhounds returning from a race at Grose Wold. The scream of distressed dogs added to the frightfulness of the scene.

An ambulance raced the injured men to the nearest hospital. Jack was badly concussed and his left thigh fractured. His mates suffered similar injuries. Having survived the war and two gunshot wounds, it seemed as though nothing could kill Jack. But the accident left him with a limp.

To make matters worse, Jack had received a letter from his employer, the Metropolitan Water, Sewerage and Drainage Board, 'regretfully' informing him that his services would be terminated due to the 'insufficiency of loan funds' to finance its major works. In October 1929 the Wall Street stock market in New York had crashed, plunging the world into the Great Depression. Many Australians were about to experience unemployment and hardship. Jack and the other members of the Chipilly Six would not dodge this bullet.

Australia was in an economic recession even before the international finance markets collapsed. In the late 1920s, the export price of Australia's most important commodities, wheat and wool, declined, while urbanisation and infrastructure development increased, financed by loans from the London banks. When the bankers ceased making loans in April 1930 and demanded repayment of the interest, the Water Board declared that it would be retrenching one thousand workers and their managers. This included Jack and Jerry: the latter was working as a chainman under Jack. A public service job was meant to be 'a job for life', but ironically, Jack's termination date was set for Anzac Day 1930. In 2019 his grand-daughter Helen unearthed the termination letter the Water Board sent to him. Her anger was raw: 'Go to war and get killed but we cannot keep you in a job!'

The impact of the global financial crash was 'immediate and savage'.[1] The ravaged faces of men who marched on Anzac Day joined the jobless queues alongside men from many walks of life in a generation that had still not recovered from the sacrifices of the war years. As the gross national product slipped, unemployment, which had averaged 8 per cent for most of the 1920s, rose to 10 per cent in 1929, 18 per cent in 1930, 27 per cent in 1931 and 28 per cent in 1932.[2] The impact of joblessness was worse than the numbers suggested as the available data only counted workers who were union members. Historian Mark Lyon found that in 1928, in response to deteriorating economic conditions, the number of ex-servicemen seeking help in finding employment from the returned services charity Legacy had tripled to five or six per week. By July 1929, Legacy's main objective of assisting the dependents of deceased servicemen was outpaced by 'induced growth' in the club's commitment to ex-servicemen requiring material relief and work.[3] By 1932–33, Leonard Arthur Robb, president of the New South Wales branch of the RSSILA, estimated that 15 000 ex-servicemen were out of work in that state alone.[4]

George Stevens and Bill Kane also lost their jobs. Harold Andrews' war injuries, and worries about the farm's income, led to him being hospitalised. Dick and Lizzie Turpin saw their hopes in Western Australia shattered.

All the Chipilly Six used their status as returned soldiers to fight for preference in employment for themselves and digger mates who had fallen on hard times. Jack was fortunate that a member of the board of the Water Board, Alderman Ben Richards, was a friend and founding sponsor of the Marrickville Anzac Memorial Club. While Jack was in hospital, Richards appeared before the board and insisted that Jack should be 'afforded time' to appeal his retrenchment. Richards told his colleagues that Jack

> … was a returned soldier having participated in the landing at Gallipoli, had been in the service for almost seven years, during which time as the result of study, he had graduated from the position of chainman to the post which he now occupied, and was, he understood, doing good work. Shortly after the issue of the notice, Hayes met with a very serious motor accident, and it was probable he would be in hospital for at least three

months. He was thus unable to make an appeal to the board for reconsideration of the notice.[5]

A number of board members were reluctant to act in Jack's favour, arguing that the company would have to pay sick leave while they waited for Jack's appeal. Others were concerned about placing the board in an 'invidious position' – and perhaps setting a precedent that other returned employees might also appeal retrenchment. But at least one, Alderman John Elder Galloway, a former trooper in the 2nd New South Wales Mounted Rifles, considered that the war service rendered by Jack 'should justify the Board in treating his case as a special one'.[6]

Galloway and Richards' attitudes prevailed. Jack made an appeal and retained his job, and kept it again during another round of 'wholesale retrenchments' the following year when the New South Wales treasury was empty and the Water Board was forced to lay off more employees. But as the economic situation worsened, Jack and all salaried public servants like him endured wage reductions, increased working hours and financial anxiety as the New South Wales and Commonwealth Labor governments grappled with how to balance the budget and avoid inflation. The following year, as many as 2500 men on wages lost their jobs with the Water Board.[7]

What happened to Jerry during these years is not known, but it is likely that as an unskilled labourer he would not have been as fortunate as Jack. At best the Water Board would have employed him on relief work at reduced wages.

*

Bill and Emma Kane were living in the small timber town of Bowraville with six kids. Bill worked as a sleeper-cutter and timber-getter. Their eldest son Arthur left school at age thirteen, after only three years of formal education, to go with his dad and cut timber in the bush. As the 1920s drew to a close, piecework as a sleeper-cutter dried up. The heyday of the expansion of the railways ended with the war years. To add to the woes of the timber-getters, the Bruce-Page Nationalist-Country Party government decimated the timber industry with a series of attacks in the Arbitration Court. In January 1929 wages were cut, the maximum permissible ratio of apprentices to men employed was increased, and the forty-four-hour week – one of the labour movement's hardest-won achievements – was increased to forty-eight hours. The timber workers went on strike, but unemployment in Sydney was already so bad that there was never a shortage of scab labour to fill their jobs. Bill's daughter Renie says that in 1929 Bill was out of work and 'went around the banks and asked them if he could clean their windows to earn some money'.[8]

The family moved to 2 Mary Street, Macksville. It was a three-bedroom fibro and timber home with an iron roof, a picket fence out the front and a veranda running around three sides of the house. A laundry was out the back, down a flight of stairs. The floors were of polished timber. There was a fuel stove in the kitchen, and a long table where the family sat together for meals. Bill and Emma put in a veggie patch, kept chooks and grew 'the biggest' macadamia tree in the backyard. The house was owned by Emma's sister and her husband, who lived next door. With a large family to feed and rent due fortnightly for the house, young Arthur got a job working in the local doctor's garden, polishing the floors on his hands and knees and helping with the washing up as the doctor and his wife entertained a lot. The money he was paid he gave to his mother. Arthur's daughter, Robyn Franks (Bill's granddaughter), remembers:

> Dad told me that Emma would sometimes give him 6 pence to go to the local picture show. They were hard times, certainly for my father, being the eldest in the family, but he said he was happy to help his dad as they worked hard to do the best for them all.[9]

*

In Young, George Stevens lost his job at Chant & Co. His employer had honoured his promise of employment on George's return from the war, but the Depression was different. Rural people had stopped spending. Thrift was a necessity. Bill Kane and George Stevens found work on government (shire) relief gangs in Macksville and Young respectively, improving roads and building culverts and bridges. As returned servicemen with gallantry medals, and being well-known sportsmen and respected workers in their local communities, they were afforded what little respect relief wages could provide and were made gangers (leading hands).

*

Harold Andrews' annual farm income hit all-time lows as the global price of wheat and domestic demand for butter plunged. Harold admitted himself to Randwick Hospital for returned servicemen in Sydney. His son Graham and grandson Peter remember it was for operations to mend his wounded leg,

UNOFFICIAL HISTORY OF THE A.I.F.

These men are convicted of having served their Country.

Smith's Weekly championed digger causes in the 1920s and 1930s.
Bill Kane, George Stevens and Dick Turpin all found work in
government relief road-making gangs during the Great Depression.

long neglected. But as an old man, Harold wrote about the
severe psychological effects of unresolved war trauma:

> … separation from family, anxiety about family;
> severe apprehension of action and 'fear-of-fear' and
> being unable to measure up to expectations of what is
> expected … as well as boredom, harsh living conditions,
> and … the realities of being in action itself.[10]

For Harold, hospitalisation was clearly more than recovery from physical wounds. He spent six weeks as a patient on 'a meagre pension of £2/4/0 a week', but could not escape the worry of the farm. 'Tension was the order of the day,' Harold remembered in 1975.[11]

*

Harold's grandson, Peter, related another experience Harold had during the Depression – a visit by a member of 'a right-wing group':

> Dad remembers when he was young in the 1930s, a chap came to see Pa, he was in uniform and Dad was impressed by the uniform so he remembered the chap, he had lunch with Pa, Dad and Nanna, whilst having lunch he tried to get Pa to join the New Guard.[12]

The New Guard was a proto-fascist movement that began in the exclusive gentlemen's clubs of Sydney and grew to a membership of at least 50 000 recruits, 20 000 of whom were classed as 'hard-core ironsides'.[13] Prominent businessmen, industrialists, professionals, public servants, clergymen and members of the pastoral elite and many ex-AIF officers from the middle- and upper-middle classes joined its ranks. Historian Keith Amos, whose book on the New Guard is still the only serious study of the organisation, found that many of these former officers were still quite young men, hardened by the war, and looking for the purpose and sacrifice that was held out as a virtue in army service but was missing from the materialistic life they found on their return. The New Guard wore uniforms, organised themselves into 'brigades' with ranking officers, used a solemn salute reminiscent of the rising fascist movements in Europe, and planned and sometimes carried out attacks on communists and striking workers.

No one excited the anger of the Guard so much as Jack Lang, the democratically elected leader of the Labor government in New South Wales. Few figures in Australian political history have been as divisive as the 'Big Fella'. Lang was born into a working-class family that had suffered greatly during the depression of the 1890s. He aroused adoration in many and outrage in others. When Lang made clear that he would put the interests of the unemployed and the working class ahead of the repayment of war debts and interest on loans from British bondholders, he attracted the wrath of conservative groups in Australian society and became a target of the New Guard. The Guard branded Lang a disloyal 'socialist' or worse, a 'communist', and depicted him as the wolf at the door of the propertied classes.

The Guard's leader, Eric Campbell, a solicitor and former AIF officer, insisted the movement was a defensive organisation. Campbell and several secretive cadres, including the self-proclaimed 'Fascist Legion', schemed to overthrow Lang.[14] Some 'revolutionary' Guardsmen boasted that they were prepared to use the bayonets and firearms stored in Victoria Barracks to do it. Lang's dictatorial style (called by his detractors 'one-man control') also put him at odds with those within his own party.[15] But throughout the Depression, his towering figure remained immensely popular among hundreds of thousands of struggling Labor voters and the unemployed. Lang was the most radical premier in the history of Australian politics. His simplistic messaging that the Depression was caused by 'money power' at home and abroad, and his compelling oratorical style that targeted the 'English' or 'overseas' or 'foreign bondholders' struck a chord with the increasing number of people battered by the Depression who were looking for someone to blame for their desperate situation.

'Should the men who did the fighting now go without the necessities of life in order that the international money ring should have its pound of flesh?' Lang asked.[16]

The New Guard's most notable 'revolutionary act' occurred at the opening of the Sydney Harbour Bridge in March 1932, when an antiques merchant and former British army officer, Francis De Groot, rode past a Light Horse guard and slashed the opening ribbon, denying Lang the privilege.

After that, Lang's chief inspector of police, William MacKay, pursued the Guard relentlessly. When a crowd of 2000 guardsmen gathered outside the courts to protest De Groot's sentence, MacKay led his baton-wielding officers into them and, according to Lang, 'kicked the Guard's backsides ... right down to George Street'.[17] Many moderate (or perhaps liberal-minded) Guardsmen began to shy away from the movement, not wishing to directly confront the police, the courts and other respectable institutions of civil life. The Guard lost further ground when the thugs of the Fascist Legion invaded the home of former communist and secretary of the Labor Council, Jock Garden. Garden was badly beaten, but his sons and the family dog fought off the attackers, and captured one whose hand the dog had bitten. The Gardens bandaged up the assailant and drove him home! The conservative press such as the Fairfax-owned *Sydney Morning Herald* continued to support the Guard, but popular papers like *Smith's Weekly* mocked the movement and labelled the New Guard and its offshoots 'a silly rabble'.[18]

The failure of Scullin's federal Labor government to deal

adequately with the Depression saw angry voters throw it out of office in 1932. Blocked by a conservative and undemocratically elected Senate, a constitution that restricted change and financiers who set strict limits to what the government could do, Scullin's Labor caucus had been 'in government, but not in power'.[19] The vacuum allowed Jack Lang in New South Wales to become the sole political voice of the embattled worker, the ordinary digger, the widow, pensioners and the unemployed.

If the New Guard schemed to depose Lang, there was no need for it. Sir Philip Game, the governor of New South Wales, did it for them. Game dismissed the premier for a direct breach of Commonwealth law after Lang refused to pay interest to overseas bond holders, and issued a proclamation ordering all state revenues to be paid to the Treasury in cash. Like the infamous events in Canberra in 1975, Game acted unconstitutionally, but the dismissal was widely admired by the ruling class. Significantly, Lang walked. By choosing to do so, the 'Big Fella' probably saved New South Wales from a bloody moment in its history. At the ensuing election, the swinging voters came out against Lang – his demagoguery and his open disdain for 'money power' and its 'convention' and 'orthodoxy' unsettled many. The Great Depression ruined the labour movement's ideal of creating a workingman's paradise. Many true believers abandoned the Labor Party, seeing more hope in kicking a can than backing another Labor government. With Lang gone, the New Guard lost much of its relevance and slipped away. Yet Keith Amos was surely correct when he concluded that the New Guard was not an aberration but a movement with 'deep roots in a conservative form of Australian patriotism'.[20]

In the dark days of 1932, Harold Andrews declined to join the New Guard. As a young ex-officer with a conservative background, he might well have considered becoming a member. Why did he refuse? Perhaps Harold thought of his mates in C Company. He finished the war as an officer but had spent most of his time with the boys in the trenches, where he learnt not to judge a man by his religion or creed. Perhaps when he said 'No' he was thinking of working-class men like the diggers he went over the top with at Chipilly – men from different backgrounds to him but brothers in war. Harold was a believer in God, King and Country, but the war taught him to see the world from other people's perspectives ('how the other half lived', as he put it) and he had a deep respect for the virtue of Australian democracy. Harold was never a fascist nor a sympathiser with such movements.

CHAPTER 24
THE BROTHERHOOD
OF THE TRENCHES

Harold threw himself into the service of others. He taught Sunday School at the Free Presbyterian Church and became president of the Hastings River sub-branch of the RSSILA. Sub-branch meetings were held at the School of Arts on High Street, Wauchope. The building contained two billiard tables, a ping-pong table and seating. Public library books were stored in the rear room. Ivy helped out in both these endeavours and organised 'socials' with other wives of returned soldiers.[1]

It was the misfortune of many old soldiers that the Great Depression fell upon them just as the full impact of their war service began to reveal itself. Most of the Six had returned from the war with serious wounds they had tried to shrug off. In 1919 they were young, single and anxious to get out of the army, and it was a working-class virtue not to accept welfare (such as an army pension) if you could make a living with your hands. But a decade after their repatriation, without wounded pensions and with their livelihoods in jeopardy, family responsibilities – and in Harold's case, a property to manage –

the psychological and physical impact of war experience and financial stress hit hard.

The returned soldiers' clubs and the RSSILA continued to clash, but were united in demanding that the Repatriation Department recognise the many afflictions killing off 'burnt-out diggers'. It was becoming clear that, beyond what the calendar and army records showed, the diggers had left many more years of their lives in the trenches. By 1934 the diggers were dying at a rate of 2000 a year at an average age of forty-five, while the average non-returned man was living to well into his sixties. By 1936, the league and the soldiers' clubs – and that great champion of the digger, Sydney's *Smith's Weekly* – were pointing out that 8000 diggers were dying each year.[2] Unemployment among returned soldiers was also a cause of distress. During the Great Depression, politicians and private employers found it impossible to keep the promise of digger preference that they had bandied about so freely during the war years when recruits were wanted.

Perhaps the most important public figure to unify the soldiers' clubs and the league was Sir Isaac Isaacs, the first Australian-born governor general, appointed by the Scullin Labor government in 1931. Issacs hosted a series of meetings that were instrumental in bringing the ex-service organisations together during the Depression years, especially on the issue of fighting for 'digger preference'.[3]

The league and the clubs cooperated on a range of 'unemployment drives'. Spokesmen from both organisations encouraged government and private business to employ old soldiers, arguing: 'The "Digger" tackled big jobs in France. He can still do big jobs in Australia. Try him. He does not want charity. He wants work.'[4]

Leonard Robb and other prominent members of the

'Keeping the spirit of Anzac Alive', George Finey, 1930.

league and the clubs movement, including Ernie Rushbrooke and George Paterson, urged employers to do more, and pressed the public to be sympathetic to the increasing prevalence of 'burnt out' and unemployed diggers. But public charity and generosity to ex-servicemen's causes was burnt out too when so many people were suffering and could ill afford to pay their bills or find food for their tables. The louder the cry for digger preference, the greater the rift became between old soldiers and other struggling sections of the community.

The brotherhood of the trenches meant that the loyalties of the Chipilly Six lay with the diggers despite whatever class or political opinions each man carried with him in civilian life. But behind that staunch loyalty lay a deep layer of family, class and community support keeping the Six grounded and connected and, indeed, loved. The strength of these connections probably assisted them to cope with the severe challenges of those days. By the time the kids of the Six had grown old enough to hear stories of the Great Depression, their parents had stopped telling them. Only the stories of the fun times, the cricket matches, threepenny dances, the infamous Bodyline Ashes tour and the big-hearted horse Phar Lap were enthusiastically passed down. But there are other sources – old photos, condolence cards, obituaries in newspapers and letters to friends – that tell us much about the tears and the anguish that the Chipilly Six tried to protect their children and grandchildren from during those years.

The Chipilly Six knew of many men and some women whose lives were cut short by the war years. The diggers' joke 'If a bloke don't get pneumonia here, there's something wrong with his ruddy lungs!' had become ironically fatal in the two decades after the war.[5] Diggers died from their wounds, the psychological trauma and depression caused by war service, and an increasing number of previously unrecognised war-related causes such as the effects of gas, the recurrence of lung disease and infection, and the dreaded 'white plague' – tuberculosis.

Macksville mourned the untimely death in 1927 of George Rowe DCM, one of the footballers Bill Kane enlisted with in 1915. Bill and old digger mates wrote 'An appreciation' of George in the local paper entitled 'Another of the old warriors "gone west"'. It is typical of the sentiment of the times:

> He was just a son of Australia
> As he faced the shot and shell,
> Fighting with stern devotion

For the land he loved so well.
Happy he lies at rest –
He had chosen the better part;
Think of him, friends, tho' in silence
Deep down in your innermost heart.
And as the ceaseless days go by
Let his children's children read
Of a brave man's fight for his native land,
Of a brave man's honoured deeds.[6]

Jack Hayes and Harold Andrews were shocked to hear of the suicide of their old mate Tom Henry Rockstroh. 'Rock' was a Marrickville boy like Jack, and the two had fought at Gallipoli together and shared a blanket and a dugout on many an awful night on the Western Front. Rock had been Harold's corporal when Harold was an inexperienced reinforcement in France in 1916 and taught him the ropes. Harold kept a portrait-size photograph of Rockstroh that remains in the Andrews family collection. It is a poignant reminder of one of Harold's treasured friendships.

Suicide among ex-servicemen was high in the 1920s and 1930s. Official suicide statistics for the years 1926 to 1932 show that as unemployment reached its peak and the struggle for survival became more desperate, the rate of suicide increased. The years of uncertainty prior to the Wall Street crash in 1929, and the year following that disaster, claimed the most lives.[7] Rock's suicide was one among many in the ranks of the old AIF. The Chipilly Six would have known of many a good bloke who went to the 'other side' by his own hand in those stricken years. Many young men survived the war but not the peace that followed it.

Marrickville mourned the death by tuberculosis of their

'Queen', Alice Cashin. The disease was prevalent in the Australian population in the 1920s and 1930s and particularly among returned soldiers and nurses.[8] Several thousand Australian soldiers returned from the trenches with TB; many thousands more developed the disease later in life. It was particularly prevalent during the Great Depression when ill-health and chronic fatigue played havoc with weary bodies. In 1934, the RSSILA claimed that in Victoria alone more than one ex-serviceman was dying each week from TB.[9] Jerry Fuller's shell-shocked brother Roy died from the disease. So did Bob Traill, the Chipilly Six's former officer. Traill survived four years of trench warfare from Gallipoli to the Somme, and major wounds, only to die of TB in what should have been the prime of his life. The Australian War Memorial in Canberra holds Traill's wartime diaries. His writing is some of the most honest, eloquent and sometimes humorous in the memorial's rich archive. Traill's diaries remind us of the greatness of that generation of young men and the nurses who served with them. Were it not for Bob Traill, we would not know half as much about the character of men like Jack Hayes and Harold Andrews, or how the diggers believed the capture of Chipilly Spur was worthy of the Victoria Cross.

CHAPTER 25
PRESIDENT JACK

When the Great Depression was at its worst, the soldiers' clubs were places where people could forget their woes for a while. May Hayes spoke with pride of the community spirit in Marrickville and surrounding suburbs like Newtown. 'They all stuck together,' she said. John Hayes, although a boy at the time, also had strong memories of the Depression: 'No one was left to go hungry in the Depression days and the hard times,' he said.

The Marrickville Anzac Memorial Club was a focal point of this ethos. The club's membership – and its supporters like Mayor Ben Richards and local member Charlie Lazzarini – contributed materially so that resources went to those that needed them. 'Many's a chook I cooked for someone that really needed it, or a leg of lamb,' May said.

Listening to John Hayes, it was clear how the Great Depression shaped the outlook of the club:

> It was strictly a club effort. Caring for each other. Comradeship if you like … I think the only way you get that sort of bond is in times of great adversity, you never

see it otherwise. In times of affluence and in times of
relatively full employment, and trying to 'keep up with
the Joneses' as the saying goes, you don't see that.

You've got to be in hard times to get that bond,
to get that link, where people care about each other,
regardless of your race or religion. Religion never
mattered. Race has never mattered. Though of course in
those days everyone was predominantly Anglo-Saxon.[1]

Jack travelled with the Marrickville Anzac Debating Club to
debate the Woy Woy club. The debate was on a topical issue:
*A Bill to Introduce Prohibition of the Manufacture and Sale of
Intoxicating Liquor.* Marrickville were to argue the case for the
prohibition of alcohol, while Woy Woy were to argue against.
The Marrickville team all enjoyed a drink or two, which made
arguing for the case of prohibition a challenge.

To demonstrate the harmful effect of alcohol, the
opening speaker for Marrickville dropped a worm into a glass
of whisky, with fatal results for the worm. The Woy Woy men
interjected, denying any comparison between the general
public and worms, and accusing the debater of spoiling a
perfectly good glass of whisky. Then they cordially invited him
to join their team to share the remainder of the bottle.

One of the Marrickville debaters spoke from great
experience about the ill-effects of the 'morning after the night
before'. He appealed to the audience to vote for prohibition
and eliminate the 'night before', so that there could be no
'mornings after'. Everybody agreed that the morning after
ought to go, but few were willing to ban the night before. The
Woy Woy team won the debate.

The teams and the audience then adjourned to the bar
where Jack gave the closing remarks. He said he couldn't

understand how his club could argue such an 'unpalatable subject', though

> … after hearing my teammate describe with harrowing detail, the awful state of a person's insides after a 'wee doch and doris', I was almost persuaded to sign the [prohibition] pledge.[2]

Jack also organised a legendary fancy dress ball at the Anzac Club, which along with the Queen of Marrickville competition became a regular on the calendar of events.

The Back to the Wazir fancy dress ball was held at the club amidst props and music reconstructing the diggers' lives in Egypt in 1914 and 1915. It was an excuse for everyone to dress up in costumes ranging from ancient Egyptian pharaohs and princesses to some of the sights the diggers had witnessed in the notorious Wazir – the brothel district of Cairo.[3] At one of these dances, a drunken ex-digger made a move on May. Jack stepped in. The other bloke said, 'Just because your initials are JC doesn't make you Jesus Christ.' Jack's granddaughter heard that Jack gave the bloke 'a bunch of fives'.

May Hayes also remembered the threepenny dances run by the Ladies Auxiliary:

> Teenagers would come to the dances. A lot of them didn't have any money so it would be six in for sixpence. Cake and coffee provided by the club – plain block pound cake and coffee out of an urn.

John Hayes was one of 'those sixteen, seventeen, eighteen year olds. [We] were the ones who enlisted in the Second World War and came back to the club when the war ended.'[4]

The club also kept up its commitment to continue the Anzac Day dawn service. In 1931 the state governor attended for the first time and special trams and trains were organised. In 1939, with the threat of war imminent, some 20 000 people were present at the dawn service at the Cenotaph. By then Jack was the president of the Marrickville Anzac Memorial Club.

The New Guard movement held little attraction for men like Jack Hayes, or bush workers like Bill Kane, George Stevens and Dick Turpin. While remaining loyal to their soldier mates, they slowly joined or re-joined the trade unions and sporting clubs in their working-class communities. This is the solidarity that John Hayes witnessed as a boy: 'Comradeship, if you like ... in times of adversity.' This sense of connection shielded many working-class men from the extremism of the New Guard. They mocked the Guard and the bogeys it created, and they typically voted for the government the New Guard imagined overthrowing. Living hand to mouth on wages, or cooking chooks at the Marrickville Anzac Memorial Club, or sharing sandwiches in your front yard with battling Aboriginal mates from the timber-getting and road-building gangs made destitute by the Depression, as Bill and Emma Kane did, made them 'of the people'. Where Eric Campbell and the New Guard saw 'Communism, anarchism and the IWW' and 'disloyalty with a Capital D', the families in this story simply endured the Great Depression.[5]

We cannot see the world exactly as they saw it at the time, nor how their sympathies may have swung between the different demands of loyalty and patriotism. But we have an insight into the predominant view in Marrickville as expressed in parliament by Jack's good mate Charlie Lazzarini, the Labor MLA. Lazzarini tore into the New Guard, calling them 'irresponsible people' and 'braggarts' who 'colluded in the backyards of their homes':

> While the leader Eric Campbell could best be described as a 'bombastic furioso' [laughter] ... the members of the New Guard had proved to the community that they were yellow to the backbone, and that one fully grown man was equal to eight of them.[6]

Most of the Chipilly Six were not political to any great extent. Though Harold, as a popular and prominent church leader and president of his local RSSILA, did publicly endorse a local Country Party candidate, LC Jordan, because

> The dairy farmers' outlook is now allied to the welfare of the working classes in as much as these classes are the biggest consumers of butter, and it is in the farmers' interests that the working classes are employed, and on such conditions and wages as will permit them to pay a fair price ... the assets of the dairy farmer not only comprise the acres of his farm, but also such conveniences as good roads, available telephones, satisfactory educational facilities, electricity for the home and power.[7]

Jack and May's granddaughter said 'all the family were Labor' and that by the time she was old enough to vote, 'You wouldn't dare vote otherwise. You'd get your head chopped off!' Bill Kane's daughter Renie said, 'Dad was a true Labor man. When each of us got to eighteen he told us how to vote.'[8] When asked, Dick Turpin's son simply said that his father voted Labor 'I should think,' as if it was a ridiculous question.

CHAPTER 26

DICK TURPIN AND THE STYX

In April 1924 Dick Turpin and his advance party met their 'groupies' at the Styx River camp. By then the Group Settlement Scheme was already in trouble. Many groupies walked off settlements around Denmark and the south-west of the state on seeing the land and realising the task ahead of them. By April 1924 it was estimated that about 30 per cent of immigrant settlers and 42 per cent of those Australian-born had walked off their holdings.[1] Those who stayed struggled to set up their blocks for the £1000 their agreement with the Western Australian government stipulated. Running costs were proving three times that. Government debt from the scheme was rising. When the Devon and Cornwall families disembarked at Fremantle, they were met by unfriendly lumpers shouting 'Go away! There's no work for you!'. The port city and Perth were full of English migrants whose dreams of a new life and a farm of their own had already been shattered.

The failures of the program came in for sharp criticism at the state election early in 1924. Mitchell lost the premiership to his Labor rival Collier. The Labor government launched a royal commission into the roll-out of the Group Settlement

Scheme but did not put a halt on migration or the land development agreement with the British government.

Despite all this, some twenty Devon and Cornwall families made their way to Denmark by train. There, a convoy of three-ton (2.7 tonne) open trucks picked them up and took them along the bumpy Scotsdale track to the land Dick and the advance party had pegged out for them. Dick met them in a clearing cut in a stand of red gums by the Styx River. The women were tired from the long journey and the questions of their hungry wide-eyed children. The men humped their families' belongings on their shoulders: mattresses, stretcher beds, pillows, clothing, and perhaps a lamp or billycan bought in haste in Albany. Dick led each family by the light of a hurricane lamp to their 'tin hut' – a temporary shelter made of galvanised iron sheets wired to a framework of saplings. Each hut contained its own wood stove for cooking and warmth. Toilets were rudimentary military-style latrines of the type Dick and some of the Tommies in the group were used to in France. Water had to be carried in kerosene tins from the Styx River about one hundred metres away; the corrupted taste reminded the old soldiers of thirst in France.

Most of the Devon and Cornwall group were capable men and women: clerks, tradesmen, artisans and their wives. But they were not bush people in the sense that Australian conditions demand. The tin huts would be their homes through their first winter in the cold and wet Great Southern forest while they built the roads and cleared the land before the ballots were handed out.

In January 1925 Premier Collier and his deputy Bill Angwin, the Minister for Lands, Immigration and Industries, visited the settlement. Collier, and his predecessor Mitchell, were notorious for visiting only successful groups and ignoring the distress of others. If this is the case, it reflects well on Dick Turpin. A fortnight after the premier's visit, Dick was asked to speak before the royal commissioners investigating the Group Settlement Scheme at a special meeting held in Denmark. The interview, as reported in the Perth *Daily News*, is the longest first-hand account of Dick speaking that exists. By all accounts, Dick was a man of few words. Even at his court-martial in France in December 1917 he refused to speak when instructed to by his commanding officers. But now Dick found his voice. He told the commissioners he had plenty of farming experience but not on dairy farms in a country lacking soil with sufficient minerals for pasture growth, such as those the group settlers encountered. Besides, he told them, the success of a farm depended on its access to markets and resources. Dick and thirteen men from the group had spent the winter 'engaged in making roads and tracks' and had given the area a new name:

> I have had to put in bridges and culverts … Some of the work done is off the main road … The settlers do not want to live in their shacks through another winter, but I understand the houses cannot be built for some time yet, at all events until the roads are made. It has cost about 30s [30 shillings] a day during the winter for carting, using one man and two horses. It is 14 miles from Denmark to Hell's Hole Corner. The settlers have asked that a sawmill should be erected in the neighbourhood, so that they may get cheap timber for their houses.

Dick said there was plenty of good jarrah on the site, as well as red gum and karri, which the men could cut themselves to build their houses. The commissioners raised the problem of the rising costs of group settlement. They asked for Dick's opinion whether the migrants could clear their twenty-five acres, build homes and dairies within the cost and time the scheme's authors demanded.

'Some may pick up the work in two years, but it may take others a lifetime,' Dick said. On the issue of clearing, Dick recommended 'blast and burn without doing any pulling':

> I blasted the trees standing. The work will be done much cheaper under the group system. Some eighteen months ago I took a contract at £8 for partial clearing, and £11 for outright clearing and made good wages. I consider we shall get our partial clearing for about £8.[2]

Dick was proud of his group. He had not experienced challenges to his authority as the foremen had complained of at other sites:

> I do not think more than one [family] will leave the group. One family has 14 acres of ground partially cleared, the work having been done by the wife and nine children. This represents an increased value of about £5 an acre to that land. The ages of the children range from 18 years to six years. They can all use an axe, even the girls.

Dick worked alongside the families, teaching them to use the broadaxe and cross-cut saw. He formed a team that used heavy slashers to clear bracken fern that stood up to twelve feet (3.6 metres) high – the children helping. The smaller timber was cut down by axe. The bigger jarrah, karri and red gums were 'blasted standing'. The following summer, the felled dry timber was set alight. Eleven of the settler families were on their own blocks. The intervening time was spent building a school and improving the bridges, culverts and tracks. Meanwhile, the women improved their homes.

In 1926 the Group opened its school. In 2018 only the original stumps remain, but one can see the view as Dick and the others would have seen it as the land falls away to the Styx River and the old timber bridge first made by Dick and the pioneers from Devon and Cornwall. The school became an important social meeting place. Mothers cooked cakes and made lemonade for socials and events. Sometimes other Group schools would visit for sports carnivals.

The Great Depression hit just as Dick and the settlers were on the verge of fulfilling their dreams. The price of butterfat, the major source of income for the settlers, halved, meaning that expenses outweighed income. Most settlers grew vegetables and kept pigs, chickens and a small dairy herd, but there was no cash on the settlements and a consequent scarcity of necessities such as dry goods, clothing and shoes. Charles Hodgson, a young man on Group 42, near Denmark, remembered:

> About this time, my brother, who was an enterprising bloke, decided to get a job and he got on his horse and rode off. He was gone three weeks away on the horse and he came back awestricken. He got into the country up through Kendenup and Mount Barker and he said, 'I got plenty of food. I have had a lovely time, I met the most beautiful dollies you have ever seen, and I've got drunk two or three times, but my God! I never got hold of a bob. There wasn't a bob to be seen as far as that horse could carry me.'[3]

Albert Gasmier, the Tealdale Group schoolteacher, wrote that children were coming to school malnourished and without shoes, and others were staying home from shame.[4] Some families walked off the land or had to suffer the indignity of the bailiff turning them out. They joined the ranks of the unemployed in Albany and Perth. Charles Wittenoom, the mayor of Albany, said that a number of destitute groupies were coming into the town. He told the Legislative Council:

> Most of these people – and this may be their own fault
> – appear to be ill nourished and in general distress,
> while some of the women seem to be absolutely
> starving … We in Albany cannot let them starve, but
> we have our own poor to look after and we cannot
> afford to maintain all those that are coming in from the
> groups.[5]

Laying fault at the feet of the groupies probably had something to do with the power of the Calvinistic message espoused by land zealots like Mitchell. It was never the failure of politicians or speculators who ignored plunging prices on exports, poor soil and drought. No, it was easier to blame a lack of moral fibre in the English settlers. The stigma of being a groupie never left some of these brave settler families.

*

The writing was on the wall for Dick and Lizzie too. Dick was away working in the bush and spent little time with Lizzie at Springdale House. The retreat fell into disuse, as few people could afford a holiday at a guest house. How did Dick and Lizzie cope?

The memories of the late Frank Gomm are illuminating. Gomm wrote that 'In 1925 and 1926 ... I got to know [Dick Turpin] very well as I camped with him in the bush [on road-building gangs]'. Gomm reckoned Dick and his wife 'drank heavy and smoked heavy'.[6] What Gomm didn't know was that Lizzie was wasting away from cervical cancer. She required medical care in Perth, but at the height of the Depression, Dick could not risk moving to the city, where the couple had no friends or contacts and the unemployment problem was even worse. So, Dick stayed in the bush. Poor Lizzie took the long train journey to the city with her son. She died of 'exhaustion' at the Home of Peace refuge in Perth and was buried in the Anglican cemetery, Karrakatta. Lizzie's boy Jack later joined the navy at Fremantle, serving as boy and man on escort and patrol duties in the Indian Ocean, and later in operations around New Britain during the Second World War, before settling in Sydney. By the time Jack left Springdale, Dick was drinking heavily.

The Group Settlement Scheme became a social and financial catastrophe. Of the 6000 families who made the trip to Australia, fewer than 300 were still on the land after the Great Depression. The loss to the state from the scheme was £6 500 000.[7] Yet it is a testament to Dick and the Devon and Cornwall group that they achieved as much as they did. Some of those first settlers, the Pomerys and Swallows, stayed on the land and still live in the district. Scores of other settler families made important contributions to Western Australian society in other fields and professions after leaving the groups.[8]

The Great Depression ended with Dick alone. He had no roots in the Great Southern but had come to love the bush there. He stayed on, and like George Stevens and Bill Kane, he used his reputation as a returned soldier, and no small amount

The opening of 'London Bridge', Scotsdale, near Denmark,
Western Australia, during the 1930s Great Depression.
Dick Turpin being carried across by one of his men.

(Courtesy of Denmark Historical Society)

of skill with the broadaxe and cross-cut saw, to become a
ganger on the relief crews of sustenance workers tasked with
opening up Western Australia. Out in the bush, the sight of
Dick Turpin on his mare Black Bess meant a good man was
coming to get a tough job done. Much of the development of
the roads and bridges in the far south of the state was down
to Dick Turpin and his crew. Today, a stone memorial to the
Tealdale Group Settlers in the lonely bush, and a dusty road
that crosses the Muir Highway near Rocky Gully named after

him, are mute acknowledgements of the pioneering spirit of Dick Turpin.

A faded photocopy of a photo donated to the Denmark Historical Society – one of the few pictures we have of Dick – shows a mate carrying him on his back over one of the many timber bridges they built in the rugged southland. It is a testament to the mateship and respect the groupies had for their foreman in what was often a thankless job against great odds. Dick was up to the task. But like the war, it took a personal toll on him.

*

The Great Depression threw down the Chipilly Six like straws. Recovery was very slow. From 1932, the worst year of the Depression, it took at least half a decade before economic conditions returned to 'normal'. In the industrial inner-city suburbs like Marrickville, the factories became more competitive because the cost of labour and raw materials fell considerably, and duties and tariffs made imported goods expensive. Marrickville entered a period of relatively full employment as the chemical, metals and textile industries took on more workers. Jack Hayes survived in his salaried job with the Water Board and began to prosper. He and May took in Jack's widowed mother Blanche – Ottie Hayes died during the Depression – and the couple began to plan their children's nest egg.

The recovery of world prices for wheat and wool was more gradual, but there was a revival of sorts as high levels of farm production and improved exports of primary goods enabled many farmers to return gradually to prosperity. Rising employment in the cities also increased the demand for butter and milk. Harold Andrews benefited from these multiple strands of recovery. George Stevens found steady work in a butcher's shop – a sure sign that consumer confidence had returned in Young. But for many men who worked with their hands, and without a trade, the years of economic uncertainty continued right up to the beginning of the Second World War.

Jerry Fuller was on wages – a hand-to-mouth existence similar to the economic uncertainty experienced by casual workers today. Yet he and Olive managed to put their children through school and university – a remarkable achievement for a working-class family at that time. Dick Turpin and Bill Kane were foremen of gangs building the roads and bridges that increasingly mobile Australians drove over each day. Did they realise that so many of those ravaged faces lining the roadside with their picks, shovels and cross-cut saws were wounded veterans of the First World War?

The 1930s were the years that the men experienced all the joys and trials of raising their children and striving for the simple security of paying the rent or pursuing the dream of owning their own home. Holidays, for those who could afford them, were simple and short, and usually involved fishing, surfing or swimming somewhere close to home.

In 1939 Australia would go to war again, and for many, army service offered a good wage to support families.

PART SIX
OLD WAR HORSES

CHAPTER 27

JERRY FULLER GOES TO THE SECOND WORLD WAR

Jerry Fuller was seldom at home. That was Olive's domain. Jerry was active in the returned soldiers' movement as secretary of the Arncliffe sub-branch of the RSSILA and a member of the Marrickville Anzac Memorial Club. But it was in returned soldiers' cricket that Jerry made his mark. In 1937–38 Jerry was player-manager of the Old War Horses – the unbeaten New South Wales returned soldiers team that toured Queensland.

In a match of 'particularly bright cricket' at Warwick on the Darling Downs, Jerry put on a 'brilliant display of aggressiveness … his square cutting and late cutting being a pleasure to watch, until … he was retired after passing his half century'.[1] He could bowl a bit, too. A cricket writer in a local rag (not *Wisden*) described him as the Clarrie Grimmett of the New South Wales team. This was high praise as Grimmett (who played thirty-seven tests for Australia) invented the 'flipper' and was one of the finest leg spinners in world cricket at the time. In reality, Jerry and the other digger cricketers were mostly in their forties and played for fun, camaraderie and the refreshments afterwards.

When the Second World War began in September 1939, Jerry was not content to see out the conflict from the stands. He signed up on 6 July 1940 at the Drill Hall, Arncliffe, claiming he was thirty-nine, which would have made him seventeen at the time of the Chipilly stunt.[2] John Hayes claimed, 'Jerry put his age up for the First World War and dyed his grey hair brown for the second.'[3] His former trade as a tailor was in demand in the army. He was made a Grade III Textile Re-fitter in the 2/3rd Australian Field Workshop, 7th Australian Division. The field workshops refitted or repaired equipment, weapons and machines – anything from boots, uniforms, small arms (revolvers, rifles and tommy guns) to heavy weapons, vehicles and tanks – Allied and captured. Almost all of the men in the 2/3rd workshop were tradesmen. And it claimed the distinction of having the highest proportion of First World War diggers in the Second AIF. It was unique also in that three men in the unit had two sons with them, and six others had one son.[4]

The 2/3rd Field Workshop disembarked at the port of Kantara, Egypt, in January 1941. Several months passed uneventfully in Australian camps near Cairo before the workshop received orders to prepare for the invasion of Greece. However, the orders were quickly withdrawn, which was undoubtedly a blessing for Jerry, as the Australian campaign in Greece swiftly became a disaster.

Jerry finally saw action when the 7th Australian Division crossed the Litani River and attacked the Vichy French force in Syria on the night of 7 June 1941. The 2/3rd Field Workshop was in the third line of the attack. The Australians advanced through a landscape of biblical sites and historic battlefields dating from the ancients to the Light Horse and the capture of Damascus in 1918. Jerry wrote of his adventures in letters and postcards to Jack, including an unauthorised visit to the Tomb of Rachel in Bethlehem, and going absent without leave to enjoy the thrills and spills of Damascus after the ancient city fell to the Allies.

The generals told the diggers the invasion of Syria (and Lebanon) would be a pushover: '... walk in, wave our hats to the Frogs, and walk on.'[5] But the Vichy French, mostly French Foreign Legionnaires and tough North Africans and Senegalese, put up a stubborn resistance, particularly when the ground suited the defenders. At one point, the legionnaires launched a counter-attack that regained much of the ground the Australians had won in the opening days of the invasion. The 7th Division fought its way along the Mediterranean coast through olive groves and Arab towns, its right flank in the jagged mountains that overlooked the brilliant blue of the Mediterranean Sea. The Australian writer Donald Stuart fought in the campaign as a machine-gunner with the Western Australians and described the 'acrid stink of goats ... the faint smell of ... olive oil, spilled, cooking fires that had died a week or more ago; and the smell that hangs in the air wherever human beings have been in trouble'.[6]

Rock falls and debris caused by enemy shelling blocked the narrow mountain roads and held up Australian armour and trucks. The Vichy French made skilful use of the rugged mountain passes and defiles to ambush Australian infantry and motorised patrols. The nasty short campaign was fought in extreme conditions that quickly wore down armour, vehicles and equipment. Jerry would have been flat out recycling and repairing mostly First World War–vintage kit.

The workshop's headquarters were at Madj al Kurum in the Jordan valley, north of the Sea of Galilee. Although behind the frontline, the unit's war diary records shellfire and the threat of Vichy French fighter bombers searching for targets.[7] Mosquitoes were another danger in the Jordan valley. In the First World War, malaria caused more casualties than Turkish bullets to the Australian Light Horseman.

Sometime during the Syrian campaign, Jerry bumped into his old C Company commander Burt Withy MC. Jerry was still a private but Withy was now a lieutenant-colonel commanding the Queensland 2/25th Infantry Battalion. Withy quickly arranged a transfer so that Jerry could join his battalion as it fought its way into Lebanon. So Jerry enjoyed the unique distinction of being Burt Withy's batman in two world wars. In Syria Withy was awarded the Distinguished Service Order (DSO) and Jerry became an honorary member of the 2/25th sergeants' mess.

The battalion was on garrison duty in Lebanon when the Japanese attacked Pearl Harbor on 7 December 1941, signalling the end of the Second AIF's war in North Africa and the Mediterranean. The 2/25th Battalion sailed for Ceylon (now Sri Lanka) just as the first Japanese troops entered Singapore. When Singapore fell, the 7th Division was ordered home to take part in the defence of Australia, and arrived in Sydney in March 1942. The campaign in Syria transformed the 2/25th from an untested battalion of inexperienced young men and a sprinkling of First World War veterans into a battle-hardened outfit eager to take on the Japanese. Jerry's battle experience would have been of great value to the young reinforcements who joined the battalion after the severe losses in the Syrian campaign. But he was discharged as medically unfit just before the battalion sailed to Port Moresby to take part in the desperate fighting on the Kokoda Track. Burt Withy continued as battalion commander at Kokoda, Imita Ridge,

Templeton's Crossing, Gorari and Gona before relinquishing command in January 1943.

The war against the Japanese was a young man's war and old diggers like Jerry and Burt Withy had already done their bit.

CHAPTER 28
BILL KANE ENLISTS AGAIN

Bill Kane enlisted just after the fall of Singapore. When asked why her dad enlisted – surely he had already done his bit in the First World War – his daughter Renie replied, 'He just realised you need men to fight,' she said. 'And besides, the Kanes were not so well off in those days. Bill was still working on the road gangs on poor wages ... If it rained the road workers did not get paid.'[1]

He was sent to the 19th Works Company – a type of army labour company working on the Darwin boom wharf. Later he told his kids that his goal was to find his way into an infantry battalion fighting in New Guinea. He arrived in Darwin on 10 November 1942 – nine months after the first Japanese bombing raids on the town – and very quickly found himself in the thick of the action.

Bill's first job was unloading timber and 44-gallon (200-litre) fuel drums from the SS *Burwah* at the boom wharf. In the oppressive heat of a Top End 'build-up' before the arrival of the wet season, the men worked shirtless, their eyes stinging with sweat. Bill had only been on the job a few days when Japanese bombers came over before dawn and dropped their 'eggs' as Bill and his team were unloading cement. The diggers heard the engines, then saw the brilliant strobes of the Darwin garrison searchlights catch the Japanese bombers against the moody grey-black sky. The Aussie anti-aircraft gunners opened up. The flash followed by the boom of the guns might have reminded Bill of the Somme and Passchendaele. The 19th Works Company war diary described how shell fragments fell among the diggers as they worked. Most of Bill's new mates on the job were very young men and it was their first time under fire. Bill and his crew cheered loudly as a Japanese aircraft fell in flames. Then some of the diggers looted ice cold beers from the ship's refrigerators while their officers were taking cover. That evening the cooks treated Bill and his mates to fish for supper: 'Gathered by the lads at the Boom Wharf this morning, being blown to the surface by the concussion of stick bombs that fell in the harbour.'[2]

About a week and half a dozen air raids later, Bill went to see an army doctor and asked to be transferred to the infantry. But the doctor was an old acquaintance from Macksville.

'He knew Daddy had a family,' Renie said. The doctor told Bill: 'Oh Bill, you're not going to the war, you're going back to Macksville,' and arranged for him to be transferred to the 11th Garrison Battalion at Adamstown.[3]

So Bill saw out the war building bunkers and coast-watching. On the weekends he'd travel home by train or on the back of a lorry. His second-youngest daughter Phyllis remembered, 'Us kids used to love it because he would bring us home a chocolate.'[4] At the end of the Second World War, Bill was fifty-two-and-a-half years old. He'd seen three years active service on the Western Front in the First World War and 625 days service at home in the second, including the bombing of Darwin. It is little wonder that he was known around Macksville as 'Digger' or 'Cobber' Kane.

CHAPTER 29
SONS OF ANZACS

By 1942, John, the son of Jack and May Hayes, and Ernie, the son of George and Carrie Stevens, were old enough to enlist. They were destined to fight a very different war from that of their fathers.

Ernie drove Matilda tanks and fought in the vicious jungle campaigns at Morobe, Buna and Sattelberg in New Guinea, and Balikpapan during the invasion of Borneo in July 1945.

John Hayes joined the Royal Australian Air Force after Jack refused to allow him to become an infantryman. He served as corporal recorder with a fighter control unit at RAAF Northern Command (NORCOM), Madang Harbour, New Guinea.

Jack's daughter Megs Hayes married a Rat of Tobruk. Dick Turpin's estranged stepson, Jack Barton, was at sea with the Royal Australian Navy. Jerry's half-brother Len was in the army in Darwin.

Harold Andrews became a captain in the Citizens Military Force in New South Wales; his son Graham was too young to enlist. In Young, Carrie and George took in American servicemen on leave.

As president of the Marrickville Anzac Memorial Club, Jack Hayes continued to serve diggers and their families, and to attend the Anzac Day dawn service at Martin Place.

After the First World War, politicians and the RSSILA identified 25 April 1915 as the birth of the nation. The architects of national mythology marked the landing at Anzac as the moment when Australia matured to take its place among the great nations on the world stage. The sentiments invoked were tied to loyalty to empire and race, linking Australia to the Mother Country and the old world. Through this national story, Australians were encouraged to reconcile the sheer scale of loss in the First World War – 59330 killed and 152171 wounded – and the burden placed on families crippled by war debts and the rising cost of living, as the price of loyalty and national prestige.

But behind the noble themes of loyalty and nation-building was deep community trauma which made Anzac Day the 'natural' platform to remember and mourn the dead, while recognising the impact of that loss on families and communities. It was the ritual of remembrance and mourning which appealed to men like Jack Hayes and the originators of the dawn service at the Cenotaph in Martin Place.

Anzac Day took on further significance during the Second World War. In 1940 and 1941 the war was a distant conflict in which young Australians once again fought in the defence of the British Empire against the old foe Germany and its retainers. Statesmen, clergymen and scribes wrote about Anzac Day unifying the generations. The 'sons of Anzacs' were fighting on the battlefields of the past against a familiar enemy.

On Anzac Day 1941, George Stevens marched in Young, where the *Young Chronicle* reported that the First World War diggers turned out with 'a few more grey hairs, and with their ranks a little thinner' but assured its readers that the old diggers felt pride that the tradition of Anzac was 'safe in [the] hands' of the 'new AIF'.[1]

In Sydney, a record crowd of 40 000 showed up for the dawn service at the Cenotaph in a remarkable contrast to the first solemn gathering in 1928. The Sydney service had evolved into something of a festival atmosphere: people brought stools, cushions and picnic blankets. Women sat and knitted khaki gifts for young soldiers, and the crowd sang popular songs in the apricot light of the street lamps while they waited for the old diggers to arrive.[2]

That Anzac Day was in sharp contrast to the one which followed in 1942 after Japan entered the war. The fall of Singapore and the sinking of the Royal Navy's Pacific fleet decapitated the British Empire in the east. The bombing of Darwin, the arrival of enemy submarines in Australian waters, the Japanese fleet in the Coral Sea and reconnaissance planes over Sydney and Melbourne changed the mood of the nation. The old assumptions that Britain would protect Australia were under threat. The war rapidly became very local and very frightening – a battle for national and racial survival. Australia had a new prime minister, the Labor leader John Curtin, who had a clear message: Australia stood alone. Curtin turned to the United States for help and warned that Australians had to be 'All-in!' to defeat the Japanese.

Fear of an enemy attack led Curtin to cancel public com-memorative events on Anzac Day 1942. The prime minister appealed to Australians:

> The fact that the enemy is on our threshold and the
> dangers to the public from warlike operations cannot

be discarded will make it desirable that any large congregations of people outside the normal should be discouraged.[3]

The RSSAILA (from 1940, the league's acronym included an extra 'A' for 'airmen'), the Legion of Returned Servicemen's Clubs (representing the independent clubs like the Marrickville Anzac Memorial Club), other returned soldiers' groups and tens of thousands of Australian families adhered to the request. The RSSAILA recommended Australians stay away and commemorate Anzac Day in their own homes. That year Anzac Day fell on a Saturday: the special buses and trams that had become a feature of the day in Australian cities were cancelled. Shops and pubs were closed, organised sport abandoned, and theatres did not open until the afternoon. Only the munition workers remained at their posts. In Sydney, the dawn service was relocated from the Cenotaph to the Savoy Theatre. A small group of 200 invited guests, including the governor of New South Wales and officials representing the British, American and Dutch East Indies, gathered for an official service that followed the traditional ritual of prayers and hymns and the bugle calls marking 'The Last Post' and 'The Rouse'. The originators, Ernie Rushbrooke and George Paterson, were absent on war service.

Despite the restrictions, four old diggers from the Marrickville Anzac Memorial Club slipped through the police barricades to lay a wreath at the Cenotaph in Martin Place. A reporter from *The Sun* had made a similar journey to see who might be there. He found the four Marrickville diggers and asked them why they had come. One replied 'To carry on, with a simple service, the torch of remembrance'. The reporter forgot to record the old soldiers' names, perhaps caught up in the emotion of the moment or perhaps not wanting to get them into trouble, given the official injunction to stay away. The four diggers laid a wreath then stood hat in hand before the solemn granite block and its two bronze figures. One of them spoke in a distinctive 'strine' with the unselfconscious authority of a senior sergeant: 'Age shall not weary them, nor the years condemn. At the going down of the sun and in the morning, we will remember them.' His voice carried across Martin Place. An American soldier on sentry duty 'whose footsteps had been echoing hollowly through the darkness, stopped abruptly and stood at attention'. It was then that one of the old diggers broke down. Finally, the four diggers left, as silently and as unpretentiously as they had arrived.[4] But in their simple act they reiterated that Anzac Day was a people's day of remembrance and mourning, and that while the ritual itself was important, the Cenotaph in Sydney had become a sacred place too. John Hayes said his father never missed a service at Martin Place.

CHAPTER 30
AT THE GOING DOWN
OF THE SUN

A few years after the Second World War, Jerry Fuller went up to Macksville on a lawn bowls tour. He asked the local bowlers if Billy Kane still lived in the district. 'I'd like to see old Bill again, we did a stunt together in France,' Jerry said. A local nicknamed 'Liftman' was playing bowls and arranged a meeting between the two friends. 'Liftman' was so impressed by the two old diggers that he wrote an article about their meeting for the *Macksville Elevator*.

> I wondered if I might sneak a story from them and even though I hung around after our game and joined in a generous application of tongue lubricator, my little mission failed. There [sic] conversation was mainly taken up with 'where's old so-and-so now?' and 'have you seen old — lately?' and 'what became of —?' and 'Do you remember that bloke —?[1]

So, history missed another opportunity to hear from the Chipilly Six first-hand. A couple of years after that happy meeting, Jerry died suddenly on 23 December 1951 from a massive stroke. He was the first of the Chipilly Six to go, and the youngest. He left behind his wife Olive and their four children, all in their twenties.

Jerry had spent most of his time at work as a draftsman under Jack, and his leisure with his old soldier friends from the first and second world wars. But Jerry's son Thomas (known as Ken), a doctor in Cessnock, was said to have Jerry's looks and larrikin personality.[2] Jerry's grandsons are proud of his war record but know very little of his experiences in the two world wars. Much of what you read here comes from the records kept by Jack Hayes and the stories of John Hayes, who broke into fond laughter at the memory of Jerry.

After the Second World War, Bill Kane went back to his job as a ganger with the Main Roads Department. A lot of the work was clearing the bush, opening up places like Taylor's Arm, Burrapine and Scott's Head that today are taken for granted.

'Daddy was away camping a lot of the time. He'd come home on the weekend,' his girls Renie and Phyllis said.

He was in poor health most of the time. His girls remembered his 'gammy leg' and the big 'butterfly shaped' scar under his right armpit caused by his gunshot wounds at Pozières and Froissy Valley. The kids grew up believing their daddy had shrapnel in a lung – he kept a small piece of jagged metal in the drawer beside his bed. His pneumonia at Liverpool Camp in 1915, gassing at Pozières and Spanish influenza in 1918 probably didn't help his long-term health:

> Working on the roads in the dust he suffered terribly
> … He'd get up in the morning and he'd always be
> vomiting. Have his breakfast and bring it up again.

But Bill refused a pension from the Repat Department. 'Daddy said "Give it to those who have lost limbs." He didn't know how things like that worked. He just soldiered on.'[3]

Bill never smoked – never wanted to due to his lung injury. But he did enjoy a beer with his mates. He was 'a very popular type of guy. I suppose you'd call him a man's man … Mum was the mainstay of the family. Mum had to take care of us and keep us fed … Mummy paid all the bills.'[4] Bill and Emma could not afford a car or truck.

On pay day (4.30 p.m. Thursdays) Emma would tell their youngest to jump on her pushbike and race Bill to pick up his pay at the post office. Otherwise Bill would come home via the pub. 'Saturday morning, Bill was lucky to get two shillings to go down for a drink.'

Daddy would be down at the pub, he would have three or four beers but would always come home. People were happy to shout him a beer. He'd come home … Listen to the [horse] races on the radio. But couldn't spend any money on the races – he didn't have any money!

… Daddy always knew what was going on. He went to work, chopped the wood, kept the chooks, and kept the garden on weekends and built a bit of furniture.

… He could always do things, always grow things.
He was never a cranky man, never scotty, he had a level head on him.[5]

Renie thought he was 'A very happy sort of a person. He'd learnt to "sing around the whistle" as a boy, and after supper on a Saturday, or on the rare nights he was home during the week, he'd pull out his whistle and sing, "When I grow too old to dream, I'll have you to remember" and other little love songs, mostly Irish. We used to get them sung to us all the time.'[6]

Her daughters recalled 'Emma was always in the kitchen baking something'. On Sunday arvos, Bill would have a lie-down. Emma would pack up his food. She used to send him away with scones, cooked-up corned meat, bottles of jam, butter and camping food. 'He'd share it with young fellas in the bush camp, who'd not brought their own.'[7] He had great friendships among ex-soldiers, the road gangs and the timber-getters of his youth. Many of the old bush workers came from Aboriginal families. Bill and Emma shared food and friendship with these people through the darkest days of the Great Depression when wealthier, supposedly 'upright' citizens turned their backs.

'Anzac Day was a big, big day. Daddy would have his shoes all clean and his hat brushed up. In the end they had him in a car because he couldn't walk.'[8] His last Anzac Day was 1954. On 26 October he died of exhaustion (or congestive cardiac failure), aged sixty-two.

The Holy Church of England, Macksville, was so packed for his funeral that people spilled out the doors and sat in cars along the street.[9] Six old digger mates carried his coffin to the cemetery. He was honoured with a lengthy obituary in the local papers:

> The Last Post has sounded for Bill Kane. He marches ahead, revered as a soldier and a man by those still in the earthly column ...[10]

Bill's medals from the First and Second World Wars were given to the Australian War Memorial by his family, along with a photograph of Bill and Emma on their wedding day, and a German 'Delta' trench knife most likely souvenired at Chipilly Spur. Bill's other papers and war mementoes were given to the Frank Partridge VC Museum in Bowraville and are still on display there. Bill had signed up in 1915 with Partridge's father, Patrick.

Among Bill's things, his children found a cutting from an edition of the RSSILA journal *Reveille*, dated 1 September 1933. It was an article written by 'Sammy' aka Sergeant Norman Langford, 1st Battalion, entitled 'Chipilly Stunt: Brave Diggers'. The opening paragraph reads:

> This is the story of how a handful of brave men, led by two sergeants, in the usual spirit of Digger adventure, were responsible for bringing off … the capture of Chipilly Spur …[11]

In the centre of the page is a postage-stamp-size photo of Company Quartermaster Sergeant Jack Hayes wearing a slouch hat.

When Bill was in the mood he told his kids war stories. Renie remembered fragments: 'Daddy and his mates had been well behind enemy lines. They stomped their feet on the cobblestones and made a lot of noise yelling at one another to make the Germans think they were a whole army coming.' Bill told Renie the Chipilly Six 'ought to have got the VC, but the officers were all dead, or too far away from the action and there wasn't one to say what Daddy [and his mates] did'.[12]

*

In 1938 Dick Turpin married Amy Warner (nee Fern), a young divorcee from a group settlement. Dick was about fifty, though he claimed to be forty on his marriage certificate. Amy was twenty-seven. She had a three-year-old son, also called Richard, from her previous marriage. As an adult, Richard spoke of his stepfather fondly and said Dick raised him as his own. Dick encouraged him to cycle and box and he became very good at both. Richard recalled that Dick was often away out bush with his work. 'He would come home on the train pulling his suitcase, poor fellow. Every Saturday he'd come home and leave again Sunday evening.'[13] Sometimes Dick would bring a hessian bag full of marron – the freshwater crayfish unique to the cool, clean rivers of the south-west.

What Richard knew about Dick was mostly second-hand: he was 'a good horseman; good on the broadaxe … a man who could improvise a lot of things' and was 'well thought of'. He remembered a story from the tail end of Dick's life: 'the old man' was ailing but a bridge needed to be built at Lower King River. Those employed to do the job had 'no clue what to do' so they 'got out the old man and he got it done in a few weeks'. 'They pulled him out of retirement,' Richard laughed, but they 'didn't overpay him!'[14]

Now in his nineties, Tom Atkinson, of Denmark, Western Australia, is perhaps the only surviving person to have worked with Dick on the road- and bridge-building gangs in the Great Southern. Tom was in charge of maintenance on the main roads and Dick was in charge of the bridge-building team.

'He was a very good boss on the bridge group. He ran the job,' Tom said. 'He looked after the men.'

On the job he was serious. I never heard him raise his
voice. In difficult situations he didn't go off his nut.
He'd just walk over quietly and attend to the problem
… At night time we'd get a bit of a fire going, sit round
the campfire, he was jovial, a bonzer old bloke.[15]

The family home was on the Albany Highway, on the edge of
the town – a two-storey duplex that Dick and Amy rented for
years. Richard said it wasn't until later that they bought the
house. 'The amount of rent that the old fella paid, he could
have bought the house.'[16]

Dick retired from the Main Roads Department in 1959.
In almost forty years on the group settlements, clearing
contracts, and road- and bridge-building gangs, he ignored
the pain caused by his war injuries. Amy said he never let
on because he feared being sacked from his position as a
foreman.[17] In his retirement Dick worried about leaving Amy
and Richard with the burden of the mortgage. In 1960, he
applied to the Commonwealth Repatriation Department for
a war pension. He claimed his left arm had become so weak
he could no longer pick up a hammer nor bend his elbow.
He'd also developed a chronic heart condition and blood
pressure, and thought his problems might be due to gunshot
and shrapnel wounds in France and the ravages of trench
warfare.

The Repatriation Department declined his claim three
times, probably because Dick refused a soldier's pension on
demobilisation in 1919. Back then he claimed he was fit and
well, despite being three times wounded in action and gassed.
He told Amy the pension the diggers were offered 'was an
insult'.[18] In 1919 he was newly married and keen to get out
of the army. He just wanted to be a provider and get by on his

own account. But the ethos and attitude of his youthful days worked against Dick when he made his claim in 1960.

The appeal process, which placed the onus of proof on the digger, brought up long-repressed memories and trauma. In one of his letters to the 'Repat', Dick wrote:

> I consider my long period of service must have been responsible for the disabilities arising since my discharge … My service as a Stretcher-bearer in France 1917 when I was subject to continual bad weather conditions in Trench warfare combined with the gunshot wound in my left arm contributed to my suffering from the above mentioned disabilities.[19]

Bringing up the ghosts of the past was not good for Dick. Amy wrote that he 'drank heavy and smoked heavy … I had to go to work at the Albany Woollen Mills to pay off the home'. He died at the Albany Regional Hospital on 4 April 1964. He was probably seventy-six but nobody really knew his age, or where he came from. Richard said his dad was 'a real good mystery man'.[20] Dick was buried in the Anglican section of the Allambie Park Cemetery, Albany, though he had been born a Catholic. The family placed a note in the *Albany Advertiser*:

> TURPIN (John Richard): April 4, 1964. A.R.H., loving husband of Amy, fond father of Dick, daughter-in-law Phyllis, loving pops of Debbie, Brett, Wayne.
>
> At the going down of the sun, we shall remember.
>
> No more pain at last.
>
> R.I.P.[21]

In 1977 Amy learnt about Dick's part in the capture of Chipilly Spur after someone in Albany showed her a copy of Captain Donovan Joynt VC's book on the Australians in 1918 – *Saving the Channel Ports*. Twenty-two years after Dick's death, Amy wrote to the Repatriation Commission to file a claim for a pension under Section 13 of the *Veterans Entitlement Act*, on the basis that Dick's death was caused by the war. The application makes difficult reading – you feel her frustration and anger at the process. Her handwriting is unschooled and honest:

> My husband had a rough time … during World War I
> and suffered the effects there after, one has to live with a
> sufferer to know.[22]

Her application was rejected. Amy worked at the mills for over twenty years before becoming an invalid pensioner. Richard said:

> In her retirement she was a very good bowls player, her
> name was on the honor [sic] board at the Emu Point
> Bowling Club … She died when she was 94, she had a
> hard life but survived.[23]

*

Carrie Stevens was the matriarch of her big family of eight children at the Stevens' home in Nasmyth Street, Young. She kept a happy home: simple, frugal and satisfied. George and Carrie became grandparents to sixteen children. Their grandson Rich says:

We were (and still are) a close family on the Stevens side – our grandparents' home at Young was the 'Spiritual Home' to the cousins while growing up, reuniting there at Christmas and other holidays.

Rich said the family gave George the nickname 'Boss' – 'kind of ironically. Mum always said that with seven women in the household he was anything but the Boss.'[24]

George had returned from the war a decorated hero, and that stood for something in a small town like Young. He made the transition back into community life seemingly without difficulty. After the Great Depression George worked as a lorry driver and then as a carter for a bakery. But he lost that job when the bakeries were consolidated during the Second World War, due to lack of workers. Fortunately, his status as a returned soldier worked in his favour. According to his son-in-law, George was laid-off on a Friday and on

Saturday afternoon … [a local businessman] Roy Hammond [a fellow First World War digger], the proprietor of Young's largest department store, Hammond and Hanlon, came into George's home and said, 'I believe you lost your job?' George said, 'Yeah.'

'Well, come down Monday and you've got a job. Don't worry about getting experience, you'll have plenty of time for that.'[25]

George worked as a shop assistant at Hammond and Hanlon's for seventeen years. On weekends he pulled beers at the bowls club to supplement his income. George did not drink very much, so serving drinks kept him socially engaged but it also kept his wages in the bank so Carrie could provide for their big family.

In April 1957, Carrie died of cancer. George took her death with 'remarkable stoicism' and no outward showing of emotion.[26] But two months afterwards, he resigned from his job because he was suffering heart trouble and arthritis of the spine. Perhaps 'Boss' was missing Carrie more than he let on, but he grew up in an age that smothered emotions.

Hammond and Hanlon gave him a £726/18/2 payout from the provident fund. Without an income and with bills to pay and the anxieties of old age, George looked to the RSSAILA for help. The sub-branch, the mayor and the local MP encouraged him to seek an ex-soldier's entitlement to medical expenses. He applied for a pension on the basis that his bronchial condition, gas, heart condition, 'poisoning' to his left leg, hip trouble and arthritis were due to war service. But like his old mate Dick Turpin, George had signed a declaration on leaving the army that stated:

I am not suffering from any disability due to or aggravated by war service, and feel fit and well.[27]

It was up to George (and his local doctor) to acquire the evidence that his conditions were war-related. George's heart condition and arthritis were common conditions likely to manifest regardless of whether a sufferer had been to war. To add to his difficulties, in 1919 the British government had destroyed the diggers' clinical records that had been held at the British Museum, without the Australian government's permission. These records covered each digger's medical history from enlistment to discharge, and might have helped

George (and Dick) make the case that their chronic ill-health was attributable to their war service.[28]

George wrote to the Repat Commission telling them that his bronchitis first occurred in 1916, 'and I was sent from Frecourt [sic] to Albert, and thence to Heily [sic] Hospital'. The osteoarthritis in his left hip originated 'in France during middle of 1917':

> I was gassed [at Hill 60] previous to the above …
> [remained in the frontline] … I am quite unable to
> work and require treatment at Concord, or elsewhere.

The Repat Commission denied his application. Arthur Fuller, the long-serving federal Labor Member in the House of Representatives, nicknamed 'Pilsener' for his resemblance to the long thin bottle, stepped in on George's behalf and wrote a letter to the War Pensions Entitlement Appeals Tribunal. Fuller claimed a long association with George and wrote, 'He is a fine man, a respected citizen who had been an excellent and brave soldier.' Fuller told the tribunal that George 'could not understand' the decision.[29]

As George waited on the outcome of his appeal, he prepared to drive with his son-in-law and daughter to enjoy his grandson Rich's birthday party at Lapstone in the lower Blue Mountains. On 11 November 1963 (Rich's birthday), somewhere between Blayney and Bathurst, Boss suffered a heart attack. A doctor stopped to help, but George was dead on arrival at Bathurst Hospital. 'So Boss never got to spend that holiday with us,' Rich said.

> Though I always remember this toy that he'd brought
> me; a little wooden train carriage with these two

bobble-headed passengers with what looked like
Christmas hats – it was painted green with some red
and white. I recall Mum kept it and gave it to my son
… when he was little.[30]

As far as his surviving daughter Florence and his grandson
Rich remember, George never mentioned Chipilly Spur nor
the war. It was George who told his kids he got his Military
Medal for 'cleaning the officer's boots'. Rich wondered how
George went back to Young after the war and 'go your whole
life and just zip it up'.[31]

But Rich did enjoy retelling a story his father Neville
told about Boss on Neville and Florence's wedding day. A
little nephew named Snapper got a hold of a garden hose and
began spraying the wedding guests. People ran about in panic
trying to protect their suits and dresses from Snapper and his
hose. But Boss kept his cool. He crept around the house and
came in behind Snapper. 'He put the bloody hose all over little
Snapper and said [laughing] "Do you like that? Are you ready
for a swim?" Poor old Snapper's mother was in tears. She had
to take him home and get him dressed again. That was Boss's
stealth-raiding stuff. He went around the back of the house
and came in behind him. The others didn't know what to do
[laughter].'[32]

*

After the war Harold lost contact with his mates from
Chipilly Spur. The last time he saw them together was in the
bitter fighting in the Froissy Valley, when four of the six fell
wounded and Harold was sent forward by his officer to see
what he could do. But his son Graham remembers that when

he was a boy in the early 1930s, the family came home from church or perhaps a fishing or camping trip up the coast one day and found a note from Jack Hayes on the front door. Jack never learnt to drive and seldom left the inner-west of Sydney, so this was a rare trip. Sadly, there was no reunion between the two old friends – but the thought that Jack had made the effort and the memory of their friendship made Harold happy.

Harold's father auctioned Coleraine in 1958. Harold put in the highest bid but his father declined. Eventually, Harold's younger brother Doug bought the farm. He had worked there while Harold was away at the war. Harold and Ivy left the farm in unhappy circumstances. They retired to a cottage named Oban at 82 High Street, Wauchope. It was previously owned by one of Ivy's uncles and named after the fishing town on the Firth of Lorne, Scotland. Harold was on a totally and permanently incapacitated pension due to repeated problems with his war injuries. Harold's grandson, Peter, remembers visits to Oban in the school holidays.

'There was always a cup of tea, scones or cake on hand should anyone drop by.' Harold and Ivy would sit on the veranda overlooking the road to Port Macquarie, where they could see Coleraine in the distance.

The couple's life revolved around family and faith: Harold became an elder of the Free Presbyterian Church and taught Sunday school to local children. He also taught his son and grandsons a love of the water and in particular fishing and surfing. Peter recounted several of his grandfather's legendary fishing exploits:

Pa was a great fisherman and one time he was coming home near King Creek bridge and saw some perch

(nowadays called bass) in the water near the bridge. He
raced home and grabbed a hand line and hooks and
returned, dug up some worms and proceeded to catch
dinner for the family. Another time he was on holiday
at Port Macquarie at the break wall and saw a lot of
tailor schooling there, he had his fishing line with him
and he had no bait so he took off his shirt and tore
a strip of white cloth off and wrapped it around the
hooks and cast into the school and managed to catch
dinner again.[33]

Harold's faith, and the comfort he found in being in the bush
or by the water – 'whether calm or rough' – probably helped

Harold Andrews and Ivy, Anzac Day 1974.
(Courtesy of Peter Andrews)

him make sense of his life experiences.[34] He also had a rich intellectual life for a man with limited schooling. Harold taught himself history and theology through vast amounts of reading. Yet his family bore witness that Harold's nightmares and war-related anxiety remained with him all his life.

In the living room at Oban there was a framed copy of Will Longstaff's famous painting commemorating the missing at Passchendaele, *The Menin Gate at Midnight* (1927), also known as *The Ghosts of Menin Gate*. The memory of the 'Dark Somme' and the long nights of agony in no man's land were with him always, but he learnt how to live with them.

In 1975 Harold began donating his war photographs, artefacts and stories to the Hastings River Historical Society. He spent a great deal of his time at the society building, writing his recollections and yarning with his niece Raelene Young. His stories stretched back to the first pioneers of the district, including his Ulster Scot ancestors on his father's side and his mother's convict heritage, his war experience, and the hard times managing the farm during the Great Depression. In his old age Harold recognised that his loyalty to the Empire and the British race were at odds with the rapidly changing culture of 1970s Australia. He was a man of his time, but some of his views would be considered deeply offensive now. In recalling the values of his youth, he worried:

> A repetition of those times and of those circumstances would mean violence in the 1970s. People seem Godless in their aim and in object, these days. There could be ultimate alienation from tradition – the tradition established by our forebears. There could be Republicanism or even a dictatorship – following on from the present-day so-called political leadership.

People are lacking (I think) the moral and spiritual values of those pioneering British stock. The bloodstream of which, like the U.S.A., and the New England stock of the 'Maryland' migration era, is being polluted to mutual degradation of the said moral and spiritual values. When man's 'word was his bond' and when God's name was revered (and not blasphemed by inference or implication in high places, this reverberating down to the hearthstones of our society) those values were important. The hearthstones of the 1970s could be empty, with the family bankruptcy which seems loom ahead![35]

Harold is unique among the digger writers of the First World War because he kept a war diary and later wrote copious notes and a detailed memoir of his war experiences – a total of sixty years of writing about and reflecting on the war. His letter to the official war historian CEW Bean on the capture of Chipilly Spur, written in 1929, is a classic for its detail and its laconic turn of phrase. One senses that Harold channelled his digger self while writing it – the reader is taken behind enemy lines while the Chipilly Six are cutting loose. There is larrikinism and adventurism in the writing (a kind of glint in the eye) that belies the reserved, ascetic values of the older man.

The letter contrasts with his feelings at dawn waiting for zero hour on the opening day of the Battle of Amiens – the day before the capture of Chipilly Spur – in which he recalled 'sitting in the fields shivering with fright'. Learning to control fear, not lack of fear, was an attribute that made the Chipilly Six such fine soldiers. The Bean letter is archived at the Australian War Memorial in Canberra. Raelene Young donated a typed copy of his war diary and 'Recollections' to the Mitchell Library in the State Library of New South Wales. Peter Andrews is the custodian of Harold's records and medals, including some remarkable souvenirs he brought home from the war, including an English officer's compass, which Harold reclaimed from a German officer he captured at Chipilly Spur.[36] Yet for all the eloquence of his diary and private papers, his grandson claimed:

> Pa didn't talk much about the war, he did say when they attacked Chipilly that he went over the top of a machine-gun nest and pointed his rifle at a German who put his hands up around his face expecting to be shot. Pa grabbed him by the scruff of the neck and pointed behind him to show the German which way to go back to the Australian [English III Corps] lines. Pa said he never forgot the look on the German's face as Pa spared his life.[37]

On 11 October 1975 Harold suffered a heart attack while travelling on a train to see Graham and his family. He died in Ivy's arms; she was always his 'rock and his strength'. He was seventy-eight years old. The Reverend J Campbell Andrews of Lilybank (Harold's nephew), conducted the funeral at the Free Presbyterian Church, Wauchope. Harold's niece Raelene wrote his obituary:

> In recent years, the body of the once-strong and courageous soldier was often racked with pain. He did not complain unduly, but bravely endeavoured to pursue his daily activities – right until the last hours of his earthly existence. His sense of humour seldom

deserted him, and many were the friends and relatives who enjoyed his company. With his keen mind, his wit and humour, his tolerance and deep understanding of human nature, he endeared himself to all who came in contact with him, especially those close to him.[38]

Harold's childhood was marked by the necessity to help his father on their dairy farm. His adulthood was dominated by the experience and memory of war. As a boy, Harold's favourite book was a worn copy of GA Henty's *In Freedom's Cause* – a popular late-nineteenth century boy's-own narrative of Robert the Bruce, King of the Scots. Young Harold read the book by a paraffin lamp in his bed at Coleraine. Most of all he admired Bruce's loyal knight, Thomas Randolph, the Earl of Moray, who, with a 'score' of brave Scots of 'sure foot and stout heart', captured Edinburgh Castle in March 1314.[39]

According to the legend, the castle, which is perched on a steep rock overlooking Edinburgh, was garrisoned by crack English soldiers and considered all but impregnable. Randolph's Scottish army bashed at the castle's main gate without success until a few daring men reconnoitred the rock face looking for an alternative way in. 'The little party of adventurers' found a steep goat track that wound its way upwards to the foot of the castle wall. In the darkness they crept along the precipice path, listening to the chatter of the sentries beyond the wall and the commotion of the fighting at the main gate. Stealthily, they climbed the wall and leapt into the keep. They landed among dozens of English soldiers and slashed them down with their heavy broadswords. The English were thoroughly confused and terrified. The small party of Scots opened the gates from within and Edinburgh Castle fell quickly to Randolph's army.

The story so inspired Harold that he visited Edinburgh Castle while on leave after his wounds at Pozières. In his diary he describes asking an elderly Scot to take him to the famous goat track, but the old man regretted that German zeppelins had destroyed it in a raid. Harold also mentioned the story of the capture of Edinburgh Castle in his memoirs, written in 1975. Yet he was too unassuming and modest to realise that he had emulated his boyhood heroes in the capture of Chipilly Spur in one of the greatest battles of the First World War.

*

Jack Hayes defied the Welsh doctors who told him in 1918 that he was not likely to live. On 8 June 1968 the governor of New South Wales, Sir Arthur Roden Cutler VC, AC, KCMG, KCVO, CBE, awarded him the British Empire Medal (Civil Division) 'For services to ex-servicemen as a life member of the Marrickville Anzac Memorial Club'.[40] Jack had joined the club as 'a very very young man', and served for more than fifty years as an honorary secretary, president (at the start of the Second World War), welfare officer, gentleman and lifelong larrikin. His wife May's service to the club and the local community was equal to Jack's. Their granddaughters treasure an old newspaper clipping featuring a photograph of Jack and May at the investiture. They are pressed together – holding each other arm in arm. 'Nana and Poppa Hayes didn't leave the end of the road very much'[41] – the Marrickville Anzac Memorial Club *was* the end of the road.

Jack and May's partnership speaks to the importance of family and community in the lives of returned service people, the virtue of mutual dependence in working-class and rural

May and Jack at Jack's investiture
for the British Empire Medal, 1968.
(Courtesy of Helen Thomson and Nola Moore)

communities, and the often unappreciated work of women
in the returned soldiers' clubs of the 1920s. The descendants
of the Chipilly Six universally agreed that their mothers and
grandmothers were the vital rocks of the family, often in
charge of the budget as well as the spirit of the home. They
were also active in their communities and had strong political
(and sometimes religious) beliefs. History has let them down
in not appreciating and highlighting their achievements and
stoicism. They lived in a time before Germaine Greer and
Anne Summers and countless activists reassessed the place of
women. Many of the children of the six whom I interviewed

agreed that, 'Mum was the mainstay of the family. Mum had to take care of us and keep us fed.'[42]

Jack and May went into retirement, he a 'healthy-looking old man', still enjoying 'ten Rothman tailor-made cigarettes and a couple of middies a day', and she 'a spritely ... old lady, mentally very aware'.[43]

Their home became 23 Renwick Street, Marrickville. Granddaughter Helen remembered it well:

> Poppa got the house because he was the only one of Blanche's kids who helped her financially ... It was a very large home and what I call a gentleman's residence with many fireplaces, a double lounge, and a long hall. Another lounge at the end of the hallway where we would watch TV and there was a coke fire, lovely and warm. Off that, two bedrooms, large kitchen which they renovated when they moved in and a large room followed from that. Bathroom which they renovated, sunroom and laundry. I just loved that home and Nana had it looking beautiful.[44]

Jack and May converted the parlour into a bedroom for Blanche (she lived to eighty-five and died in 1961). Their oldest daughter Megs and her husband Warren also lived in the Renwick Street home. Often on Saturday nights Jack and May entertained friends from the club or Charlie and Myra Lazzarini. Nanna 'liked a glass of sherry and was famous for saying "just the one", then the same next time! ... They had high standards (dress and manners) but they loved a good time!'[45]

Jack kept a small garden and grew orchids and staghorn ferns – it was something he picked up from his father Ottie

Hayes, who won prizes for his orchids in Bathurst before the First World War. Jack also made his own mustard and sauces and taught himself to paint landscapes in watercolours – though sadly none have survived.

In retirement his old wounds began to wear him down. He complained to his doctor that the pain around the scar on his chest and abdomen would 'come and go'. For three or four days at a time he would have to 'rest from gardening', go inside and 'move about the house'. The pain was worse at night. His GP diagnosed right inguinal hernia, hiatus hernia and diabetes mellitus. Jack wrote to the Repat Department and successfully sought assistance: 'I have tried not to worry the Department with my complaints as I had a rather comfortable position for many years, but as I am now retired I find it difficult to meet expenses for medical treatment.'[46]

Jack and May outlived their beloved daughter Megs and her husband Warren, and suffered the loss of a granddaughter at a tragically young age. Jack kept going until time, and probably grief, caught up with him. He died aged eighty-two, on 19 September 1977, after a short spell in hospital.

He was buried at Woronora Cemetery, Sutherland, in a small quiet ceremony. Most of his First World War mates were long dead or too frail to attend. At the time there remained only forty-eight First World War diggers who were members of the Marrickville Anzac Memorial Club. There was no lofty obituary for Jack. One of Jack's last duties at the club before his death was to give the toast to special guests, including local councillors, a sergeant from the Salvos and the local Labor representatives F Daly MHR and TJ Cahill MLA (both Marrickville to their bootstraps) at the tenth Old and Bold and Widows invitation luncheon for First World War families. Among the treasured possessions Jack kept from that day was his stained beer coaster with the club logo bearing an inscription he had inspired: 'Love thy neighbour and go home quietly'.

John Hayes said his father was 'A man who loved his fellow man – he cared about people, and wouldn't ask anyone to do anything that you're not game enough to do yourself.'

> As a young boy I could put my clenched fist into the hole in his chest. Such a wound would usually kill. He had been shot at close range, but he was not destined to die. Jack's life revolved around his past soldier friends.[47]

In the Marrickville Anzac Memorial Club Jack found a purpose and meaning to his life. As an original digger he was a custodian of the Anzac tradition. But what sustained him were the ideals of volunteerism and self-sacrifice that were the digger virtues he most admired during the war. In May he met a woman with a similar upbringing and values to himself. With May as his soulmate, he recovered his self-worth and the ethos of his working-class community that placed a high premium on giving a helping hand. These were the values of the labour movement and the neighbourhoods they lived in throughout their lives.

Historians of the Anzac tradition sometimes unfairly characterise the old diggers of the First World War as triumphant nationalists or deeply conservative – or as victims who struggled to live up to the Anzac myth. Jack was none of those.

Part of Jack's legacy is the dawn service at Martin Place. Its origins are clouded in myth but it is clear that the Marrickville Anzac Memorial Club played a leading role in the first dawn service and in maintaining the tradition. Men and women like Ernie Rushbrooke, George Paterson, and Jack's close friends Jim Davidson of the 1st Battalion and Matron Alice Cashin, have not been acknowledged by historians. They were the leaders of a distinctively working-class movement of independent returned soldiers clubs that responded to the legacy of war service with the ethos of volunteerism that had inspired the diggers.

In time the Marrickville Anzac Memorial Club faded away. Changing immigration patterns after the Second World War saw Marrickville transform into a vibrant multicultural suburb comprising Italian, Greek and later Vietnamese and Middle Eastern new arrivals. The club lost relevance. The unspoken heroes in such profound demographic shifts are the old residents who face change in their long-established communities with equanimity and tolerance. John Hayes worried that the older way of life was gone, but he also called it inevitable. In 1980 the original club building on Garners Avenue was destroyed by fire. The club reopened within eighteen months, but the rise of the pokies and bad debts saw it lose money and eventually go under. The club went into voluntary administration in 2008 with $2.7 million in debts and, finally, obliteration. Its memorabilia were reportedly auctioned.

It was an ignominious end to a once celebrated club. Today, there is not even a plaque to mark the place where so many diggers and their families gathered to rebuild their community, remember their dead and help those 'not as fortunate as themselves who were doing it tough'.

For Stan Maxwell, an old Korean War digger who was the nephew of Joe Maxwell VC, the closing down of the club was 'the worst thing that ever happened'. He remembered Jack Hayes and knew the origin story of the club and the first dawn service.

John Hayes had sat at the feet of Jerry Fuller and Jack as a boy and listened to their war stories. In 1945 he returned from New Guinea and became a member of the Marrickville Anzac Memorial Club in his own right. He had privileged access to the thoughts of diggers who served in the First and Second World Wars, Korea and Vietnam. Many of the old diggers believed that Jack and his mates would have got the Victoria Cross for the capture of Chipilly Spur had there been an Australian officer there to witness it. But not wearing the VC did not bother Jack. He was an experienced frontline soldier. He knew that decorations were largely a matter of luck. Every Anzac Day, Jack would tuck his Distinguished Conduct Medal in his pocket after the march – 'he didn't show it off'. In his own eyes he was not a hero. He was serene in the knowledge that he had known many brave men who did not wear a ribbon to show it.

The events at Chipilly Spur became a weight on Jack's shoulders. As he grew older the exhilaration of the raid and the admiration of diggers who knew the story drained him. He told John that the memory of the blue-eyed German in the first post he rushed that hectic afternoon on 9 August 1918 kept him awake at night. When Jack leapt into the enemy's dugout, the German fired first and missed. Jack raised his rifle and put a bullet through the blue-eyed German. They were so close they could have touched each other. The Chipilly Six were on fire that day and Jack was their Horatius – a whole British Corps followed in the six Australians' wake. But years afterwards, Jack regretted that moment in the German post. Thinking about his former soldier self, he wished he could have spared the blue-eyed German's life.

'He had a high regard for the Germans ... He saw them as men doing the same job as him,' John recalled. But Jack was too good a soldier to hesitate. Back then it was kill or be killed: 'you or me', as Harold Andrews put it.

Jack would say, 'We went over the top first, and the rest followed so we couldn't stop!'[48]

AFTERWORD

The Chipilly Six were distinctively Australian young men: the grandsons of a mixture of convicts, pioneer settlers, and the English and Irish rural poor. They were born in the depression of the 1890s and grew up in hardship with minimal educational opportunities. They were destined to become experienced and exceptional soldiers. They fulfilled the standard of manly courage taught in their school history books, when Horatius held the bridge in the brave days of Rome.

Unlike many of their mates, they did not die in battle. Their legacy was not a cold memorial stone in France. Their cross would be the struggle of the daily grind with the Anzac legend on their shoulders. When Harold Andrews met his old friend and platoon commander Bob Traill in a Sydney street in 1919, the two held each other and prayed 'There but for the grace of God go I'.[1] They were yet to come to terms with being survivors. Poor Bob Traill was dead within years of that fateful meeting, another victim of tuberculosis brought home from the war. The Chipilly Six, like many veterans, carried survivor guilt as one does a wound.

They returned to a nation anxious about the new Spanish influenza and venereal disease, and fearful of new ideas like

Jack's beer coaster.
(Courtesy of Helen Thomson)

Bolshevism. Their communities were fraught by industrial strikes and sectarianism. After the joyful welcome home, they found some of the fear and anxiety directed at them. They joined soldiers' clubs and organisations to champion their rights and ensure that the government would fulfil the promises it made to them when they went to war in 1914. And perhaps more importantly, to continue to emulate the spirit of comradeship that they valued so much in the trenches. They created families and returned to work, meaningful community life and old loyalties. No sooner had they found their feet as providers than the Great Depression blew them down again. The Second World War took their sons to new battlefields, and some of the six fought in that war too. What they seem to have retained in common was their attachment to the AIF, personal integrity, and the support of loving families built around strong women who were independent, resilient and resourceful.

Australians viewed the First World War as a nation-defining experience. It led to an immense array of sources on soldiers' lives and battles. We could fill a football stadium with books written about Australian soldiers at war. But the history of what happened after the First World War is much more difficult to write, poorly understood and often misinterpreted. The families of service people will tell you that the experience of war does not end, it continues. The challenge for the next generation of historians – and for the families of those who serve – is to record and understand what happens when young Australians return from service.

The Chipilly Six were exceptional soldiers, and ordinary survivors of an extraordinary generation. Their time seems like a vanishing world, yet the experiences that shaped the Chipilly Six's lives continue to resonate today.

AUTHOR'S NOTE

The Chipilly Six had been largely forgotten when I began to unearth their story in my first book, *Stealth Raiders*. In writing this account, I followed their footsteps from Australia to Gallipoli and on to the Somme, to Chipilly Spur and beyond. I visited their home towns and talked to their children.

One evening, I sat down in my office with a cup of tea and rang eighty-three-year-old John Hayes, son of Company Quartermaster Sergeant Jack Hayes, the leader of the Chipilly Six. I wanted to know dozens of details about his father. John was up for a yarn. He poured himself a whisky – he 'always had a nightcap', he told me. I gulped my tea and we got into it. John's stories inspired this book.

The first thing John told me was 'My father loved people. He loved his fellow man'. Jack called the 1st Battalion, the 'pride of the line'.

'He wasn't very popular with his commanding officer. He didn't want to be an officer. He wanted to be with the men. That's all he wanted. Dad just loved those men.'[1]

Later, when the family lent me Jack's war diaries, I appreciated how accurate John's memory was of his father's attitude to army life. Jack's diaries are full of amusing references to coming 'a Gutzer' or a 'Capital G' in some run-in with an officer, or celebrating a 'stunt' or a 'rolling barrage' if he and his mates got away with going absent without leave for a few drinks, or a game of two-up or bridge. The mindless supervision of the parade ground irked Jack but he enjoyed responsibility.

Jack was the type of man to whom others were immediately attracted. A generous-hearted Australian of Irish descent, his sympathies lay with ordinary people. The Hayes family have photos of Jack's war that record some of the people he met and his attitude to them: smiling and joking beside hawkers selling pieces of the pyramids, rubbing shoulders with an old peasant on Lemnos Island in the Mediterranean. As a company quartermaster sergeant whose job was to feed 200 men, he had a knack for getting treats from tight-fisted madams and soldier-wise mademoiselles in the billets of France and Flanders.

I enjoyed several conversations with Jack's son, yarning about his dad and the war, including the firsthand accounts that led me to believe Jack Hayes was pivotal in the instigation of the original Anzac Day dawn service that Australians continue to observe each year.

Sadly, John Hayes died while I was writing this book. He had shared openly with me his father's story and there was so much more I wanted to ask. It is to him, and the other children and descendants of the Chipilly Six who contributed to this book, that I owe my sincere thanks.

ACKNOWLEDGEMENTS

My foremost thanks are to the family members of the Chipilly Six, in particular the late John Hayes and his daughters Helen Thomson and Nola Moore; Graham and Peter Andrews and Roger Wilson; Renie Channells, Phyllis Saul, Grahame Tricker, Deb and Karen Regan and Robyn Franks; Rich Baker, Florence Baker and the late Neville Baker; Lisa Sinclair, Mark Deacon and Rick Dollemore; and Richard Turpin.

The work of historians Ross McMullin and Bill Gammage led me to the story of the Chipilly Six. Ross McMullin's short newspaper article published in 2008, 'Diggers did it all on their own at Chipilly' argued that the capture of Chipilly Spur was 'a compelling example' of the influence of the Australian soldier in 1918 'on the destiny of the world.' In the preface to the illustrated edition of *The Broken Years: Australian Soldiers in the Great War*, (2010), Bill Gammage regretted not having written more about the capture of Chipilly Spur. Gammage argued that what Jack Hayes and his mates achieved at Chipilly Spur was 'among the AIF's most extraordinary achievements' and that neglecting the story of the Chipilly Six 'flaws all the many now popular judgements of the quality of the First AIF.' It was my privilege that Ross and Bill encouraged and supported me to correct that neglect. Bill urged me to 'bore into it' and generously read and advised me on numerous drafts. Dr Peter Stanley also advised and encouraged me.

A grant from the Australian Army History Unit allowed me to access sources held in institutions throughout Australia and the United Kingdom. In the UK, Dr Bart Zielinski researched the private papers of English soldiers who fought at Chipilly held by the Imperial War Museum. Dr Aaron Pegram researched and copied documents held by the Australian War Memorial. Historian and soldier Trevor Lynch connected me with the descendants of Bill Kane and introduced me to his deep knowledge of Macksville and the Nambucca area. Bill Phippen and Trevor Edmonds, Australian Railways Historical Society (NSW), answered my questions on the 1917 railways strike and the working conditions of railwaymen, be they 'Lily White' or 'Loyalist'.

In Western Australia, Ross and Bev McGuinness from the Denmark Historical Society, provided me with sources and images relating to the Group Settlement Scheme. Ross and Bev also put me in contact with Tom Atkinson, Dick Turpin's oldest suriving mate. Tom shared his memories of working with Dick on the road and bridge building gangs in the Great Southern.

I would also like to thank Heather Campbell for proofreading my drafts; Diane McCarthy of the Marrickville Historical Society; Terry Overton for allowing me access to his extensive Stevens family history; the staff at the Frank Partridge VC Museum, Bowraville; Rob Cramb and Ian Ronayne enlightened me to the presence of Australian soldiers farming on Jersey in 1919. Keith Amos answered my questions on the New Guard. Darren Mitchell's thought-provoking PhD thesis 'Anzac Rituals – Secular, Sacred, Christian' gave me a deeper understanding of the Anzac Day dawn service. Lawrie Daly shared anecdotes of Marrickville identities including CC Lazzarini. Paul Wilson at the Powerhouse

Museum went out of his way to make the long-silent May Hayes oral history tapes available.

It has been a pleasure to work with NewSouth Publishing to bring this story to readers. I would especially like to thank Harriet McInerney for her support of the Chipilly Six manuscript and her vision to see it through to this book. Thank you also to Sophia Oravecz, project editor, and Joumana Awad for their enthusiasm and interest in the characters, which has greatly contributed to the aesthetic of the book. Linda Funnell was an astute and thorough editor who I enjoyed working with, and thank you to Peter Long for designing the cover and to Josephine Pajor-Markus for drawing the maps.

My final thank you is to my family. My dad, Ken, who travelled to many of the battlefields with me, and in particular Anna, who has lived with the Chipilly Six for as long as me, and whom I love.

NOTES

Introduction

1   Monash, *The Australian Victories in France in 1918*, p. 115.

2   See *Sydney Morning Herald*, Wednesday, 31/12/1919, p. 8.

3   Actually, published in Supplement to the *Edinburgh Gazette*, 5/2/1919, p. 622.

4   Published in *The Times* and reported in Australia in the *Newcastle Sun*, 29/12/1919, p. 5.

5   Cutlack, *The Australians*, p. 260 and 'Chipilly Spur ... Clearing Up Discussion', *Sydney Morning Herald*, 1/1/1920, p. 4.

6   Martin, *Londoners on the Western Front*, p. 161.

7   Grey, *The 2nd City of London Regiment (Royal Fusiliers) in the Great War (1914-1919)*, pp. 350–351.

8   Van Every, *The AEF in Battle*, p. 226.

9   <en.wikipedia.org/wiki/Joseph_B._Sanborn>

10   Martin, *Londoners on the Western Front,* p. 160.

11   Huidekoper, *The History of the 33rd Division AEF*, p. 413.

12   The history of the 124th IR states that some of the defenders on the ridge were 'seized with panic' when they saw tanks assembled (near the Bray-Corbie Road) and then found the view shut out by smoke. Whereas in the area the six-man patrol was operating, the history of the 120th IR states that its men withdrew 'under pressure of a hostile encircling movement on the south'. The history of the 479th IR also attributes the capture of the ridge to an encircling movement from the south. See Bean, *Official History*, Vol. VI, pp. 652–653. The 131st US Regiment also reported on the Australian outflanking movement from the south in Van Every, *The AEF in Battle*, p. 226.

13   Awards: Hayes DCM, Andrews DCM, Fuller, Kane and Stevens MM, Turpin MSM.

14   Barwick, D 4/9/1918, MLMSS1493.

15   Hayes, Citation DCM, AWM28/1/44 Part1.

16   Andrews, M 1975, MLDOC2745.

17   See Mastriano, *Alvin York*.

18 Traill, D 16/8/1918, AWM2DRL/0711.
19 McCarthy, *Gallipoli to the Somme*, pp. 347–48.
20 Pers comm, Rich and Florence Baker, 21/2/2018.

Chapter 1: Jack Hayes
1 Clune, *Rascals, Ruffians & Rebels of Early Australia*, pp. 144-64.
2 Day, *Chifley*, 2002, p. 63.
3 'Cadets at the Range', *The National Advocate*, 9/9/1912, p. 3.
4 'Turkish Delight: What Private Hayes Stopped', *The National Advocate*, 9/6/1915, p. 4.
5 This quote comes from a letter to his mother published in 'One of the Unlucky Ones', *Sun*, 1/7/1915, p. 5.
6 Barwick, D 6/8/1916, MLMSS1493.
7 Hayes, D 19/7/1916.
8 Hayes, D 22/7/1916. The battalion went over the top just after midnight on 23/8/1916, but Hayes wrote up the event in his diary under the date 22/8/1916.
9 Hayes, D 18-22/8/1916.
10 By 8/2/1918, only 69 originals were left in the battalion. See 1 Bn War Diary, AWM4/23/18/28.
11 Hayes, D 24-25/7/1916.
12 Pers comm, John Hayes, 7/7/2013; Barwick D, 7/12/1917, MLMSS1493.
13 Barwick, D 28/11/1916, MLMSS1493.
14 Hayes, D 28-30/11/1916.
15 Hayes notebook, Ypres 6/9/1916, courtesy of Helen Thomson and Nola Moore.
16 Gammage, *The Broken Years*, p. 239.
17 Hayes, D 21/4/1917 and 23-26/5/1917.
18 Hayes, D 1-3/6/1917.
19 Barwick, D April 1918 and 2/11/1917, MLMSS1493.
20 Hayes, D 19/3/1916; 18-22/8/1916; 10/9/1916.
21 Andrews, D 11/11/1917, MLMSS7504.
22 Andrews, D 11/11/1917, MLMSS7504; Hayes, D 11/11/1917.
23 McMullin, *Will Dyson*, p. 199.
24 Godfrey, D 04/05/1918, AWM 3DRL/3318.

Chapter 2: Harold Andrews
1 Andrews, M 1975, MLDOC2745.
2 Andrews, M 1975, MLDOC2745.
3 Andrews, D 24/7/1916.
4 Andrews, M 1975, MLDOC2745.
5 Andrews, M 1975, MLDOC2745.
6 Way, L 15/9/1916, courtesy of Peter Andrews.

7   Edwards, MS, AWMPR89/050.
8   Traill, D 3/8/1918, AWM2DRL/0711.
9   Traill, D 14/4/1918, AWM2DRL/0711.
10   In Yule (ed), *Sergeant Lawrence Goes to France*, p. 171.
11   Handwritten note in margin of his personal copy of Stacy et al, *The History of the First Battalion AIF 1914–1919*. Courtesy of Peter Andrews.
12   Andrews, M 1975, MLDOC2754.

Chapter 3: George Stevens
1   'Local News', *Camden News*, 16/4/1908, p. 5 and pers comm, Terry Overton (Stevens family historian), 2/2/2018.
2   *New South Wales Register of Coroners' Inquests, 1821–1937*, re: Henry Stevens, date of inquest 17/05/1893.
3   Pers comm, Terry Overton, 02/02/2018.
4   Pers comm, Rich Baker interview with N Baker, 23/8/2019 and FM Baker (nee Stevens) 25/08/2019.
5   'Lodge Cricket', *Young Chronicle*, 19/4/1913, pp. 2–3.
6   <www.edwardianpromenade.com/fashion/the-clothes-the-man-cricket>.
7   'The Kangaroos Visit to Young', *Young Witness*, 10/12/1915, p. 2.
8   'The Kangaroos Visit to Young', *Young Witness*, 10/12/1915, p. 2.
9   'Visit of the Kangaroos: Young Gives Welcome', *Young Chronicle*, 14/12/1915, p. 3.
10   'To the Boys of Young: Appeal for Recruits', *Young Witness*, 31/12/1915, p. 4.
11   Bean, *Official History*, Vol. III, 1941, p. 894.
12   Barwick, D, 5/11/1917, MLMSS1493.
13   GA Stevens letters and postcards, undated c. 1916–1918, courtesy of R Baker.
14   Pers comm, Florence Baker (nee Stevens), 25/08/2019.
15   Edwards, MS, AWMPR89/050.
16   EH Hinton, Red Cross File, AWM 1DRL/0428.
17   Hayes, D 10/10/1917.

Chapter 4: Jerry Fuller
1   Pers comm, Mark Deacon, 12/2/2019.
2   Pers comm, John Hayes, 23/9/2012.
3   Emily Dive Death Certificate NSW BDM Reg. No. 1369/1900.
4   Pers comm, Lisa Sinclair, 15/4/2020.
5   5083 Fuller, recordsearch.naa.gov.au
6   Traill, D 7/7/1918, AWM2DRL/711.
7   CB Withy, Citation MC, AWM28 1/41 Part 1 and Traill, D 7/6/1918, AWM2DRL/711.
8   Andrews, D 6/11/1917, MLMSS7504.

Chapter 5: Billy Kane

1   See, for instance, *Mount Alexander Mail,* 14/2/1891, p. 2; 17/9/1892, p.2; 2/4/1897, p. 2 and 7/4/1897.
2   'Death Through a Brawl,' *Mount Alexander Mail*, 22/11/1880, p. 2.
3   'Death Through a Brawl,' *Mount Alexander Mail*, 27/11/1880, 2 and 'Items of News,' *Mount Alexander Mail*, 28/2/1881, p. 2.
4   'Castlemaine Police Court', *Mount Alexander Mail*, 17/9/1892, p. 2.
5   'Railway Sleepers: The Allen Taylor Contract', *Clarence and Richmond Examiner,* 4/2/1915, p. 6.
6   'Farewell to Recruits', *Nambucca and Bellinger News*, 13/8/1915, p. 4.
7   'With The Anzacs on The Western Front', *Sydney Mail,* 27/9/1916, p. 14.
8   Kane, L 12/7/1916, courtesy of Phyllis Saul and Deb Regan.
9   Hayes, D 29/6/1916.
10 Kane, L 12/7/1916.
11 Kane, L date unknown, courtesy of Phyllis Saul and Deb Regan.
12 'Castlemaine Soldiers', *Bendigo Independent*, 7/11/1916, p. 8 and *Bendigo Advertiser,* 4/9/1916, p. 5.
13 'Letters from the Front', *Nambucca and Bellinger News*, 29/9/1916, p. 4.
14 Kane, L date unknown.
15 In Gammage, *The Broken Years,* p. 210.
16 Administrative Staff, Headquarters 1st Australian Division, War Diary, 8/6/1917, AWM4 1/43/29.
17 'Guide to Management and Care of Horses and Harness (1915)', <collection.nam.ac.uk/detail.php?acc=1994-06-217-8>.

Chapter 7: 'Some worthwhile souvenirs'

1   From 7–14/8/1918, the Australian Corps suffered 6491 casualties, a quarter of its strength on entering the battle. <www.anzacsinfrance.com/1918/>.
2   McMullin, *Pompey Elliott*, pp. 464–465.
3   Ludendorff, in Bean, *Official History*, Vol. VI, p. 614.
4   A summary of the science of artillery in 1918 is in Hart, *1918: A Very British Victory*, pp. 310–312.
5   von Bose, *The Catastrophe of 8 August 1918*, p. 152.
6   War Diary, 15 Australian Infantry Battalion, Appendix 1, 'Narrative of the attack by 15th Battalion on Cerisy-Gailly, 8th August 1918', AWM4 23/2/41.
7   Traill, D 8/8/1918, AWM 2DRL/0711.
8   McConnel, D 8/8/1918, AWM 2DRL/0029.
9   Andrews, L 29/12/1929, AWM 1DRL 0043.
10 Andrews, L 29/12/1929, AWM 1DRL 0043.
11 2/10 Bn War Diary, August 1918, '2/10th Battalion, London Regiment. Summary of Operations. Sailly Laurette and Chipilly.

August 3 to 12, 1918: Third Phase. The Capture of Chipilly Spur', p. 11 in W0/95/30009, p. 121 of 199.

12 Andrews, L 29/12/1929, AWM 1DRL 0043.

13 Brig Gen IG Mackay DSO and Bar, CMG, CdG, MID, 1 Bde, University lecturer, of North Geelong, Vic. E 27/8/1914, aged 32, RTA 3/1/1920.

14 See 1 Bn War Diary, 9/8/1918, AWM4/23/18/34; 2/10 Bn War Diary, August 1918, 'Summary of operations', p. 11 in WO/95/30009, pp. 121–122 of 199.

15 Bean, *Official History,* Vol VI, p. 650.

16 Hart, *1918: A Very British Victory*, pp. 341–342.

17 1 Bn War Diary, 9/8/1918, AWM4/23/18/34. In 1929 Andrews wrote that the permission came through at 2 p.m. but contemporary accounts put it after the British attack commenced at 4 p.m.

18 'Private George Stevens Settling Accounts for His Pals', *Young Witness*, 29/10/1918, p. 4.

Chapter 8: The six 'cut loose'

1 2/Lt (A/Capt) JS Berrell, 2/7 Bn, London Regt, attd. 2/10 Bn.

2 2/10 Bn War Diary, August 1918, 'Summary of Operations', p. 11 in W0/95/30009, pp. 121–122 of 199; 1 Bn War Diary, August 1918, App 8, AWM4/23/18/34.

3 1 Bn War Diary, August 1918, App 8, AWM4/23/18/34.

4 Andrews, L 29/12/1929, AWM1DRL 0043.

5 Andrews, L 29/12/1929, AWM1DRL 0043.

6 2/10 Bn War Diary, August 1918, 'Summary of operations', p. 13 in W0/95/30009, p. 123 of 199.

7 The 2/10 Bn's war diary states that the party [actually led by Hayes] 'had worked through the smoke barrage faster than was anticipated'. 2/10 Bn War Diary, August 1918, 'Summary of operations', p. 13 in WO/95/30009, p. 123 of 199; Andrews, L 29/12/1929, AWM1DRL/0043.

8 Hayes marksmanship: 1 Bn War Diary, August 1918, App 1, 'Five rounds application' and '10 rounds 'rapid', AWM4/23/18/34; Barwick, D 30/11/17, 'the day when C Coys crack shots went shooting', MLMSS1493.

9 Andrews, M 1975, MLDOC2754.

10 Andrews, L 29/12/1929, AWM1DRL 0043.

11 Andrews, L 29/12/1929, AWM1DRL 0043.

12 41 Bn War Diary 9/8/1918, AWM4/23/58/22.

13 Deitz, D 9/8/1918, AWMPR01937.

14 Andrews, L 29/12/1929, AWM1DRL/0043.

15 Barwick, D 15/4/1918, MLMSS1493.

16 Barwick, D 15/4/1918, MLMSS1493.

17 Andrews, M 1975, MLDOC2754.

18 Hayes, Citation DCM, AWM28/1/44Part1.

19 Andrews, L 29/12/1929, AWM1DRL/0043.

20 1 Bn War Diary, August 1918, App 8, AWM4/23/18/34; Andrews, L 29/12/1929, AWM1DRL/0043.
21 Andrews, L 29/12/1929, AWM1DRL/0043.
22 Andrews, L 29/12/1929, AWM1DRL/0043.
23 The history of the 202nd RIR, claims its I Bn and elements of III/137 IR received orders to withdraw and make a front along the Meaulte-Etinehem Road. See Bean, *Official History*, Vol VI, pp. 652–653.
24 Andrews, L 29/12/1929, AWM1DRL/0043.
25 421370 Sergeant HL Darby DCM, of Ipswich, Eng. Citation DCM in *Supplement to the London Gazette*, 15/11/18, p. 13439; 2/10 Battalion War Diary, August 1918, 'Summary of Operations', p. 13 in W0/95/30009, p. 123 of 199.
26 Andrews, L 29/12/1929, AWM1DRL/0043.
27 1 Bn War Diary, August 1918, App 8, AWM4/23/18/34; Van Every, *The AEF in Battle*, p. 226.
28 Andrews, L 29/12/1929, AWM1DRL/0043.
29 'Glowing in terms' in Andrews, M 1975 MLDOC2754; Bean, *Official History*, Vol VI, n22, p. 652. A copy of part of Berrell's note and correspondence regarding its removal from the 1st Bn War Diary can be found at AWM27/354/254 Folios 1 and 2. The author wishes to thank Dr Peter Stanley for finding the latter source.
30 Andrews, L 29/12/1929, AWM1DRL/0043.
31 26 unwounded and 2 wounded prisoners brought through 1 Bde HQ. 1 Bn War Diary, August 1918, App 8, AWM4/23/18/34.
32 50 Bn War Diary, 9/8/1918, AWM4/23/67/26.
33 I Beckett, 'Butler, Sir Richard Harte Keatinge', *Oxford Dictionary of National Biography*.
34 Andrews, L 29/12/1929, AWM1DRL/0043.
35 Sound, Catalogue No. 9420, William Arthur Gillman (interviewed by Peter Hart).
36 'Private George Stevens Settling Accounts for His Pals', *Young Witness*, 29/10/1918, p. 4.
37 GA Stevens, Citation MM, AWM28 1/47 Part 1.
38 Traill, D 16/8/1918, AWM2DRL/0711.

Chapter 9: The Chipilly Six's last battle
1 Andrews, M 1975, MLDOC2754.
2 1 Bn War Diary, August 1918, App 14, AWM4 23/18/34.
3 Stacy et al, *The History of the First Battalion AIF 1914–1919*, p. 106.
4 Andrews, M 1975, MLDOC2754 and handwritten note in margin of his personal copy of Stacy et al, *The History of the First Battalion AIF 1914–1919*.
5 Bean, *Official History*, Vol. VI, p. 736.
6 Andrews, M 1975, MLDOC2754.

7   Graham and Peter Andrews, pers comm, 09/02/2018.
8   Andrews, M 1975, MLDOC2754.

Chapter 10: Jack Hayes' wounding
1   Pers comm, John Hayes, 7/07/2013.
2   Andrews, M 1975, MLDOC2754.
3   McConnel, D 23-24/08/1918, AWM 2DRL/0029.
4   National Archives Australia, repatriation cases (Boer War and WW1), Jack Charles Hayes (948), Series No. 138, Control Symbol M42224, Item Barcode 31810206.
5   G Stulc, 'The Antecedents and Evolution of Abdominal Surgery for Trauma in World War One', p.27. <history.army.mil/curriculum/wwi/docs/AdditionalResources/presentations/Antecedents and Evolution_Abdominal_Surgery_for_Trauma_in_WWI.pdf>.

Chapter 11: Dick Turpin's redemption
1   Andrews, M 1975, MLDOC2754.
2   Chapman, *Iven G Mackay*, pp. 112–113.
3   1st Battalion, Field General Court Martial, held on 15th October, 1918, *AWM 51/122 Part 1*.
4   JR Turpin, Citation MSM, AWM28 1/49 Part 1.
5   JR Turpin, Citation, Meritorious Service Medal, AWM28 1/49 Part 1.
6   Edwards, MS, AWM PR089/050.
7   Chapman, *Iven G Mackay*, p. 113.
8   Chapman, *Iven G Mackay*, pp. 113–114.

Chapter 12: The war is over
1   (3232) Andrews, <recordsearch.naa.gov.au>.
2   HD Andrews, Citation, Distinguished Conduct Medal, AWM28 1/44 Part 1.
3   Edwards, MS, AWM PR089/050.

Chapter 13: A changed Australia
1   Andrews, M (c. July 1919), 1975, MLDOC2754.
2   Bean, *Official History*, Vol. VI, Appendix.
3   Ward, *A Nation for a Continent*, p. 98.
4   Garton, *The Cost of War*, p. 12.
5   In Garton, *The Cost of War*, p. 15.
6   Tiveychoc (RE Lording), *There and Back*.
7   Thompson, *Bill Harney's War*, p. 52.
8   Larsson, *Shattered Anzacs*, p. 241 refers to *Medical Journal of Australia*, 24/2/1945, p. 197.
9   Murray, *The Confident Years*, pp. 9–10.

10   Lake, *Getting Equal*, 1999, pp. 1–16.
11   Murray, *The Confident Years*, p. 16.

Chapter 14: The return of Private Jerry Fuller MM
1   Barry, *The Great Influenza*, p. 5.
2   A young Sergeant Major, Alfred Ellis, 35th Battalion, labourer, of
      West Maitland, suffering from pneumonic influenza – probably picked
      up in Broadmeadows Camp, or Melbourne.
3   'At the Cricket Ground', *Sun*, 12/2/1919, p. 5.
4   'At the Cricket Ground', *Sun*, 12/2/1919, p. 5.
5   <adb.anu.edu.au/biography/lee-george-leonard-7146>
6   'The Men's Complaints Stated to General Lee', *Sydney Morning
      Herald*, 12/2/1919, p. 8.
7   'At the Cricket Ground', *Sun*, 12/2/1919, p. 5.
8   'Argyllshire Troops March Out. 900 Men go to Cricket Ground.
      Ugly Situation Ends Quietly', *Sydney Morning Herald*, 12/2/1919,
      p. 8
9   'At the Cricket Ground', *Sun* 12/2/1919, p. 5.
10   *Sydney Morning Herald*, 12/2/1919, p. 8.
11   'At the Cricket Ground', *Sun*, 12/2/1919, p. 5.
12   'The Argyllshire', *Daily Telegraph*, 10/2/1919, p. 4.

Chapter 15: Private Billy Kane MM returns to Congarinni
1   'Mamari Arrives: A Splendid Trip', *Age*, 5/2/1919, p. 8.
2   After Bill's death, the Kane family donated to the AWM this photo
      and some artifacts Billy brought back from the war: Wedding photo,
      AWM P04445.001; medals, AWM REL32849.001-005; dagger,
      AWM REL32850.
3   'Mothers' Badge Successful Function', *Nambucca and Bellinger News*,
      2/7/1920, p. 4.
4   'Eight Hour Day Sports', *Nambucca and Bellinger News*, 5/10/1923,
      p. 2.
5   'Nambucca and Bellinger News', *Nambucca and Bellinger News*,
      14/12/1928, p. 4.

**Chapter 16: The return of Company Quartermaster Sergeant Jack
      Hayes DCM**
1   'By Land and Sea', *Daily Advertiser*, 12/2/1919, p. 2.
2   Pers comm, John Hayes, 28/9/2012.
3   Ben Chifley in <adb.anu.edu.au/biography/chifley-joseph-benedict-
      ben-9738>.
4   Edmonds, *The Strike That Never Ended*.
5   Pers comm, Trevor Edmonds, 26/04/2021.
6   Pers comm Bill Phippen, 14/08/2018.

7   National Archives Australia, repatriation cases (Boer War and WWI), Jack Charles Hayes (948), Series No. 138, Control Symbol M42224, Item Barcode 31810206.
8   Hayes D.
9   Pers comm, John Hayes, 28/9/2012.
10   *Sydney Morning Herald*, 20/4/1923, p. 8.
11   'Cashin, Alice Alanna (1870–1939)', <adb.anu.edu.au/biography/cashin-alice-alanna-12842>.
12   'Queen of Marrickville', *Sun*, 14/10/1924, p. 6.
13   Ramsland, *Venturing into No Man's Land*, pp. 4–5. Thank you to David Cranage for this story.
14   Edwards, MS AWMPR89/050.
15   An extract from the first report on the Marrickville Anzac Memorial Fund, given by Foundation Secretary CV Harold in 1920, in '75 Good Years', *Club Digest*, November–December, 1996, p. 17.
16   Pers comm, John Hayes, 28/9/2012.

Chapter 17: The return of Private George Stevens MM
1   Ronayne, *Jersey Evening Post*, 16/7/2009.
2   Pers comm, Rob Cramb, 25/5/2021.
3   'Stevens-Hinton', *Young Witness*, 28/11/1919, p. 6.
4   'Personal', *Young Witness*, 26/10/1920, p. 2.

Chapter 18: The homecoming of Lieutenant Harold Andrews DCM
1   These are the scores as Harold remembered them. However, in Fielding, *Comrades in Arms and Rugby*, the following scores are given: AIF 21 Second Army 6; AIF 41 RAF 0. Marcus Fielding, pers comm, 5/6/2020.
2   Andrews, M 1975, MLDOC2745.
3   Andrews, M 1975, MLDOC2745.
4   Andrews, M 1975, MLDOC2745.
5   Andrews, M 1975, MLDOC2745.
6   Pers comm, Graham and Peter Andrews, 29/4/2021.
7   R Wilson, unpublished manuscript, 'The Andrews of Coleraine … and the Wilsons of Willsbro', 2012, p. 98.

Chapter 19: The return of Lance Corporal Dick Turpin MSM
1   'Denmark Notes', *Albany Despatch*, 26/1/1922, p. 3; see also 'Denmark Notes', *Albany Advertiser*, 3/8/1921, p. 2].
2   Bolton, *A Fine Country to Starve In*, p. 22.
3   Bolton, *A Fine Country to Starve In*, p. 50.
4   Bolton, *A Fine Country to Starve In*, p. 25.
5   Bolton in Hunt (ed.), *Westralian Portraits*, p. 165.
6   Bolton, *A Fine Country to Starve In*, p. 34.

Chapter 20: Soldiers' clubs vs the league

1   Marrickville Anzac Memorial Club Golden Anniversary Booklet, 1921–1971.

2   Pers comm, Lawrie Daly, 31/07/2018.

3   Pers comm, John Hayes, 28/9/2012.

4   'Heroic Padre: Tribute to Father Clune by Australian V.C.', *Western Champion*, 28/10/1932, p. 8.

5   'Chaplain-Major Francis Clune, C.P. Welcomed at Marrickville', *Catholic Press*, 4/9/1919, p. 25.

6   The foundation committee members were: JW Morris, Dr RB Trindall, LM Mudge, JS Davidson (Hon. Treasurer), JEP Cox, S Ismay, FJ Coogan, CV Harold (Hon. Secretary), Ald. B Richards, JP (Mayor Trustee), JH Dolphin (Trustee), HT Seymour (President), VC Davis, TE Knight TH Roberts, AG Platt, V McFarlane, CB Surbey, RT Williams, *Marrickville Anzac Memorial Club Golden Anniversary Souvenir Booklet*, 1921–1971.

7   'Bally War Is Over: Diggers at Play: No More Soldiering For Them: Reunion Plans', *Labor Daily* 18/11/1930, p. 5.

8   At the time, the League was known as the Returned Soldiers' Association (RSA).

9   Pers comm, Bill Gammage, 4/06/2021.

10   Crotty and Larsson, *Anzac Legacies*, p. 167.

11   'Join up with the Clubs!', *Smith's Weekly*, 14/7/1928), p. 22.

12   As distinct from the Australian Legion of Ex-Servicemen and Women, which formed in 1944 and had no connection to the older soldiers clubs.

13   'Country Soldiers Sticking to Labor', *Daily Standard*, 28/5/1919, p. 4.

14   'Diggers Annoyed: Mr RFH Green's Criticism', *Casino and Kyogle Courier and North Coast Advertiser*, 19/7/1930, p. 6 and 'Mr Green Explains: Statement in Parliament', *Northern Star*, 28/7/1930, p. 9.

15   'Soldiers' Clubs and League', *Evening News*, 14/12/1927, p. 12.

16   *Marrickville Anzac Memorial Club Golden Anniversary 1921–1971 Souvenir Booklet*, 1971.

17   Pers comm, Helen Thomson, 03/12/2017.

Chapter 21: Jack meets May

1   Pers comm, Helen Thomson, 19/5/2021.

2   Pers comm, Helen Thomson, 2/1/2019.

3   Lang, *The Great Bust*, p. 6.

4   MRS/278-27, Powerhouse Museum Record Series (Item), Audiocassette, interview with May Hayes (for exhibition 'Australian Communities' – Community Focus exhibition on Marrickville, 1989), 30/11/1988.

5   'They Say', *National Advocate*, 15/12/1917, p. 1.

6   'They Say', *National Advocate*, 1/12/1917, p. 1.
7   In Larsson, *Shattered Anzacs*, p. 85.
8   In Larsson, *Shattered Anzacs*, pp. 82–86.
9   'Sanitation. Technical College. Annual Prize Giving', *Sydney Morning Herald*, 12/6/1925, p. 13.
10 Hayes, private papers, courtesy of Helen Thomson.
11 Pers comm., Helen Thomson, 28/5/2019.
12 MRS/278-27, Powerhouse Museum Record Series (Item), Audiocassette, interview with May Hayes (for exhibition 'Australian Communities' – Community Focus exhibition on Marrickville, 1989), 30/11/1988.

Chapter 22: The first Anzac Day dawn service

1   Pers comm, John Hayes, 20/8/2012. The Gallipoli Club was formed in 1934. John refers to an earlier association of Gallipoli veterans.
2   'Men, Women Spend Night in Martin Place: Early Arrivals for dawn service', *Truth*, 25/4/1948, p. 2 and Frank Grose Papers, State Library of NSW, 2GB Radio Community Chest Annual Report, 30/6/1948, p. 35.
3   'The dawn service in Sydney: How It Started', Marrickville Anzac Memorial Club, 1981.
4   The exception is Darren Mitchell's excellent PhD thesis *Anzac Rituals – Secular, Sacred, Christian*.
5   'Millions of Boxes George Paterson and His Fag Papers', *Smith's Weekly*, 19/2/1938, p. 16.
6   'The Last to Leave Anzac', *Farmer and Settler*, 4/4/1916, p. 3.
7   Stickley wrote an account of the Gallipoli campaign which is held by the Australian War Memorial in Canberra: AWM 2DRL/0570.
8   'The dawn service in Sydney: How It Started', Marrickville Anzac Memorial Club, 1981.
9   The 20th Anniversary of Anzac: Photographs taken during the Dawn Ceremony of Remembrance 4.30 a.m. – Anzac Day, 1935, presented to the Mitchell Library by The Australian Legion, photographs courtesy of 'The Sun', p. 2 and 'Silent Tribute: At Early Dawn: Impressive Ceremony', *Sydney Morning Herald*, 26/4/1928, p. 11.
10 'Silent Tribute: At Early Dawn: Impressive Ceremony', *Sydney Morning Herald*, 26/4/1928, p. 11.
11 Captain W.E. Stroud, 11th Battalion, WA.
12 'Silent Tribute: At Early Dawn: Impressive Ceremony', *Sydney Morning Herald*, 26/4/1928, p. 11.
13 The story of the Cenotaph is told in vivid detail in Lang, *The Great Bust*, pp. 283–289.
14 Inglis, *Sacred Places*, p. 285.

Chapter 23: The Great Depression

1   Schedvin, *Australia and the Great Depression*, p. 47.
2   Schedvin, *Australia and the Great Depression*, p. 47.
3   Lyons, *Legacy*, pp. 36–38. See also Hilmer Smith, *History of the Legacy Club of Sydney*, Appendix A, p. 222.
4   'Returned Soldiers' League Statewide Employment Drive,' *Nepean Times*, 28/1/1933, p. 6.
5   Excerpt from Sydney Water, Sewerage and Drainage Board meeting, 16/4/1930, courtesy of Jack's granddaughter Helen Thomson.
6   Excerpt from Sydney Water, Sewerage and Drainage Board meeting, 16/4/1930, courtesy of Jack's granddaughter Helen Thomson.
7   'Wholesale Retrenchment. Water and Sewerage Board Workers', *The Australian Worker*, 25/3/1931, p. 12.
8   Pers comm, Renie Channells, 30/9/2020.
9   Pers comm, Robyn Franks, 26/04/2021.
10 Andrews, M 1975, MLDOC2745.
11 Andrews, M 1975, MLDOC2754.
12 Pers comm, Peter Andrews, 29/5/2019.
13 Amos, *The New Guard Movement*, p. 38.
14 Amos, *The New Guard Movement*, pp. 1–2 and pp. 55–78.
15 Including Jack Hayes' friend CC Lazzarini.
16 In Cannon, *The Human Face of the Great Depression*, p. 187. See also Ward, *A Nation for a Continent*, pp. 181–182.
17 Amos, *The New Guard Movement*, p. 84.
18 'New Guard Is Now a Silly Rabble: Colonel Campbell's Microphone Mania', *Smith's Weekly*, 9/4/1932, p. 7.
19 Day, *Chifley*, pp. 271–272.
20 Amos, *The New Guard Movement*, p. 2.

Chapter 24: The brotherhood of the trenches

1   W Godfrey, *Lest We Forget: The History of the Hastings River Sub-Branch of the Returned Soldiers and Sailors Imperial League of Australia*, Wauchope, 1975, p. 17.
2   Blaikie, *Remember Smith's Weekly*, p. 157.
3   'Ex-Service Men Joint Conference', *Labor Daily*, 19/9/1931, p. 6.
4   'Returned Soldiers' League State Wide Employment Drive', *Nepean Times*, 28/1/1933, p. 6.
5   Blaikie, *Remember Smith's Weekly*, p. 153.
6   'An Appreciation', *Nambucca and Bellinger News*, 30/9/1927, p. 4.
7   Baker, *Depressions*, p. 71.
8   Larsson, *Shattered Anzacs*, p. 205.

Chapter 25: President Jack

1   MRS/278-27, Powerhouse Museum Record Series (Item), Audiocassette, interview with May Hayes (for exhibition 'Australian Communities' – Community Focus exhibition on Marrickville, 1989), 30/11/1988.

2   'Forum Club Debate Marrickville Anzac Debating Club Visits Woy Woy', *Gosford and Wyong District Advocate*, 5/11/1931, p. 21.

3   'Diggers Go Back to Egypt Novel Marrickville Entertainment', *Daily Telegraph*, 17/6/1932, p. 7 and MRS/278-27, Powerhouse Museum Record Series (Item), Audiocassette, interview with May Hayes (for exhibition 'Australian Communities' – Community Focus exhibition on Marrickville, 1989), 30/11/1988.

4   MRS/278-27, Powerhouse Museum Record Series (Item), Audiocassette, interview with May Hayes (for exhibition 'Australian Communities' – Community Focus exhibition on Marrickville, 1989), 30/11/1988.

5   In Amos, *The New Guard Movement*, p. 10.

6   'New Guard and Maroubra Assault', *Newcastle Morning Herald and Miners' Advocate*, 12/5/1932, p. 7. In 1925 Lazzarini became chief secretary in Lang's first cabinet. But he later clashed with Lang and was left out of Lang's ministry. Nevertheless, Lazzarini kept winning the Marrickville seat and remained in parliament. During the Depression years he 'maintained his rage' against Lang's one-man control and was a chief instigator of the 'industrial group' which broke away from Lang. See <adb.anu.edu.au/biography/lazzarini-carlo-camillo-7129>.

7   'The Elections Mr LC Jordan Puts His Case', *Port Macquarie News and Hastings River Advocate*, 20/5/1944, p. 3. See also 'State Elections, 27 May, 1944', *Port Macquarie News and Hastings River Advocate*, 27/5/1944, p. 5.

8   Pers comm, Renie Channells, 30/09/2021.

Chapter 26: Dick Turpin and the Styx

1   Bolton, *A Fine Country to Starve In*, p.46.

2   'Views of a Foreman', *Daily News*, 22/1/1925, p. 3.

3   Bolton, *A Fine Country to Starve In*, p. 175.

4   In Bev McGuinness, *100 Years of Chalk and Dust: Denmark 1896 to 1996*, Denmark: Cinnamon Coloureds and the Denmark Historical Society, 1996, p. 81.

5   In Bolton, *A Fine Country to Starve In*, p. 60.

6   NAA repatriation files, 7061 JR Turpin, Series No. K60, Control Symbol C27503 and M27503; Series No. 878/1, Control Symbol H27503.

7　'The Groupies: Crushed Hopes of Early Settlers Who Reaped a Bitter Harvest', *Big Weekend*, 13/9/1997, pp. 5–6 and <www.slwa. wa.gov.au/dead_reckoning/government_archival_records/d-j/group_ settlement55e9.html?SQ_DESIGN_NAME=print>.

8　See, for instance, 'The Groupies: Crushed Hopes of Early Settlers Who Reaped a Bitter Harvest', *Big Weekend*, 13/9/1997 or <denmarkhistoricalsocietywa.org.au>.

Chapter 27: Jerry Fuller goes to the Second World War

1　'Fast Scoring by Digger Batsmen 511 Runs in Six Hours NSW Tourists Win', *Warwick Daily News*, 1/1/1938, p. 6 and *Nowra and Shoalhaven News*, 1/2/1939, p. 11.

2　NX53406, Fuller, <recordsearch.naa.gov.au>.

3　Pers comm, John Hayes, 28/9/2012.

4　AWM, O21876.

5　Long, *Australia in the War of 1939–1945*, p. 345.

6　Stuart, *Crank Back on Roller*, p. 1.

7　2/3rd Field Workshop, War Diary, June–July 1941, AWM52 14/2/3.

Chapter 28: Bill Kane enlists again

1　Pers comm, Renie Channells, 30/9/2020.

2　19 Works [Employment] Company War Diary 23-24/11/1942, AWM52, 22/1/26.

3　Pers comm, Renie Channells, 30/9/2020.

4　Pers comm, Phyllis Saul, 27/10/2018.

Chapter 29: Sons of Anzacs

1　'In Honour of the Anzacs: Young Residents Unite in Paying Annual Tribute: Traditions safe in hands of New AIF', *Young Chronicle*, 26/4/1940, p. 1.

2　'40000 stand before Cenotaph at Dawn, Deeper Significance to Early Service', *The Sun*, 25/4/1941, p. 3.

3　'Anzac Day and May Day', *The Bulletin*, Vol. 63, No. 3248, 13/5/1942, p. 6.

4　'Old Diggers Miss Historical Service at the Cenotaph', *The Sun*, 25/4/1942, p. 3.

Chapter 30: At the going down of the sun

1　In Lynch, *Nambucca Anzacs*, p. 338.

2　Pers comm, Lisa Sinclair, 20/11/2019.

3　Pers comm, Renie Channells, 30/9/2020.

4　Pers comm, Renie Channells 30/9/2020.

5　Pers comm, Phyllis Saul, 27/10/2018.

6 Pers comm, Renie Channells, 30/9/2020.
7 Pers comm, Renie Channells, 30/9/2020.
8 Pers comm, Phyllis Saul, 27/10/2018.
9 Pers comm, Robyn Franks, 2/5/2021.
10 'Obituary, Mr William Henry Kane, M.M.', *The Nambucca Heads Coaster*, 27/10/1954, p. 2.
11 'Chipilly Stunt: Brave Diggers', *Reveille*, 1/9/1933, p. 23 and in Lynch, *Nambucca Anzacs*, p. 338.
12 Pers comm, Renie Channells, 30/09/2020.
13 Pers comm, Richard Turpin, 29/1/2018.
14 Pers comm, Richard Turpin, 29/1/2018.
15 Pers comm, Tom Atkinson, 7/2/2019.
16 Pers comm, Richard Turpin, 21/8/2018.
17 Pers comm, Richard Turpin, 21/8/2018.
18 National Archives of Australia, repatriation cases (Boer War and WWI), John Richard Turpin, 7061, Series Nos. K60 and PP878/1; Control Symbols: C27503; M27503/1 and H27503.
19 National Archives of Australia, repatriation cases (Boer War and WWI), John Richard Turpin, 7061, Series Nos. K60 and PP878/1; Control Symbols: C27503; M27503/1 and H27503.
20 Pers comm, Richard Turpin, 21/8/2018.
21 In National Archives of Australia, repatriation cases (Boer War and WWI), John Richard Turpin, 7061, Series Nos. K60 and PP878/1; Control Symbols: C27503; M27503/1 and H27503.
22 In National Archives of Australia, repatriation cases (Boer War and WWI), John Richard Turpin, 7061, Series Nos. K60 and PP878/1; Control Symbols: C27503; M27503/1 and H27503.
23 Pers comm, Richard Turpin, 28/01/2020.
24 Pers comm, Rich Baker, 16/3/2021.
25 Pers comm, Neville Baker, 23/8/2019.
26 Pers comm, Rich Baker, 1/11/2021.
27 National Archives of Australia, repatriation cases (Boer War and WWI), George A. Stevens, 5094, Series No. C138; Controls Symbols: R77221; M77221 and C77221.
28 See Garton, *The Cost of War*, pp. 110–118.
29 National Archives of Australia, repatriation cases (Boer War and WWI), George A Stevens, 5094, Series No. C138; Controls Symbols: R77221; M77221 and C77221.
30 Pers comm, Rich Baker, 1/11/2021.
31 Pers comm, Rich Baker, 21/02/2018.
32 Pers comm, Rich Baker, 23/8/2019.
33 Pers comm, Peter Andrews, 24/3/2021.
34 Andrews, M 1975, MLDOC2754.
35 Andrews, M 1975, MLDOC2754.

36 Harold also 'souvenired' an Iron Cross First Class from a German officer.

37 Pers comm, Peter and Graham Andrews, 17/3/2018.

38 In Andrews, M 1975, MLDOC2754. Reportedly published in the *Hastings Shire Gazette and Port Macquarie News*, 11/12/1975.

39 Henty, *In Freedom's Cause*, pp. 284–295.

40 Private papers of Jack Hayes: Governor General Commonwealth of Australia, Honours and Awards, 8/6/1968, certificate (courtesy of Nola Moore).

41 MRS/278-27, Powerhouse Museum Record Series (Item), Audiocassette, interview with May Hayes (for exhibition 'Australian Communities' – Community Focus exhibition on Marrickville, 1989), 30/11/1988 and Pers comm, Helen Thomson, 19/4/2020.

42 Pers comm, Renie Channells, 30/09/2020.

43 National Archives of Australia, repatriation cases (Boer War and WWI), Jack Charles Hayes, 948, Series No. C138; Controls Symbols: H42224 part 1 and 2 and M42224.

44 Pers comm, Helen Thomson, 3/8/2018.

45 Pers comm, Helen Thomson, 19/04/2020.

46 National Archives of Australia, repatriation cases (Boer War and WWI), Jack Charles Hayes, 948, Series No. C138; Controls Symbols: H42224 part 1 and 2 and M42224.

47 Pers comm, John Hayes, 20/8/2012.

48 Pers comm, John Hayes, 28/9/2012 and 7/7/2013.

Afterword

1 Andrews, M 1975, MLDOC2754.

Author's note

1 Pers comm, John Hayes, 28/09/2012.

BIBLIOGRAPHY

ARCHIVAL SOURCES

Official records

Australian War Memorial, Canberra
AWM1 Australian Red Cross Society Wounded and Missing Enquiry
Bureau Files, 1914–18 War.
AWM4 AIF Unit War Diaries.
AWM8 Unit Embarkation Nominal Rolls.
AWM28 Recommendation Files for Honours and Awards AIF 1914–1918
War.
AWM38 CEW Bean papers.
AWM43 Biographical Indexes of CEW Bean for 1914–18 War.
AWM47 Herbertson Papers (German Material).
AWM52 WW2 Unit War Diaries.
AWM93 AWM Registry Files.

Battye Library, State Library of Western Australia, Perth
Records relating to the Group Settlement Scheme.

Marrickville Council Library and History Services
Records of the Marrickville Anzac Memorial Club.

National Archives, Australia
B2455 First Australian Imperial Force Personnel Dossiers (1914–20).
B884 Australian Army Personnel Records (1939–46).
A6770 Navy Personnel Records.
A9301 Air Force Personnel Records.
A471 Court Martial Records.
B73; C138; K60 & PP878/1 Repatriation Cases (Boer War and WWI).

The National Archives, London
WO95 First World War and Army of Occupation War Diaries.
WO372 British Army Medal Index Cards 1914–1920.
WO374 British Army Service Records 1914–1919.

New South Wales State Archives and Records
NSW Railway employee's superannuation record cards.
NSW Government Gazette and Annual Reports.

Australian Railway Historical Society (NSW), Alexandria, Sydney
NSWGR&T permanent employee records [Hayes] 1890–1938.

Private records

Australian War Memorial, Canberra
1DRL/0043 Letter of Harold Dudley Andrews.
PR01937 Diary of Claude Reilly Deitz.
PR089/050 Manuscript of Albert William Edwards.
3DRL/3318 Diary of George William Godfrey.
PR87/018 Letters of Paul Reginald Johanesen.
2DRL/0666 Manuscript of Norman Langford.
2DRL/0029 Memoirs and papers of Kenneth Hamlyn McConnel.
3DRL/6551 Papers of Bertie Stacy.
2DRL/0711 Diaries of Sydney Robert Traill.

Frank Partridge VC Military Museum, Bowraville
WH Kane collection.

Imperial War Museum, London
IWM Doc. 9889 Private papers of 2nd Lieut. AR Armfield.
IWM Doc. 6621 Private papers of WG Bishop.
IWM Doc. 14150 Private papers of Lieutenant General Sir Richard Butler KCB, KCMG.
IWM Doc. 16460 Private papers of John Jones.
IWM Doc. 22166 Private papers of Joseph Nosbert Saunders.
IWM Doc. 17119 Private papers of Robert Hutton Bembridge.
IWM Doc.17191 Private papers of R Bright.
IWM Doc.7922 Private papers of Bertie Frederick John Chapman.
IWM Doc. 12494 Private papers of Private Cyril Thomas Newman.
IWM Sound, Catalogue No. 9420, William Arthur Gillman (interviewed by Peter Hart).

Mitchell Library, (Records of the European War Collecting Project), State Library of NSW, Sydney
ML MSS 7504; MLDOC 2754 Memoirs of Harold Dudley Andrews.
ML MSS 1493/1 Diaries of Archibald Barwick.
ML MSS 1224 Letters of Harry Joseph Cave.
ML MSS 1143 Diary of Harold Mercer.

Frank Grose Papers, 2GB Radio Community Chest Annual Report, 30/6/1948.

940.939/A The 20th Anniversary of Anzac: Photographs taken during the Dawn Ceremony of Remembrance 4.30 a.m. – Anzac Day, 1935, presented to the Mitchell Library by The Australian Legion, photographs courtesy of 'The Sun'.

National Library of Australia, Canberra

NP 940.477994 The Australian Legion of Ex-Service Clubs: Constitution, Rules and Objects, Sydney, 1939.

Powerhouse Museum, Sydney

MRS/278-27, interview with May Hayes (for the exhibition 'Australian Communities' – Community Focus exhibition on Marrickville, 1989), 30/11/1988.

Private papers

Papers, photos and diaries of Harold Dudley Andrews, courtesy of Graham and Peter Andrews.

Papers and photos of Albert 'Jerry' Fuller, courtesy of Lisa Sinclair, Mark Deacon and Rick Dollemore.

Papers, photos and diaries of Jack Charles Hayes, courtesy of Helen Thomson, Nola Moore and the late John Hayes.

Papers and photos of William Henry Kane, courtesy of Phyllis Saul, Renie Channells, Robyn Franks, Deb Regan, Karen Regan and Grahame Tricker.

Material relating to the Marrickville Anzac Memorial Club, courtesy of Diane McCarthy.

Papers and photos of George Albert Stevens, courtesy of Florence, Neville and Rich Baker, and Terry Overton.

Papers and photos of John Richard 'Dick' Turpin, courtesy of Richard Turpin.

Papers and photos relating to Dick Turpin and the Group Settlement Scheme courtesy of Ross and Bev McGuinness (Denmark Historical Society).

R Wilson, unpublished manuscript, *The Andrews of Coleraine ... and the Wilsons of Willsbro*.

Published sources

Adam-Smith, P, *Hear the Train Blow: Patsy Adam-Smith's Classic Autobiography of Growing Up in the Bush*, Nelson, Melbourne, 1981.

Aitken, A, *Gallipoli to the Somme: Recollections of a New Zealand Infantryman*, Oxford University Press, London, 1963.

Amos, K, *The New Guard Movement 1931–1935*, Melbourne University Press, Carlton, 1976.

Baker, C, *Depressions: 1890s, 1930s: A Social History*, Oxford University Press, Melbourne, 1982.

Barry, JM, *The Great Influenza: The Story of the Deadliest Pandemic in History*, Penguin Books, New York, 2018.

Barton, P, *Passchendaele: Unseen Panoramas of the Third Battle of Ypres*, Constable, London, 2007.

Bean, CEW, *The Official History of Australia in the War of 1914–1918: The Story of ANZAC from the Outbreak of War to the End of the First Phase of the Gallipoli Campaign, May 4, 1915*, Vol. I, 11th edn, Angus & Roberston, Sydney, 1941.

— *The Official History of Australia in the War of 1914–1918: The Story of ANZAC from 4 May, 1915, to the Evacuation of the Gallipoli Peninsula*, Vol. II, 11th edn, Angus & Robertson, Sydney, 1941.

— *The Official History of Australia in the War of 1914–1918: The AIF in 1916*, Vol. III, 12 edn, Angus & Robertson, Sydney, 1941.

— *The Official History of Australia in the War of 1914–1918: The Australian Imperial Force in France, 1917*, Vol. IV, 11th edn, Angus & Robertson, Sydney, 1941.

— *The Official History of Australia in the War of 1914–1918: The Australian Imperial Force in France During the Main German Offensive, 1918*, Vol. V, 8th edn, Angus & Robertson, Sydney, 1941.

— *The Official History of Australia in the War of 1914–1918: The Australian Imperial Force in France During the Allied Offensive, 1918*, Vol. VI, 1st edn, Angus & Robertson, Sydney, 1942.

Bean, CEW, *Anzac to Amiens*, Penguin Books, Ringwood, [1946]1993.

Beaumont, J and A Cadzow (eds), *Serving Our Country: Indigenous Australians, War, Defence and Citizenship*, NewSouth, Sydney, 2018.

Belford, WC, *'Legs-Eleven': Being the Story of the 11th Battalion AIF in the Great War*, Imperial Printing Company, Perth, 1940.

Bennett, C, *Rough Infantry: Tales of World War II*, Warrnambool Institute Press, Brunswick, 1984.

Blaikie, G, *Remember Smith's Weekly*, Rigby Ltd, Melbourne, 1967.

Blair, D, *Dinkum Diggers: An Australian Battalion at War*, Melbourne University Press, Carlton, 2001.

Bolton, GC, *A Fine Country to Starve In*, UWA Press, Nedlands, 1972.

Bond, B, et al, *'Look to Your Front': Studies in the First World War*, Spellmount, Staplehurst, 1999.

Booker, M, *The Great Professional: A Study of W.M. Hughes*, McGraw-Hill Book Company, Sydney, 1980.

Bradshaw, J, *Jinkers & Whims: A Pictorial History of Timber-Getting*, Vivid Publishing, Fremantle, 2012.

Brophy, J and E Partridge, *The Long Trail: Soldiers' Songs & Slang 1914–18*, Sphere Books Ltd, London, 1969.

Brown, M, *The Imperial War Museum Book of 1918: Year of Victory*, Sidgwick & Jackson, London, 1998.

Burke, D, *Making the Railways*, State Library of NSW Press, Sydney, 1995.

Butler, AG, *Official History of the Australian Army Medical Services in the War of 1914–1918*, Vols. 1–3, Australian War Memorial, Melbourne, 1940.

Cameron, DW, *The August Offensive at Anzac, 1915*, Australian Army History Unit, Canberra, 2011.

Cameron, S, *Lonesome Pine: The Bloody Ridge*, Big Sky Publishing, Newport, 2013.

Campbell, E, *The Rallying Point: My Story of the New Guard*, Melbourne University Press, Carlton, 1965.

Cannon, M, *The Human Face of the Great Depression*, Today's Australia Publishing Company, Mornington, 1997.

Carroll, B, *Earning a Crust: An Illustrated Economic History of Australia*, Reed, Sydney, 1977.

— *Between the Wars: An Illustrated History of Australia 1919–1939*, Cassell Australia Ltd, North Ryde, 1980.

Cashman, R and C Meader, *Marrickville Rural Outpost to Inner City: A Social History of Marrickville and the Former Municipalities of Newtown, Camperdown, Petersham, and St Peters*, Hale & Iremonger, Alexandria, [1990]1997.

Cave, N, *Battleground Europe: Hill 60*, Leo Cooper, Barnsley, [1998]2009.

Chapman, I, *Iven G Mackay: Citizen and Soldier*, Melway, Melbourne, 1975.

Charlton, P, *Pozieres: Australians on the Somme 1916*, Methuen Haynes, North Ryde, 1986.

Clark, M, *A Short History of Australia*, Mentor, London, [1963]1969.

Clune, F, *Saga of Sydney*, Halstead, Sydney, 1961.

— *Rascals, Ruffians & Rebels of Early Australia*, Angus & Robertson, North Ryde, 1987.

Cooper, R, *A Short History of the Village of Wauchope*, Vols. 1 & 2, Wauchope District Historical Society, Wauchope, 2001 and 2005.

Cowen, Z, *Isaac Isaacs*, Oxford University Press, Melbourne, 1967.

Crawford, RM, *Australia*, Hutchinson of Australia, Richmond, [1952]1970.

Crisp, LF, *Ben Chifley: A Political Biography*, Angus & Robertson, Melbourne, [1961]1977.

Crotty, M and M Larsson, *Anzac Legacies: Australians and the Aftermath of War*, Australian Scholarly Publishing, North Melbourne, 2010.

Cutlack, FM, *The Australians: Their Final Campaign, 1918*, Samson, Low Marston & Co, London, 1919.

Daley, P, *Beersheba: Travels Through a Forgotten Australian Victory*, Melbourne University Press, Carlton, [2009]2017.

Damousi, J and J Smart (eds), *Contesting Australian History: Essays in Honour of Marilyn Lake*, Monash University Publishing, Clayton, 2019.

Dando-Collins, S, *Heroes of Hamel: the Australians and Americans Whose WW1 Victory Changed Modern Warfare*, Penguin Random House, North Sydney, 2018.

Dawes, JNI and LL Robson, *Citizen to Soldier: Australia Before the Great War – Recollections of Members of the First A.I.F.*, Melbourne University Press, Carlton, 1977.

Day, D, *Chifley: A Life*, Harper Perennial, Sydney, [2001]2007.

Dennis, P and J Grey (eds), *1918 Defining Victory*, Chief of Army History Conference 1998, Army History Unit, Department of Defence, Canberra, 1999.

Dunne, D (compiler), *Precious Memories: A Photographic History of the Nambucca Shire*, The Printery, Nambucca Heads, 2001.

Edge, J, *My Early Years Down Under*, Edgerton, Hastings, 2009.

Edmonds, T, *The Strike That Never Ended: The Great NSW Railways Strike of 1917 and the Decades it Influenced*, Transport Heritage NSW, Eveleigh, 2017.

Ekins, A, 'Fighting to Exhaustion: Morale, Discipline and Combat Effectiveness in the Armies of 1918', in *1918 The Year of Victory: The End of the Great War and the Shaping of History*, Exisle, Auckland, 2010.

Essex-Clark, J, *Hassett: Australian Leader*, Australian Military History Publications, Loftus, 2005.

Fielding, M, *Comrades in Arms: The Remarkable Achievements of the 1919 Australian Imperial Force Rugby Union Squad*, Superscript Publishing, Melbourne, 2018.

Fitchett, WH, *Deeds that Won the Empire: Historic Battle Scenes*, Smith Elder & Co., London, 1904.

Fitzpatrick, B, *The Australian People 1788–1945*, Melbourne University Press, Carlton, 1946.

— *A Short History of the Australian Labor Movement*, Macmillan, South Melbourne, [1940]1968.

Fitzpatrick, G (compiler), *Anzac Day: Past and Present*, Australian War Memorial Education Service, Canberra, 1992.

Foott, B, *Dismissal of a Premier: (The Phillip Game Papers)*, Morgan Publications, Sydney, 1968.

Fox, L (ed.), *Depression Down Under*, Hale and Iremonger, Sydney, [1989]1992.

Frances R and B Scates (eds), *Beyond Gallipoli: New Perspectives on ANZAC*, Monash University Publishing, Clayton, 2016.

Furphy, J, *Such is Life: Unemployed at Last*, Text Publishing, Melbourne, [1903]2013.

Gabbedy, JP, *The Forgotten Pioneers: Axemen – Their Work Times and Sport*, Fremantle Arts Centre Press, 1981.

— *Group Settlement Part I: Its Origins, Politics and Administration*, UWA Press, Crawley, 1988.

— *Group Settlement Part II: Its People, Their Life and Times: An Inside View*, UWA Press, Crawley, 1988.

Gadsby, B (compiler), *'The Top End': Burrapine Thumb Creek*, Macksville and District History Group, Macksville, 2003.

Gammage, B, *The Broken Years: Australian Soldiers in the Great War*, Melbourne University Press, Carlton, [1974]2010.

Garton, S, *The Cost of War: War Return and the Re-shaping of Australian Culture*, Sydney University Press, [1996]2020.

Glynn, S, *Urbanisation in Australian History, 1788–1900*, Nelson, Melbourne, 1970.

Golding, P, *They Called Him Old Smoothie: John Joseph Cahill*, Australian Scholarly Publishing, North Melbourne, 2009.

Grey, WE, *The 2nd City of London Regiment (Royal Fusiliers) in the Great War (1914–1919)*, Headquarters of the Regiment, London, 1929.

Griffith, P, *Battle Tactics of the Western Front: The British Army's Art of Attack 1916–18*, Yale University Press, London, 1994.

Grimwade, F Clive, *The War History of the 4th Battalion the London Regiment (The Royal Fusiliers) 1914–1919*, Headquarters of the 4th London Regiment, London, 1922.

Hall, RJ, *The Australian Light Horse*, W.D. Joynt & Company Pty Ltd, Blackburn, 1968.

Harney, WE, *Bill Harney's War*, Currey O'Neil, Melbourne, 1983.

Harris, G (compiled and updated by R. McGuinness), *Past Times of Denmark Western Australia*, Denmark Historical Society, Denmark, 2018.

Hart, P, *1918: A Very British Victory*, Phoenix, London, 2008.

Harvey, NK, *From Anzac to the Hindenburg Line: The History of the 9th Battalion A.I.F.*, The Naval and Military Press, Uckfield, [1941]2009.

Henty, GA, *In Freedom's Cause: A Story of Wallace and Bruce*, Dover Publications Inc, New York, [1894]2004.

Hesketh-Prichard, H, *Sniping in France: How the British Army Won the Sniping War in the Trenches*, BCA, London, 1994.

Hilmer Smith, E, *History of the Legacy Club of Sydney*, Legacy Club of Sydney, Sydney, 1944.

Hobsbawm EJ and G Rudé, *Captain Swing*, Penguin Books, Harmondsworth, [1969]1985.

Holbrook, C, *Anzac: The Unauthorised Biography*, NewSouth, Sydney, 2014.

Huidekoper, FL, *The History of the 33rd Division A.E.F.*, Illinois State Historical Library, Springfield, 1921.

Hunt, L (ed.), *Westralian Portraits*, UWA Press, Crawley, 1979.

Hyde, R, *Nor the Years Condemn*, University of Otago Press, Dunedin, [1938]1995.

Inglis, KS, *Sacred Places: War Memorials in the Australian Landscape*, 3rd ed., Melbourne University Press, Carlton, 2001.

Iremonger, J, J Merritt and G, Osborne (eds) *Strikes: Studies in Twentieth Century Australian Social History*, Angus &Robertson, Melbourne, 1973.

James, R, *Australia's War With France: The Campaign in Syria and Lebanon, 1941*, Big Sky Publishing, Moss Vale, 2017.

Jauncey, LC, *The Story of Conscription in Australia*, Macmillan, South Melbourne, [1935]1968.

Johnston, G, *My Brother Jack*, Harper Collins, Sydney, [1964]2013.

Johnston, M, *The Silent 7th: An Illustrated History of the 7th Australian Division 1940–46*, Allen & Unwin, Crows Nest, 2005.

Jordan, L, *Stealth Raiders: A Few Daring Men in 1918*, Vintage Penguin Random House, North Sydney, 2017.

Joynt, WD, *Saving the Channel Ports: 1918 After the Breach of 5th Army*, Wren Publishing, North Blackburn, 1975.

Kelly, M, *A Certain Sydney 1900: A Photographic Introduction to a Hidden Sydney*, Doak Press, Paddington, n.d.

Kiernan, C (ed.), *Ireland and Australia*, Angus & Robertson, North Ryde, 1984.

Kristianson, GL, *The Politics of Patriotism: The Pressure Group Activities of the Returned Servicemen's League*, ANU Press, Canberra, 1966.

Lack, J (ed.), *Anzac Remembered: Selected Writings of K.S. Inglis*, The History Department, University of Melbourne, Melbourne, 1998.

Lake, M, *Getting Equal: The History of Australian Feminism*, Allen & Unwin, Crows Nest, 1999.

Lang, JT, *The Great Bust: The Depression of the Thirties*, McNamara Books, Katoomba, [1962]1980.

— *I Remember*, McNamara's Books, Katoomba, [1956]1980.

Larsson, M, *Shattered Anzacs: Living with the Scars of War*, UNSW Press, Sydney, 2009.

Lawrence, DH, *Kangaroo*, The Text Publishing Company, Melbourne, [1923]2018.

Lewis, T, *A War at Home: A Comprehensive Guide to the First Japanese Attacks on Darwin*, Northern Territory Library and Information Service, Darwin, [1999]2010.

Lloyd, C and J Rees, *The Last Shilling: A History of Repatriation in Australia*, Melbourne University Press, Carlton, 1994.

Long, G, *Australia in the War of 1939–1945, Series One: Army, Volume II, Greece, Crete and Syria*, Adelaide, 1953.

Louis LJ and I Turner, *The Depression of the 1930s*, Cassell, Stanmore, [1968]1979.

Lynch, TG, *Nambucca Anzacs: Servicemen and Women of the Nambucca District in the First World War, 1914–1918, and Beyond*, Longueville Media, Double Bay, 2013.

Lyons, M, *Legacy: The First Fifty Years*, Lothian Publishing Company, Melbourne, 1978.

Macintyre, S, *A Concise History of Australia*, 5th ed., Cambridge University Press, Cambridge, 2020.

Main, JM, *Conscription: The Australian Debate, 1901–1970*, Cassell, North Melbourne, 1970.

Martin, D, *Londoners on the Western Front: The 58th (2/1st London) Division in the Great War*, Pen & Sword, Barnsley, 2014.

Mastriano, DV, *Alvin York: A New Biography of the Hero of the Argonne*, University of Kentucky Press, Kentucky, 2014.

Matthews, H, *Saints and Soldiers: With the Men Over There*, W.F. Floessell, Sydney, 1918.

Maude, AH, *The History of the 47th (London) Division 1914–1919*, The Naval & Military Press, Uckfield, [1922]2009.

Maynard, J, *The Unseen Anzac: How an Enigmatic Polar Explorer Created Australia's World War I Photographs*, Scribe, Melbourne, 2015.

McAllester, J and S Trigellis-Smith, *Largely a Gamble: Australians in Syria June–July 1941*, Headquarters Training Command Australian Army, Sydney, 1995.

McCarthy, D, *Gallipoli to the Somme: The Story of C.E.W. Bean*, John Ferguson, Sydney, 1983.

McGuinness, R, *Elleker Denmark Nornalup: The Railway Extended West but Never Met …*, 2nd ed., Bev and Ross McGuinness, Denmark, 2015.

McKernan, M, *Australians at Home World War II*, The Five Mile Press, Scoresby, 2014.

McKernan, M and M Browne (eds), *Australia Two Centuries of War & Peace*, Australian War Memorial in association with Allen & Unwin, Canberra, 1988.

McMullin, R, *Will Dyson: Australia's Radical Genius*, Scribe, Melbourne, 2006.

McMullin, R, *Pompey Elliot*, Scribe, Melbourne, 2002.

McNair Scott, R, *Robert the Bruce: King of the Scots*, Canongate, Edinburgh, 1996.

McWilliams, J and RJ Steel, *Amiens Dawn of Victory*, Dundurn Press, Toronto, 2001.

Mead, G, *The Doughboys: America and the First World War*, Allen Lane, London, 2000.

Meader, C, R Cashman and A Carolan, *Marrickville People and Places: A Social History of Marrickville, Newtown, Camperdown, Petersham, Stanmore, St Peters, Tempe & Dulwich Hill*, Hale & Iremonger, Sydney, 1994.

Mitchell, B, *The Australian Story and its Background*, Cheshire, [1965]1971.

Mitchell, GD, *Backs to the Wall: A Larrikin on the Western Front*, Allen & Unwin, Crows Nest, [1937]2007.

Monash, J, *The Australian Victories in France in 1918*, Angus & Robertson, Sydney, [1920]1936.

Montgomery, AA, *The Story of the Fourth Army in the Battles of the Hundred Days: August 8th to November 11th*, Hodder & Stoughton, London, 1919.

Murdoch, W and A Mulgan (compilers), *A Book of Australian and New Zealand Verse*, 4th edn, Oxford University Press, Melbourne, 1950.

Murray, R, *The Confident Years: Australia in the Twenties*, Allen Lane, Ringwood, 1978.

Nairn, B, *Civilising Capitalism: The Labor Movement in New South Wales 1870–1900*, ANU Press, Canberra, 1973.

Nairn, B, *The Big Fella: Jack Lang and the Australia Labor Party 1891–1949*, Melbourne University Press, Carlton, 1986.

Newton, LM, *The Story of the Twelfth: A Record of the 12th Battalion A.I.F During the Great War of 1914–1918*, 12th Battalion Association, Hobart, 1925.

Nichols, GHF (Quex), *The 18th Division in the Great War*, The Naval & Military Press, Uckfield, [1922]2004.

— *Pushed and the Return Push*, The Naval and Military Press, Uckfield, [1919]2009.

Ollif, L, *Louisa Lawson: Henry Lawson's Crusading Mother*, Rigby, Melbourne, 1978.

Palmer, V, *The Legend of the Nineties*, Currey O'Neil, South Yarra, 1954.

Payton, P, *'Repat': A Concise History of Repatriation in Australia*, Department of Veteran's Affairs, Canberra, 2018.

Pedersen, PA, *Monash as Military Commander*, Melbourne University Press, Carlton, 1985.

Pook, H, *A Worker's Paradise? A History of Working People in Australia, 1788–1901*, Oxford University Press, Melbourne, 1981.

Potts, D (ed.), *In and Out of Work: Personal Accounts of the 1930s*, The History Institute, Carlton, 1988.

Poyser, H, *The Story of Kentdale: Pictures and Recollections of a Group 110 Settler*, Denmark Historical Society, Denmark, 2018.

— *Somewhere in the West: A Personal Account of Growing Up in Kentdale Western Australia 1924–1934 Under the Group Settlement Scheme*, Denmark Historical Society, Denmark, 2012.

Pugsley, C, *The ANZAC Experience: New Zealand, Australia and Empire in the First World War*, Reed Military, Auckland, 2004.

Ramsland, J, *Venturing into No Man's Land: Joseph Maxwell VC World War I Hero*, Brolga Publishing, Melbourne, 2012.

Rhodes, C, *Undaunted: The History of the Nambucca River Co-operative Society Limited*, Nambucca River Co-operative Society Ltd., Lismore, 2002.

Richards, T, *Wallaby Warrior: The World War I Diaries of Australia's Only British Lion*, Allen & Unwin, Crows Nest, 2013.

Rickard, J, *Class and Politics: New South Wales, Victoria and the Early Commonwealth, 1890–1910*, ANU Press, Canberra, 1976.

Robbins, S, *British Generalship on the Western Front 1914–18: Defeat into Victory*, London, 2005.

Robertson, J, *Anzac and Empire: The Tragedy & Glory of Gallipoli*, Hamlyn, Port Melbourne, 1990.

Robson, LL, *Australia & the Great War*, Macmillan, South Melbourne, [1970]1976.

Roper, M, *The Secret Battle: Emotional Survival in the Great War*, Manchester University Press, Manchester, 2009.

Ross, J, *The Myth of the Digger: The Australian Soldier in Two World Wars*, Hale & Iremonger, Sydney, 1985.

Ruhen, O, *The Rocks Sydney*, Rigby Ltd, Sydney, 1966.

Russell, E (ed.), *Victorian and Edwardian Sydney from Old Photographs*, John Ferguson, Sydney, 1975.

Russell, WB, *There Goes a Man: The Biography of Sir Stanley G. Savige*, Longmans, Melbourne, 1959.

Ruwoldt, R, *Darwin's Battle for Australia*, Vol. 2, Darwin Defenders 1942–45 Incorporated, Clifton Springs, 2009.

Schedvin, CB, *Australia and the Great Depression: A Study of Economic Development and Policy in the 1920s and 1930s*, Sydney University Press, Sydney, 1970.

Seal, G, *Inventing Anzac: The Digger and National Mythology*, University of Queensland Press, St Lucia, 2004.

Sekuless, P and J Rees, *Lest We Forget: The History of the Returned Services League 1916–1986*, Rigby, Dee Why West, 1986.

Shaw, AGL, *The Story of Australia*, Faber and Faber, London, [1955]1983.

Shaw, IW, *Pandemic: The Spanish Flu in Australia 1918–1920*, Woodslane Press, Warriewood, 2020.

Sheffield, G and D Todman, *Command and Control on the Western Front: The British Army's Experience 1914–18*, Spellmount, Staplehurst, 2004.

Simkins, P, *From the Somme to Victory: The British Army's Experience on the Western Front*, Praetorian Press, Barnsley, 2014.

Smith, FB, *The Conscription Plebiscites in Australia 1916–17*, 3rd edn, Victorian Historical Association, Melbourne, 1971.

Spearitt, P, *Sydney Since the Twenties*, Hale and Iremonger, Sydney, 1978.

Stacy, BV, FJ Kindon and HV Chedgey, *The History of the First Battalion, AIF 1914–1919*, First Battalion Association, Sydney, 1931.

Stanley, P, *Men of Mont St Quentin: Between Victory and Death*, Scribe, Carlton, 2009.

— *Bad Characters: Sex, Crime, Mutiny, Murder and the Australian Imperial Force*, Pier 9, Millers Point, 2010.

Stead, C, *Seven Poor Men of Sydney*, The Miegunyah Press, Carlton, [1934]2015.

Stevenson, R, *To Win the Battle: The 1st Australian Division in the Great War, 1914–1918*, Cambridge University Press, Melbourne, 2013.

Stuart, D, *Crank Back on Roller*, Georgian House, Melbourne, 1979.

Stuart-Smith, S, *The Well Gardened Mind: Rediscovering Nature in the Modern World*, William Collins, London, 2021.

Summers, A, *Damned Whores and God's Police: The Colonization of Women in Australia*, Penguin Books, Ringwood, 1975.

The Forty-First: Being a Record of the 41st AIF During the Great War, compiled by members of the Intelligence Staff, St Maxen, 1919.

Thomson, A, *Anzac Memories: Living with the Legend*, Monash University Press, Clayton, [1996]2013.

Thompson, EP, *The Making of the English Working Class*, Penguin Books, London, [1963]2013.

Thompson, J, *Bill Harney's War*, Currey O'Neil, South Yarra, 1983.

Tiveychoc, A (RE Lording), *There and Back: The Story of an Australian Soldier 1915–1935*, Halstead Printing, Sydney, 1935.

Townsend, N, *Valley of the Crooked River: European Settlement on the Nambucca*, New South Wales University Press, Kensington, 1993.

Turner, I, *Industrial Labour and Politics: The Labour Movement in Eastern Australia 1900–1921*, The Australian National University, Canberra, 1965.

Tyrrell, I, *River Dreams: The People and Landscape of the Cooks River*, UNSW Press, Sydney, 2018.

USA General Staff, *Histories of Two Hundred and Fifty-one Divisions of the German Army Which Participated in the War* (1914–1918), Chaumont, 1919.

Vader, J, *Red Cedar: The Tree of Australia's History*, Reed Books, Frenchs Forest, 1987.

Van Every, D, *The AEF in Battle*, D. Appleton and Co, New York, 1923.

von Bose, T (Translated by D Pearson, P Thost & T Cowan), *The Catastrophe of 8 August 1918*, Big Sky Publishing, Newport, 2019.

Ward, R, *The Australian Legend*, Oxford University Press, Melbourne, 1958]1989.

— *A Nation for a Continent: The History of Australia 1901–1975*, Heinemann Educational, Richmond, [1977]1981.

Watson, D, *Brian Fitzpatrick: A Radical Life*, Hale & Iremonger, Sydney, 1979.

Whitaker, A, *Marrickville Pictorial History*, Kingsclear Books, Alexandria, 2006.

Williams, M, *Australia in the 1930s*, Trocadero Publishing, Sydney, 1985.

Yockelson, MA, *Borrowed Soldiers: Americans Under British Command 1918*, University of Oklahoma Press, Norman, 2008.

Yule, P (ed.), *Sergeant Lawrence Goes to France*, Melbourne University Press, Melbourne, 1987.

FILM

Dennison, R (director), Mutiny *on the Western Front*, Orana Films, 1979.

NEWSPAPERS

Age, Melbourne, 5/2/1919.
Albany Advertiser, 3/8/1921.
Albany Despatch, 26/1/1922.
The Australian Worker, Sydney, 25/3/1931.
Bendigo Advertiser, 4/9/1916.
Bendigo Independent, 7/11/1916.
Big Weekend, WA, 13/9/1997.
Camden News, 16/4/1908.
Casino and Kyogle Courier and North Coast Advertiser, 19/7/1930.
Catholic Press, 4/9/1919.
Clarence and Richmond Examiner, 4/2/1915.
Daily Advertiser, Wagga Wagga, 12/2/19.
Daily News, Perth, 22/1/25.
Daily Standard, 28/5/1919.
Daily Telegraph, Sydney, 10/2/19; 17/6/1932.
Edinburgh Gazette, 5/2/1919.
Evening News, Sydney, 14/12/1927.
Farmer and Settler, 4/4/1916.
Gosford and Wyong District Advocate, 5/11/1931.
Hastings Shire Gazette, 11/12/1975.
Jersey Evening Post, 16/7/2009.
Labor Daily, Sydney, 18/11/1930; 19/9/1931.
Mount Alexander Mail, 22/11/1880; 27/11/1880; 28/2/1881; 14/2/1891; 17/9/1892; 2/4/1897 & 7/4/1897.
Nambucca and Bellinger News, 13/8/15; 29/9/1916; 2/7/20; 5/10/23; 30/9/27; 14/12/28.
The Nambucca Heads Coaster, 27/10/1954.
The National Advocate, Bathurst, 9/9/1912; 9/6/1915; 1/12/1917; 15/12/1917.
Nepean Times, 28/1/1933.
Newcastle Morning Herald and Miners' Advocate, 12/5/1932.
Newcastle Sun, 29/12/1919.
Northern Star, 28/7/1930.
Nowra & Shoalhaven News, Nowra, 1/2/1939.

Port Macquarie News and Hastings River Advocate, 20/5/1944; 27/5/1944; 11/12/1975.
Smith's Weekly, Sydney, 14/7/28; 9/4/1932; 19/2/1938.
Sun, Sydney, 1/7/1915; 12/2/19; 14/10/24; 25/4/1941; 25/4/1942.
Sydney Mail, 27/9/1916; 19/2/1919.
Sydney Morning Herald, 31/12/1919; 12/2/19; 1/1/1920; 20/4/1923; 12/6/1925; 26/4/1928.
Truth, Sydney, 25/4/1948.
Warwick Daily News, 1/1/1938.
The West Australian, 23/8/2008.
Western Champion, 28/10/1932.
Young Chronicle, 19/4/1913; 14/12/1915; 26/4/1940.
Young Witness, 10/12/1915; 31/12/1915; 29/10/1918; 28/11/19; 26/10/20.

JOURNALS AND ARTICLES IN JOURNALS

Association of Returned Sailors' and Soldiers' Clubs of New South Wales, *The Rising Sun*, Vol. I, No. 1–2, September–December, 1928.
'The Dawn Service in Sydney: How It Started', Marrickville Anzac Memorial Club, 1981.
Marrickville Anzac Memorial Club Golden Anniversary Souvenir Booklet, 1921–1971.
Returned Services League of Australia, New South Wales Branch, *Reveille: Official Journal of the NSW Branch R.S.S.I.L.A.*, 1930–1945.
Returned Services League of Australia, ACT Branch, *Stand-To, Journal of the Australian Capital Territory Branch R.S.S.A.I.L.A.*, 1950–1965.
Amos, K, 'A Note on the Social Composition of the New Guard', *Armies of the Night, Armies of the Right*, Conference Organised by Andrew Moore, 25 August 1979.
Bongiorno, F, R Frances & B Scates, 'Labour and Anzac: An Introduction,' *Labour History*, No. 106, May 2014, pp. 1–17.
Clissold, B, '… that six-man patrol', *Sabretache*, Vol. XXX1, April/June 1990.
Cooksey, R (ed.), 'The Great Depression in Australia', *Labour History*, No. 17, Australian Society for the Study of Labour History, Canberra, 1970.
Crotty, M & M Edele, 'Total War and Entitlement: Towards a Global History of Veteran Privilege', *Australian Journal of Politics and History*, 2013, pp. 15–32.
Deery, P & F Bongiorno, 'Labor, Loyalty and Peace: Two Anzac Controversies of the 1920s', *Labour History*, No. 106, May 2014, pp. 205–228.
Duffett, R & M Roper, 'Making Histories: The Meeting of German and British Descendants of World War One Veterans in "No Man's Land", Bavaria 2016', *The Public Historian*, Vol. 40, February 2018, No. 1, pp. 13–34.

Dyrenfurth, N, 'Labor and the Anzac Legend, 1915–1945', *Labour History*, No. 106, May 2014, pp. 163–188.

Garton, S, 'Demobilization and Empire: Empire Nationalism and Soldier Citizenship in Australia After the First World War – in Dominion Context', *Journal of Contemporary History*, Vol. 50, No. 1, January 2015, pp. 124–143.

Garton, S, 'War and Masculinity in 20th Century Australia', *Journal of Australian Studies*, 22–56, 1998, pp. 85–96.

Inglis, KS, 'The Anzac Tradition', *Meanjin Quarterly*, March, 1965.

Kirk, N, 'Australians for Australia: The Right, the Labor Party and Contested Loyalties to Nation and Empire in Australia 1917 to the Early 1930s', *Labour History*, No. 91, November 2006, pp. 95–111.

Lake, M, 'The Militarisation of Australian Historical Memory', March 2006 (available online).

McQueen, H, 'The "Spanish Influenza" Pandemic in Australia: 1912–1919', Jill Roe (ed.), *Social Policy in Australia Some Perspectives 1901–1975*, Cassell, Stanmore, 1976, pp. 131–147.

Moore, A, 'The New Guard and the Labour Movement 1931–1935', *Labour History*, No. 89, November 2005, pp. 55–72.

Oliver, B, 'Disputes, Diggers and Disillusionment: Social and Industrial Unrest in Perth and Kalgoorlie 1918–1924', paper in special issue: J. Gregory (ed.), *Western Australia Between the Wars, 1919–1939*, pp. 19–28.

Quartly, M, 'Making Working-Class Heroes: Labor Cartoonists and the Australian Worker, 1903–16', *Labour History*, No. 89, November 2005, pp. 159–178.

Roberts, J, 'The Front Comes Home: Returned Soldiers and Psychological Trauma in Australia During and After the First World War', *Health and History*, Vol. 17, No. 2, 2015, pp. 17–36.

Roper, M & R Duffett, 'Family Legacies in the Centenary: Motives for First World War Commemoration Among British and German Descendants', *History & Memory*, vol. 30, No. 1, Spring/Summer 2018, pp. 76–115.

Roper, M, 'The Bush, the Suburbs and the Long Great War: A Family Memoir', *History Workshop Journal*, 2018, pp. 1–25.

Scates, B, 'The Unknown Sock Knitter: Voluntary Work, Emotional Labour, Bereavement and the Great War', *Labour History*, No. 81, November 2001, pp. 29–49.

Serle, G, 'The Digger Tradition and Australian Nationalism', *Meanjin Quarterly*, June, 1965.

Thomson, A, Anzac Memories: Putting Popular Memory Theory into Practice in Australia', *Oral History*, Vol. 18, No. 1, Spring 1990, pp. 25–31.

— 'Memory as a Battlefield: Personal and Political Investments in the National Military Past', *The Oral History Review*, Vol. 22, No. 2, Winter 1995, pp. 55–73.

Wise, N, '"In Military Parlance I suppose we were mutineers": Industrial Relations in the Australian Imperial Force During World War I', *Labour History*, No. 101, November 2011, pp. 161–176.

— 'The Myth of Classlessness in the Australian Imperial Force', *Australian Historical Studies,* 43, 2012, pp. 287–302.

— 'Job Skill, Manliness and Working Relationships in the Australian Imperial Force During World War I', *Labour History*, No. 106, May 2014, pp. 99–122.

— 'Fighting a Different Enemy: Social Protests Against Authority in the Australian Imperial Force During World War I', *IRSH*, 52, 2007, pp. 225–241.

— 'The Lost Labour Force: Working Class Approaches to Military Service During the Great War', *Labour History*, No. 93, November 2007, pp. 161–176.

Zino, B, '"A Lasting Gift to His Descendants": Family memory and the Great War in Australia', *History and Memory*, Vol. 22, No. 2, Fall/Winter, 2010, pp. 125–146.

THESES

Gammage, W, *The Genesis of the Anzac Ethos: Australian Infantry in France and Belgium During the Great War; and Some Attitudes and Values Relating to the Military Experience of the First A.I.F.*, Honours thesis, The Australian National University, Department of History, 1965.

Mitchell, D, *Anzac Rituals – Secular, Sacred, Christian*, thesis submitted for the degree of Doctor of Philosophy, University of Sydney, 2020.

Sheldon, PM, *Maintaining Control: A History of Unionism Among Employees of the Sydney Water Board*, thesis submitted for the degree of Doctor of Philosophy, University of Wollongong, 1989.

PERSONAL COMMUNICATIONS AND CORRESPONDENCE

Graham Andrews, Peter Andrews and Roger Wilson regarding Harold Andrews.

Lisa Sinclair, Mark Deacon and Rick Dollemore regarding Jerry Fuller.

Ross and Bev McGuinness regarding the Group Settlement Scheme, Denmark, WA.

The late John Hayes, Helen Thomson and Nola Moore regarding Jack Hayes.

Renie Channells, Phyllis Saul, Robyn Franks, Deb Regan, Karen Regan and
    Grahame Tricker regarding Bill Kane.
Trevor Lynch regarding Bill Kane and the history of the Nambucca region.
Lawrie Daly regarding the history of Marrickville, CC Lazzarini and the
    Australian Labor Party.
Diane McCarthy regarding the history of Marrickville and the Marrickville
    Anzac Memorial Club.
Keith Amos regarding the New Guard.
Trevor Edmunds regarding the 1917 NSW Railways strike.
Bill Phippen (Australian Railway Historical Society NSW) regarding the
    railway careers of Jack Hayes and Jack Slocombe.
Florence Baker, the late Neville Baker, Rich Baker and Terry Overton
    regarding George Stevens.
Richard Turpin and Tom Atkinson regarding Dick Turpin.

FIELDWORK

Archival research at IWM, London and National Archive, Kew: May 2012
    and Chipilly Spur battlefield May–June 2012.
Fieldwork and archival research in Western Australia, New South Wales,
    Victoria and Canberra (2012–2021).

ONLINE SOURCES

Ancestry: <www.ancestry.com.au>.
Anzac Day Dawn Service Trust: <www.anzacdaydawnservice.org.au>.
Australian Dictionary of Biography: <adb.anu.edu.au>.
Australian War Memorial: <www.awm.gov.au>.
British Army Groom: <collection.nam.ac.uk/detail.
    php?acc=1994-06-217-8>.
Citations for gallantry in the London Gazette the and Edinburgh Gazette,
    1914–1920: <www.thegazette.co.uk>.
The Denmark Historical Society: <denmarkhistoricalsocietywa.org.au>.
Edwardian cricket and fashion: <www.edwardianpromenade.com/fashion/
    the-clothes-the-man-cricket>.
Evolution of abdominal surgery WW1: <history.army.mil/curriculum/wwi/
    docs/AdditionalResources/presentations/Antecedents and Evolution_
    Abdominal_Surgery_for_Trauma_in_WWI.pdf>.
National Archives of Australia: <www.naa.gov.au>.
National Library of Australia: <www.nla.gov.au/>.
NSW Births, Deaths and Marriages: <www.nsw.gov.au/births-deaths-
    marriages>.
Oxford Dictionary of National Biography: <www.oxforddnb.com/>.

Bibliography

The State Library of NSW: <www.sl.nsw.gov.au/contact-us/mitchell-library>.
The State Library of Western Australia: <slwa.wa.gov.au>.
WA Births, Deaths and Marriages: <www.wa.gov.au/organisation/department-of-justice/the-registry-of-births-deaths-and-marriages>.

INDEX

Index

Index